Public Debt and Economic Growth

Dynamic Modeling and Econometrics in Economics and Finance

VOLUME 11

Aims and Scope

The series will place particular focus on monographs, surveys, edited volumes, conference proceedings and handbooks on:

- Nonlinear dynamic phenomena in economics and finance, including equilibrium, disequilibrium, optimizing and adaptive evolutionary points of view; nonlinear and complex dynamics in microeconomics, finance, macroeconomics and applied fields of economics.
- Econometric and statistical methods for analysis of nonlinear processes in economics and finance, including computational methods, numerical tools and software to study nonlinear dependence, asymmetries, persistence of fluctuations, multiple equilibria, chaotic and bifurcation phenomena.
- Applications linking theory and empirical analysis in areas such as macrodynamics, microdynamics, asset pricing, financial analysis and portfolio analysis, international economics, resource dynamics and environment, industrial organization and dynamics of technical change, labor economics, demographics, population dynamics, and game theory.

The target audience of this series includes researchers at universities and research and policy institutions, students at graduate institutions, and practitioners in economics, finance and international economics in private or government institutions.

Public Debt and Economic Growth

by

Alfred Greiner

Bielefeld University, Germany

and

Bettina Fincke

Bielefeld University, Germany

Springer

Prof. Dr. Alfred Greiner
Department of Business Administration
and Economics
Bielefeld University
Universitätsstr. 25
33615 Bielefeld
Germany
agreiner@wiwi.uni-bielefeld.de

Dipl.-Vw. Bettina Fincke
Department of Business Administration
and Economics
Bielefeld University
Universitätsstr. 25
33615 Bielefeld
Germany
bfincke@wiwi.uni-bielefeld.de

ISSN 1566-0419
ISBN 978-3-642-26924-0 e-ISBN 978-3-642-01745-2
DOI 10.1007/978-3-642-01745-2
Springer Dordrecht Heidelberg London New York

Printed on acid-free paper

Springer is part of Springer Science+Business Media (www.springer.com)

Preface

Public debt has become an important problem for most industrialized countries over the last decades. In Europe many economies are characterized by public debt to GDP ratios that have been rising almost monotonously since World War II. The USA were successful in reducing their public debt to GDP ratio in the aftermath of the Second World War but currently face tremendous public deficits that will raise their debt ratio in the near future. Therefore, the problem of public debt is not only of interest to economics professionals but also to policymakers who bear responsibility for the evolution of public debt in the countries. In an inter-temporal framework two problems arise within that context: First, the question of whether a given time path of public debt has been sustainable comes up. The answer to that question is crucial since it yields information about whether a given debt policy can go on or whether it has to be changed and if so how urgent the need for change is. Second, the question arises which effects public deficits and public debt have on the growth rates of economies. Of course, these two problems are interrelated and should not be treated separately.

In this book we intend to address the problem of public debt and economic growth where we pay special attention to sustainability of government debt. The theoretical framework we resort to in our analysis is the basic infinite horizon model of economic growth with optimizing agents. Growth is endogenous and sustained growth results either from positive externalities of private capital or from government investment in a productive public capital stock.

This book builds in part on research papers by ourselves. The motivation to write this monograph was that a book allows to give a more comprehensive view of the effects of public deficits and public debt. In contrast to publications in form of papers it is possible to get more into the details and also to be more precise about the effects that ensue when certain assumptions are changed and replaced by other ones. We have also benefitted from earlier joint work with Peter Flaschel, Göran Kauermann, Uwe Köller and Willi Semmler whom we owe our thanks.

Parts of the material in this book were presented at conferences, workshops and university seminars. Valuable comments that are gratefully acknowledged were provided by participants in the International Workshop on Advances in Macrodynamics at Bielefeld University, in the Conference on The Institutional and Social Dynamics of Growth and Distribution, Lucca, Italy, in the 64th Congress of the International Institute of Public Finance, Maastricht, in the ZEW Conference on Economic Growth in Europe, Mannheim, in the World Bank workshop on Modeling Fiscal Policy, Public Expenditure and Growth Linkages, Washington, D.C., in the Symposium on Nonlinear Dynamics and Econometrics, London, and in the DIW annual workshop on macroeconometric modelling, Berlin, as well as in seminars at the Université du Luxembourg, at the Vienna University of Technology and at the Université Paris 1 Panthéon-Sorbonne. We also have to thank a referee for taking time to read our manuscript and for giving helpful hints and suggestions. Finally, some of the research has been performed as contribution to the International Research Training Group "Economic Behavior and Interaction Models" that is financially supported by Deutsche Forschungsgemeinschaft (DFG) under GRK1134/1. We thank the DFG for that support.

Bielefeld

Alfred Greiner
Bettina Fincke

Contents

Chapter 1
Introduction and Overview

The question of how public debt affects economies has had a long tradition. In the 19th century David Ricardo set up what nowadays is called the Ricardian equivalence theorem. According to that theorem budget deficits today require higher taxes in the future when a government cuts taxes without changing present or future public spending. Given that households are forward looking they will realize that they have to pay higher taxes in the future so that their total tax burden remains unchanged. As a consequence, households will reduce their consumption and increase savings in order to meet the future tax burden.

The Ricardian equivalence theorem is based on the inter-temporal budget constraint of the government and on the permanent income hypothesis. The first principle states that public debt must be sustainable in the sense that outstanding debt today must be equal to the present value of future government surpluses. The second principle states that households do not base their consumption on current income but on permanent income so that they will not raise consumption as long as their income increases only temporarily. The Ricardian equivalence theorem is intuitively plausible but rests on assumptions that may be difficult to find in real world economies, such as the absence of distortionary taxation or the non-existence of capital market imperfections, just to mention two.

In the 1970s it was the Keynesian view that dominated economics. According to that approach market economies are inherently unstable and, in particular, not capable of generating an aggregate demand that is high enough to guarantee full employment in an economy. Consequently, the government has to intervene in order to assure that demand is sufficiently large so that labour demand rises and approaches its full employment level. In addition, according to that view public debt does not pose a problem if the government runs into debt in the home country. This holds because no resources are lost and public deficits just imply a reallocation of resources from taxpayers to bondholders.

The aspect of inter-generational redistribution is also the justification for the so-called golden rule of public finance. According to that rule, governments should finance public investments that yield long-term benefits by public deficits in order to make future generations contribute to the financing. Since future generations will

A. Greiner, B. Fincke, *Public Debt and Economic Growth,*
Dynamic Modeling and Econometrics in Economics and Finance 11,
DOI 10.1007/978-3-642-01745-2_1, © Springer-Verlag Berlin Heidelberg 2009

benefit from today's investment, their contribution to the financing is justified. Otherwise, the current generation would have to bear all the costs but benefit only to a certain degree which is considered as unfair.

As a consequence of the predominant Keynesian view in the 1970s public debt rose considerably over that period. Further, the rise in public debt often was even larger than the growth rate of the gross domestic product (GDP) in many countries so that the ratio of public debt to GDP increased, too. This evolution has raised the question of whether the time path of public debt is sustainable. In economics, a great many studies have been undertaken that address this question starting with the seminal paper by Hamilton and Flavin (1986).[1]

In this book our goal is to analyze effects of public debt using modern models of economic growth. Starting point of the analysis is the inter-temporal budget constraint of the government. When dealing with the question of under which conditions a given path of public debt is sustainable we do not consider the central bank of an economy. Hence, we neglect the possibility that a government can use seignorage or inflation to reduce the stock of real public debt. We do this because central banks are independent and governments should not rely on central banks to reduce public debt when deciding about debt and deficits.

In addition, by abstracting away from monetary policy in the economy and by requiring that the inter-temporal budget constraint of the government must always be fulfilled, we neglect the possibility of non-Ricardian regimes that may characterize economies. The distinction between Ricardian and non-Ricardian regimes is based on the fiscal theory of the price level. According to that theory, the inter-temporal budget constraint of the government must hold for some paths of the price level but not for all, in contrast to the budget constraint of private agents. If the latter holds, the government follows a non-Ricardian policy and the inter-temporal budget constraint of the government only holds in equilibrium. If the inter-temporal budget constraint holds for any price path, and not only for the equilibrium price path, the government pursues a Ricardian fiscal policy. For contributions as regards the fiscal theory of the price level see for example Leeper (1991), Sims (1994) and Woodford (1994). However, the fiscal theory of the price level is controversial and has been criticized, for example in the contribution by Buiter (2002) and in the paper by McCallum (2003). For a survey of the fiscal theory of the price level as well as for further studies criticizing that theory see McCallum and Nelson (2006).

Chapter 2 first theoretically analyzes conditions that must be fulfilled such that a given time path of public debt complies with the no-Ponzi game condition so that public debt is sustainable. Particular emphasis is put on the reaction of the primary surplus to public debt, relative to GDP respectively, and how this is related to sustainability. That chapter, then, empirically tests for selected developed and developing countries whether public debt has been sustainable.

The following chapters analyze the impact of public debt on economic growth given the assumption that the primary surplus relative to GDP is a positive function of the debt to GDP ratio. Chapters 3 and 4 posit that the economy is characterized

[1] See Chap. 2.1 for further references.

by full employment. Chapter 3 studies an endogenous growth model assuming that public spending is a mere waste of resources while Chap. 4 presumes that the government can invest in a productive public capital stock.

Chapter 5 allows for unemployment and studies the role of public debt, where two situations are distinguished. First, real wages are sufficiently flexible so that employment equals its natural level. Second, real wages are rigid so that the level of employment is below its natural level. Again, an endogenous growth model is assumed where the government invests in a productive public capital stock. Chapter 6, finally, summarizes the main findings of this book and points out in brief the effects of public debt in market economies.

Chapter 2
Sustainability of Public Debt

2.1 Theoretical Considerations

Modern research on sustainability of debt policies that applies statistical tests has started with the contribution by Hamilton and Flavin (1986) who analyzed whether the series of public debt in the USA contains a bubble term. Since then a great many papers have been written that try to answer the question of whether given debt policies can be considered as sustainable. The interest in that question is in part due to the fact that the latter question is not only of academic interest but that it has practical relevance, too. Hence, if tests reach the conclusion that given debt policies cannot be considered as sustainable governments should undertake corrective actions.

An important role in many of those studies on sustainability plays the interest rate, an aspect that was pointed out by Wilcox (1989) for example. Recalling that the inter-temporal budget constraint of the government requires that the present value of public debt asymptotically converges to zero, the role of the interest rate that is resorted to in order to discount the stream of public debt becomes immediately clear. Therefore, tests have been conceived that reach results which are independent of the interest rate. One such test is to analyze whether public deficits inclusive of interest payments grow at most linearly, as suggested by Trehan and Walsh (1991). If that property is fulfilled a given series of public debt is sustainable because any time series that grows linearly converges to zero if it is exponentially discounted, provided the real interest rate is positive. Denoting by B public debt and by r the interest rate, another test proposed by Trehan and Walsh (1991) is to analyze whether a quasi-difference of public debt, $B_t - \vartheta B_{t-1}$ with $0 \leq \vartheta < 1 + r$, is stationary and whether public debt and primary surpluses are co-integrated. If government debt is quasi-difference stationary and public debt and primary surpluses are cointegrated, public debt is sustainable. Hence, these two tests present alternatives where the outcome is independent of the exact numerical value of the interest rate. A survey of analyses that tested on sustainability of debt policies can be found in Afonso (2005), Neck and Sturm (2008) or Bohn (2008).

Another test that has received great attention in the economics literature is the one proposed by Bohn (1995). There, it is suggested to test whether the primary

A. Greiner, B. Fincke, *Public Debt and Economic Growth*,
Dynamic Modeling and Econometrics in Economics and Finance 11,
DOI 10.1007/978-3-642-01745-2_2, © Springer-Verlag Berlin Heidelberg 2009

surplus relative to GDP is a positive and at least linearly rising function of the debt to GDP ratio. If that property holds, a given public debt policy can be shown to be sustainable. This test is very plausible because it has a nice economic intuition: if governments run into debt today they have to take corrective actions in the future by increasing the primary surplus. Otherwise, public debt will not be sustainable. Testing real world debt policies for that property one can indeed find evidence that countries behave like that (see for example Bohn 1998, for the USA and Ballabriga and Martinez-Mongay 2005; Greiner et al. 2007, or Fincke and Greiner 2008, for selected countries of the euro area).

From a statistical point of view, a rise in primary surpluses as a response to higher government debt implies that the series of public debt relative to GDP should become a mean-reverting process. This holds because higher debt ratios lead to an increase in the primary surplus relative to GDP, making the debt ratio decline and return to its mean. However, mean-reversion only holds if the reaction coefficient, determining how strongly the primary surplus reacts as public debt rises, is sufficiently large, as will be shown in detail in this section.

In this section, our goal is to elaborate on that test from a theoretical point of view. In particular, we are interested in the behaviour of the debt to GDP ratio when governments pursue sustainable debt policies. For example, one question we address is whether a sustainable debt policy is compatible with a rising debt to GDP ratio. Another question we study is whether sustainability can be given if the government does not react to rising debt ratios and whether there probably exists a critical initial debt ratio that makes a sustainable debt policy impossible.

2.1.1 Public Debt and the Primary Surplus

We consider a real economy and we posit that the government cannot use seignorage or inflation to reduce its outstanding debt. We do this because, as already mentioned in the introduction to this book, modern economies are characterized by independent central banks so that governments cannot control the money supply. Thus, governments cannot rely on money creation to reduce outstanding public debt.

Starting point for the analysis of sustainability of public debt, then, is the accounting identity describing the accumulation of public debt in continuous time described by the following differential equation:

$$\dot{B}(t) = r(t)B(t) - S(t), \tag{2.1}$$

with $B(t)$ real public debt[1] at time t, $r(t)$ the real interest rate, $S(t)$ the real government surplus exclusive of interest payments on public debt and the dot over a variable stands for the derivative with respect to time d/dt. A government is said to follow a sustainable debt policy if the present value of public debt converges

[1] Strictly speaking, B should be real public net debt.

to zero asymptotically, that is if it does not play a Ponzi game. This implies that $\lim_{t\to\infty} e^{-C_1(t)} B(t) = 0$ holds, with $C_1(t) = \int_0^t r(\mu)d\mu$ the discount rate (see for example Blanchard and Fischer 1989, Chap. 2).

Now, assume that the government in the economy chooses the primary surplus to GDP ratio, $s(t) = S(t)/Y(t)$, such that it is a positive linear function of the debt to GDP ratio, $b(t) = B(t)/Y(t)$, and of an autonomous term that is independent of public debt, $\phi(t)$ (see Bohn, 1995, 1998, Canzoneri et al. 2001, or Greiner, 2008a, 2008b). The primary surplus ratio, then, can be written as

$$s(t) = \psi(t)b(t) + \phi(t), \tag{2.2}$$

where $\psi(t)$ is the coefficient determining how strong the primary surplus reacts to changes in the public debt ratio and that is time-varying. It should be noted that any non-linear model can be approximated by a linear model with time-varying coefficients. Further, the approximation is good if the parameter changes smoothly (cf. Granger 2008). Thus, the modelling in (2.2) can be justified and there does not seem to be the need for a more general function describing the response of the primary surplus to public debt.

The term $\phi(t)$ is also time dependent and it is influenced by other economic variables, such as social spending or transitory government expenditures in general. As concerns $\phi(t)$ we suppose that it is bounded by above and below by a certain finite number that is constant over time. Since $\phi(t)$ gives the autonomous part of the primary surplus relative to GDP, that assumption is obvious and realistic. We should also like to point out that $\phi(t)$ cannot be completely controlled by the government. The government can influence that parameter to a certain degree but it has not complete control over it because $\phi(t)$ is also affected by the business cycle for example that can affect temporary government outlays.

In the next subsection, we analyze conditions that must be fulfilled such that the inter-temporal budget constraint of the government holds and how the debt to GDP ratio evolves in that case.

2.1.2 Conditions for Sustainability of Public Debt

Before we start our analysis we make two additional assumptions. First, we posit that the interest rate on government bonds exceeds the growth rate of GDP on average so that $\int r(\mu)d\mu > \int g(\mu)d\mu$, with g denoting the growth rate of GDP. We make this assumption because otherwise the inter-temporal budget constraint would not pose a problem for the government since it can grow out of debt in that case. In addition, this condition is fulfilled for countries of the euro area at least since the 1980s. Second, we neglect the case where public debt becomes negative meaning that the government would be a net lender. This is done for reasons of realism because a situation with negative public debt is of less relevance for real world economies.

In our analysis of sustainable debt policies we are particularly interested under which conditions sustainability of public debt is given and in the question of whether a sustainable debt policy is compatible with a rising debt to GDP ratio. To study those questions, we distinguish between two cases. First, we analyze the situation where the government sets the primary surplus according to (2.2), with $\psi(t) \neq 0$. Second, we study the case where the primary surplus does not react to variations in the debt ratio, implying that $\psi(t) = 0$ holds. In the latter case, we posit in addition that the government sets the primary surplus relative to GDP equal to its maximum value.

2.1.2.1 The Primary Surplus as a Function of Public Debt

In this subsection, we posit that the primary surplus is given by (2.2), with $\psi(t) \neq 0$. To study sustainability of public debt, we combine (2.1) and (2.2) yielding

$$\dot{B}(t) = (r(t) - \psi(t))B(t) - \phi(t)\,Y(t). \tag{2.3}$$

With (2.3), the debt to GDP ratio evolves according to

$$\frac{\dot{b}}{b} = \frac{\dot{B}}{B} - \frac{\dot{Y}}{Y} \tag{2.4}$$

which is equivalent to

$$\dot{b}(t) = (r(t) - \psi(t))b(t) - \phi(t) - g(t)\,b(t). \tag{2.5}$$

With these two equations, we can derive our first result in proposition 1.[2]

Proposition 1 *A strictly positive reaction coefficient on average so that $\int_0^t \psi(\mu)d\mu = \infty$ holds for $t \to \infty$ guarantees sustainability of public debt.*

For $\int_0^t \psi(\mu)d\mu > (=) \int_0^t (r(\mu) - g(\mu))d\mu$, the debt to GDP ratio converges to zero (remains constant) and it diverges for $\int_0^t \psi(\mu)d\mu < \int_0^t (r(\mu) - g(\mu))d\mu$, for $t \to \infty$ respectively.

Proof See the appendix to this section. □

This proposition demonstrates that a positive reaction coefficient on average is sufficient for sustainability of public debt.[3] If the reaction coefficient is strictly negative on average, the discounted value of public debt diverges to infinity. But Proposition 1 also shows that a positive value of the reaction coefficient does not necessarily

[2]In this book we consider deterministic economies. Sustainability of public debt with an additive stochastic term is briefly discussed in the appendix to this section.

[3]The first part of this proposition has already been shown by Bohn (1995) for a model formulated in discrete time.

imply that the debt to GDP ratio remains constant or that it asymptotically converges to zero. Only if the reaction coefficient exceeds the positive difference between the interest rate and the GDP growth rate on average, convergence can be guaranteed. Otherwise, the debt to GDP ratio diverges to infinity.

An immediate consequence of Proposition 1 is that a bounded public debt to GDP ratio guarantees sustainability of public debt when the government sets the primary surplus according to the rule given by (2.2). The reason for that outcome is that, given (2.2), a bounded debt to GDP ratio implies that the average reaction coefficient ψ is strictly positive. This is sufficient for the inter-temporal budget constraint to be fulfilled. We state this result as a corollary to Proposition 1.

Corollary 1 *A bounded debt to GDP ratio is sufficient for the inter-temporal budget constraint to hold if the government sets the primary surplus according to the rule given in* (2.2).

Proof According to Proposition 1 the debt to GDP ratio remains bounded if and only if $\int_0^t \psi(\mu)d\mu \geq \int_0^t (r(\mu) - g(\mu))d\mu$ holds for $t \to \infty$. Since the average interest rate exceeds the average GDP growth rate by assumption, $\int_0^t \psi(\mu)d\mu > 0$ must hold for $t \to \infty$ which assures sustainability of public debt according to Proposition 1. □

With the result of Proposition 1, one could reach the conclusion that a sustainable debt policy is compatible with a continuously rising debt to GDP ratio, in case the reaction coefficient ψ is positive on average but smaller than the difference between the average interest rate and the average growth rate, $r - g$. However, when the government sets the primary surplus according to rule (2.2), that possibility is not given as Proposition 2 demonstrates.

Proposition 2 *If the government pursues a sustainable debt policy and sets the primary surplus according to the rule given by* (2.2), *the debt to GDP ratio remains bounded.*

Proof Assume that $b(t) \to \infty$. According to (2.2) this implies $s(t) \to \infty$ which, however, is excluded because the primary surplus cannot become larger than GDP implying that $s(t) < 1$ must always hold. □

The result in Proposition 2 is simply due to the fact that the primary surplus must be financed out of the GDP so that the ratio of the primary surplus to GDP must be smaller one. Consequently, when the government pursues a sustainable debt policy and raises the primary surplus relative to GDP as the debt to GDP ratio increases, the debt ratio must remain bounded in the long-run.

Hence, a situation may be observed where the debt to GDP ratio rises over a certain time period although the primary surplus positively reacts to higher public debt. Such an evolution of public debt may be compatible with a sustainable debt policy but it cannot go on forever. Sooner or later, the public debt to GDP ratio must become constant or decline. Otherwise, sustainability is not given.

2.1.2.2 The Primary Surplus Independent of Public Debt

In our considerations up to now, it was assumed that the government sets the primary surplus according to the rule specified in (2.2). However, one could argue that governments can perform sustainable debt policies without reacting to higher public debt if they only chose the primary surplus sufficiently high, independent of public debt. Further, a situation is feasible where the government cannot react to higher debt since there is no scope for it because the primary surplus relative to GDP has already reached its upper bound. In both cases the reaction coefficient $\psi(t)$ would be zero.

In order to analyze that case we set $\psi(t) = 0$ and we denote by $m < 1$ the constant upper bound of the primary surplus to GDP ratio. In addition, we assume that the government sets the primary surplus to GDP ratio equal to that maximum value for all times, that is $s(t) = m$ for all t. Thus, the evolution of public debt is described by

$$\dot{B}(t) = r(t)\,B(t) - m\,Y(t) \tag{2.6}$$

and the debt to GDP ratio evolves according to

$$\dot{b}(t) = r(t)\,b(t) - m - g(t)\,b(t). \tag{2.7}$$

Given (2.6) and (2.7), we can derive Proposition 3.

Proposition 3 *Assume that the initial debt to GDP ratio exceeds a certain threshold. Then, a sustainable debt policy is excluded.*

If the initial debt to GDP ratio is smaller than or equal to the critical threshold, the government can pursue a sustainable debt policy. In this case, the debt to GDP ratio converges to zero.

Proof See the appendix to this section. □

Proposition 3 states that a sustainable debt policy cannot be pursued if the initial debt to GDP ratio is larger than a certain critical value. The critical value is given by $b_{crit} = m \int_0^\infty e^{-(C_1(\mu) - C_2(\mu)) dv} d\mu$, with $C_1(\mu) = \int_0^\mu r(v) dv$, $C_2(\mu) = \int_0^\mu g(v) dv$, and depends on how large the primary surplus relative to GDP can maximally become, m, and on the average difference between the interest rate and the growth rate, $r - g$. Hence, countries that do not stabilize their debt to GDP ratio but instead let it grow for a longer time period face the risk that they find themselves in a situation where they cannot react to higher debt to GDP ratios by raising their primary surplus relative to GDP. Then, it may become impossible to pursue a sustainable debt policy, independent of how large the primary surplus relative to GDP is set. In this case, the public debt to GDP ratio becomes unbounded asymptotically.

The proposition also demonstrates that the government can control public debt if it chooses the maximally possible value of the primary surplus, m, provided the initial debt to GDP ratio is not too large, that is if it is smaller than the critical value b_{crit}. In that case, sustainability of public debt is guaranteed and the debt to GDP ratio asymptotically converges to zero. Of course, convergence to zero is only given if the government always sets the primary surplus equal to its maximum value m and does not switch to a different debt policy.

2.1.3 Conclusion

In this section, we have studied conditions under which governments can pursue sustainable debt policies. When the interest rate exceeds the growth rate of GDP on average, a given debt policy is sustainable if the primary surplus relative to GDP is a positive and at least linearly rising function of the debt to GDP ratio. If a government pursues such a policy the debt ratio remains constant in the long-run or it converges to zero. We could also demonstrate that a public debt to GDP ratio which rises in the long-run is not compatible with a sustainable debt policy. Further, a stationary debt ratio guarantees sustainability of public debt if the government increases its primary surplus as public debt rises.

If the primary surplus relative to GDP does not react to a rising debt ratio, a sustainable debt policy is excluded if the initial debt to GDP ratio exceeds a certain threshold, independent of how large the primary surplus is chosen.[4] If the initial debt to GDP ratio is smaller than the critical value it is possible that public debt remains sustainable provided the ratio of the primary surplus relative to GDP is sufficiently large. In that case, the debt ratio asymptotically converges to zero if the government sets the primary surplus relative to GDP equal to its maximum value for ever.

This first section has provided theoretical considerations as regards sustainability of public debt. In the remainder of this chapter, we want to analyze empirically how governments react to public debt and to find whether the time series of public debt can be considered as sustainable taking data over a certain time horizon. The empirical tests are first undertaken for selected developed economies and, second, for developing countries.

Another motivation for that test is the following. If the primary surplus is a positive function of public debt, this will have effects for public spending and, as a consequence, for economic growth.

2.1.4 Appendix

Proof of Proposition 1 To prove that proposition we note that the evolution of public debt is given by (2.3). Integrating that equation and multiplying the resulting

[4] Of course, the primary surplus is bounded by above.

expression by $e^{-\int_0^t r(\mu)d\mu}$ to get present values gives,[5]

$$e^{-C_1(t)}B(t) = e^{-C_3(t)}B(0) - Y(0)e^{-C_3(t)} \int_0^t e^{-C_1(\mu)+C_2(\mu)+C_3(\mu)}\phi(\mu)d\mu, \tag{A2.1}$$

with

$$\int_0^t r(\mu)d\mu \equiv C_1(t), \int_0^\mu r(\nu)d\nu \equiv C_1(\mu), \int_0^\mu g(\nu)d\nu$$
$$\equiv C_2(\mu), \int_0^\mu \psi(\nu)d\nu \equiv C_3(\mu).$$

For $\lim_{t\to\infty} C_3(t) = \lim_{t\to\infty} \int_0^t \psi(\nu)d\nu = \infty$, the first term on the right hand side in (A2.1), that is $e^{-C_3(t)}\,B(0)$, converges to zero.

The second term on the right hand side in (A2.1) can be written as

$$\frac{Y(0)\int_0^t e^{-C_1(\mu)+C_2(\mu)+C_3(\mu)}\phi(\mu)d\mu}{e^{C_3(t)}} \equiv K_1(t).$$

If $\int_0^\infty e^{-C_1(\mu)+C_2(\mu)+C_3(\mu)}d\mu$ remains bounded $\lim_{t\to\infty} C_3(t) = \infty$ guarantees that K_1 converges to zero. If $\lim_{t\to\infty} \int_0^\infty e^{-C_1(\mu)+C_2(\mu)+C_3(\mu)}d\mu = \infty$, applying l'Hôpital gives the limit of K_1 as

$$\lim_{t\to\infty} K_1(t) = \lim_{t\to\infty} \frac{e^{-C_1(t)+C_2(t)}}{\psi(t)}.$$

Since $-C_1(t) + C_2(t) < 0$ we can find a constant $k > 0$ such that $K_1 \le e^{-kt}/\psi(t)$. The right hand side in the former inequality does not converge to zero if $\psi(t)$ converged to zero exponentially. However, in that case $\lim_{t\to\infty} \int_0^t \psi(\mu)d\mu < \infty$ would hold. Consequently, in case that $\lim_{t\to\infty} \int_0^t \psi(\mu)d\mu = \infty$ holds, $\psi(t)$ cannot decline exponentially, and $K_1(t)$ converges to zero.

These considerations demonstrate that the inter-temporal budget constraint holds for $\lim_{t\to\infty} \int_0^t \psi(\mu)d\mu = \infty$ which means that the reaction coefficient $\psi(t)$ is positive on average.

The debt ratio is obtained from (2.5) as

$$b(t) = e^{(C_1(t)-C_2(t)-C_3(t))}b(0) - e^{(C_1(t)-C_2(t)-C_3(t))}$$
$$\times \int_0^t e^{-(C_1(\mu)-C_2(\mu)-C_3(\mu))}\phi(\mu)d\mu.$$

That expression shows that the debt ratio diverges to plus or minus infinity in case of $\int_0^t \psi(\mu)d\mu < \int_0^t (r(\mu) - g(\mu))d\mu$, while it remains constant or converges to zero in all other cases. □

[5]Equation (A2.1) illustrates that a government can grow out of debt when $g > r$ holds with $\phi > 0$.

Proof of Proposition 3 To prove that proposition we note that the present value of public debt is now obtained from (2.6) as

$$e^{-C_1(t)}B(t) = B(0) - mY(0)\int_0^t e^{-(C_1(\mu)-C_2(\mu))}d\mu.$$

The inter-temporal budget constraint is fulfilled for $\lim_{t\to\infty} e^{-C_1(t)}B(t) = 0$ which implies $b(0) = m\int_0^\infty e^{-(C_1(\mu)-C_2(\mu))}d\mu$. If the initial debt to GDP ratio, $b(0)$, is larger than $m\int_0^\infty e^{-(C_1(\mu)-C_2(\mu))}d\mu$ sustainability of public debt is excluded.

The debt to GDP ratio is obtained from (2.7) as

$$b(t) = e^{(C_1(t)-C_2(t))}\left(b(0) - m\int_0^t e^{-(C_1(\mu)-C_2(\mu))}d\mu\right).$$

If the inter-temporal budget constraint holds we have $b(0) = m\int_0^\infty e^{-(C_1(\mu)-C_2(\mu))}d\mu$ and, thus, $\lim_{t\to\infty} b(t) = 0$. □

2.1.4.1 Public Debt Accumulation with a Stochastic Disturbance

Assume that the evolution of public debt is described by a stochastic differential equation with an additive noise. Equation (2.3), then, can be written as,

$$dB_t = (h(t)B_t - \phi(t)Y(t))dt + \sigma\, dW_t,$$

with $h(t) \equiv r(t) - \psi(t)$ and W is a Wiener process with constant diffusion σ which is set equal to one, $\sigma = 1$. Solving that equation yields

$$B_t = e^{\int_0^t h(\tau)d\tau}\left(B_0 - \int_0^t e^{-\int_0^\tau h(\mu)d\mu}\phi(\tau)Y(\tau)d\tau + \int_0^t e^{-\int_0^\tau h(\mu)d\mu}dW_\tau\right)$$

with B_0 public debt at time $t = 0$. Multiplying both sides by the discount factor $e^{-\int_0^t r(\tau)d\tau}$ and rewriting gives

$$e^{-C_1(t)}B_t = e^{-C_3(t)}B_0 - Y_0 e^{-C_3(t)}\int_0^t e^{C_3(\tau)}e^{C_2(\tau)}e^{-C_1(\tau)}\phi(\tau)d\tau + e^{-C_3(t)}\int_0^t e^{C_3(\tau)}e^{-C_1(\tau)}dW_\tau \qquad \text{(A2.2)}$$

with

$$\int_0^t \psi(\tau)d\tau \equiv C_3(t),\ \int_0^\tau \psi(\mu)d\mu \equiv C_3(\tau),$$

$$\int_0^\tau g(\mu)d\mu \equiv C_2(\tau),\ \int_0^\tau r(\mu)d\mu \equiv C_1(\tau),$$

where g gives the growth rate of Y. The first two terms are as in (A2.1) above so that we do not have to consider them again.

The third term on the right hand side in (A2.2) is stochastic with the expected value equal to zero. Defining the third term as $X_t(\omega) \equiv e^{-C_3(t)} \int_0^t e^{C_3(\tau)} e^{-C_1(\tau)} dW_\tau(\omega)$, the second moment can be written as

$$E[X_t^2(\omega)] = E\left[\left(\frac{\int_0^t e^{C_3(\tau)} e^{-C_1(\tau)} dW_\tau(\omega)}{e^{C_3(t)}}\right)^2\right] = \left(\frac{\int_0^t E[e^{2C_3(\tau)} e^{-2C_1(\tau)}] d\tau}{e^{2C_3(t)}}\right),$$

because $E[(\int_0^t e^{C_3(\tau)} e^{-C_1(\tau)} dW_\tau(\omega))^2] = \int_0^t E[(e^{C_3(\tau)} e^{-C_1(\tau)})^2] d\tau$.

Since the mean of the realized real interest rate is strictly positive, we can find a constant $\bar{r} > 0$ so that $-C_1(\tau) = -\int_0^\tau r(\mu) d\mu \leq -\int_0^\tau \bar{r}\, d\mu$. Then, we can write

$$\frac{\int_0^t e^{2C_3(\tau)} E[e^{-2C_1(\tau)}] d\tau}{e^{2C_3(t)}} \leq \frac{\int_0^t e^{2C_3(\tau)} e^{-2\bar{r}\tau} d\tau}{e^{2C_3(t)}}.$$

If $\int_0^t e^{2C_3(\tau)} e^{-2\bar{r}\tau} d\tau$ remains bounded and if $\lim_{t\to\infty} C_3(t) = \infty$ holds, the expression converges to zero. If $\int_0^t e^{2C_3(\tau)} e^{-2\bar{r}\tau} d\tau$ diverges, applying l'Hôpital gives the right hand side as $e^{-2\bar{r}t}/2\psi(t)$ showing that $\psi(t)$ must not converge to zero faster than $e^{-2\bar{r}t}$ if that term is to converge to zero asymptotically. Now, assume that $\psi(t)$ declines exponentially. This would imply that $\lim_{t\to\infty} C_3(t) = \lim_{t\to\infty} \int_0^t \psi(\tau) d\tau < \infty$ holds. Consequently, if $\lim_{t\to\infty} C_3(t) = \infty$ holds, $\psi(t)$ cannot decline exponentially so that the expression $E[X_t^2(\omega)]$ converges to zero.

2.2 Empirical Results for Developed Countries: Euro Area Countries and the USA

The growth of the public debt level is an important factor that affects the budget plan of a government. Without balanced budgets the ensuing deficits accumulate and lead to a rise of public debt in individual countries. Over the last decades a lot of European countries and, to a smaller degree, the USA have suffered from permanent and in part high public deficits. This trend has represented a serious problem from the economic and political point of view, especially for members of the European Monetary Union. Countries in the euro area have to stick to the Convergence Criteria of the Maastricht Treaty of the European Union and to the Stability and Growth Pact that imposes limitations with respect to fiscal policies.

In order to account for the size of the different countries in the European Union, public debt is usually expressed in terms of ratios, mostly relative to GDP. This measurement is also resorted to in the Convergence Criteria of the Maastricht Treaty of the European Union, which limits public deficits to three percent of GDP and public debt to 60 percent of GDP.[6] In the early 2000s these criteria had been frequently violated by France, Germany and Portugal for example.

As pointed out in the last section, an important aspect in this context is the question of whether governments are able to respond in a sustainable way to the above mentioned tendency of persistent budget deficits and growing levels of debt. Here, it is important to recall that the concept of sustainability is well compatible with indebtedness in the short run but it requires that the present value of debt converges to zero asymptotically. This raises the question of how governments react to higher debt levels, which options they have to respond and if these actions are still effective.

Therefore, the starting point of our analysis is the test, where the response of the primary surplus relative to GDP with respect to public debt relative to GDP is analyzed. We take data until 2006 and we allow for a time varying coefficient giving the reaction of the primary surplus to GDP ratio to variations in the debt ratio. Applying that estimation strategy, we are able to find whether the response of governments with respect to public debt have changed over time besides detecting whether the coefficient is positive at all. Thus, we intend to contribute to the literature that goes beyond OLS estimation in that area and that tries to find structural breaks, threshold or possible non-linearities (see for example Bajo-Rubio et al. 2004; Martin 2000; Payne et al. 2007, or Westerlund and Prohl 2008).

Additionally, based on our theoretical analysis of Sect. 2.1, we argue that performing that test alone may not be sufficient to answer the question of whether a given fiscal policy is sustainable. As we have shown theoretically, this holds because a positive reaction coefficient does not necessarily imply that the debt ratio remains bounded which, however, must hold asymptotically. Therefore, we analyze in addition whether the total deficit of the government is stationary which is a sufficient condition for sustainability of public debt if the interest rate is positive.

The countries we consider in our study are Austria, France, Germany, Italy, the Netherlands and Portugal for the euro area and the USA. France, Germany and Italy are included because they are the largest economies in the euro area. Austria and Portugal are included because the evolution of their debt ratios with a sharp increase during the 1970s and a stabilization in the 1990s can be seen as characteristic for many euro area countries. The Netherlands, finally, have undertaken substantial macroeconomic reforms in the mid 1980s to early 1990s.

2.2.1 The Primary Surplus and Public Debt

In this subsection we apply a test that implements the theoretical considerations to data for six selected euro area countries and for the USA. We analyze the correlation between the primary surplus and the public debt all measured as ratios to GDP. For the selected countries it has been checked in advance whether the long-term interest

[6] See European Union (1992) Title VI Chap. 1, Art. 104c, Sect. 2 and Protocol 5 on the excessive deficit procedure.

rate exceeds the growth rate of GDP. For the euro area countries under consideration, this holds at least on average. In the USA, the real return on government bonds has been smaller than the real growth rate of GDP over the time period from 1916 until 1995 (see Bohn 1998). Over the shorter time period 1974 to 2003, we consider in our study, it turns out that this also holds, with the difference being slightly negative (−0.004).

We begin with a description of its public debt ratio and its primary surplus ratio for each selected country. To implement the test we estimate the following equation,

$$s(t) = \psi(t)\,b(t) + \phi^T Z(t) + \epsilon(t), \tag{2.8}$$

with $s(t)$ the primary surplus to GDP ratio and $b(t)$ the public debt to GDP ratio at time t. $Z(t)$ is a vector of variables that includes 1 in its first element, for the intercept, and additional variables in its other elements, that influence the primary surplus ratio. $\epsilon(t)$ is an error term, which is assumed to be i.i.d. $N(0, \sigma^2)$.

The variables included in $Z(t)$ are motivated by the tax smoothing hypothesis according to which public deficits should be used in order to keep tax rates constant which minimizes the excess burden of taxation (cf. Barro 1979). Hence, normal expenditures should be financed by regular revenues and deficits should be incurred to finance unexpected spending. However, that rule is not robust in the sense that the situation of an economy does not affect optimal tax rates. For example, Bohn (1990) shows that in a stochastic economy tax rates should be smoothed over states of nature as well as over time. Consequently, the primary surplus should also react to variations in outstanding public debt.

In our estimations we take account of the tax smoothing hypothesis. Therefore, we include a business cycle variable, YVar, that accounts for fluctuations in revenues. In addition, we include the surplus of the social insurance system relative to GDP, Soc, because governments often subsidize social insurances when revenues of social insurances fall short of expenditures. Finally, the real long-term interest rate, int, can affect the primary surplus ratio, too, although it does not affect the primary surplus ratio directly. But, since the government cannot run overall deficits arbitrarily, the interest payments of the government will also affect the primary surplus. Thus, high real interest rates imply that the debt service of the government is large which tends to reduce the primary surplus ratio. On the other hand, high real interest rates may characterize booms with high tax revenues which tend to raise the primary surplus ratio. Therefore, the sign of the coefficient of the real interest rate cannot be determined theoretically.

Further, for the estimation the lagged debt ratio $b(t-1)$ is used in order to take account of problems of endogeneity. Thus, (2.8) can be written as

$$s(t) = \phi_0 + \psi(t)b(t-1) + \phi_1\,\mathrm{Soc}(t) + \phi_2\,\mathrm{int}(t) + \phi_3\,\mathrm{YVar}(t) + \epsilon(t). \tag{2.9}$$

In order to estimate time-varying coefficients we resort to penalized spline (p-spline) estimation that is more robust than OLS estimation (for a brief introduction to penalized spline estimation see Appendix A. A more thorough treatment can be found in Hastie and Tibshirani (1990) or Ruppert et al. 2003).[7] This allows to estimate the reaction coefficient $\psi(t)$ in (2.9) as a function of time showing how that coefficient evolves over time.

2.2.1.1 Austria

Figures 2.1 and 2.2 show the public debt to GDP ratio, measured as general government gross financial liabilities as percentage of GDP, and the primary surplus ratio for the years from 1975 to 2005 for Austria.[8]

As Figs. 2.1 and 2.2 show, Austria has faced a steady increase of public debt within the last 30 years. Especially we recognize a sharp rise from 1975 to the late 1980s. Possible reasons for this might be the aftermath of the first and second oil crisis and the recessions they initiated.[9] For that time period the trend is accompanied by persistent primary deficits. This stage is followed by a period of fiscal discipline and a decline in public debt relative to GDP approximately until 1992 and positive primary surpluses. Afterwards another steep rise of the public debt ratio begins which ends in 1996. This may be due to the recession in the early nineties. From about that time onwards, the debt level has stayed around 70 percent of GDP. This comes along with primary surpluses for the corresponding period.

Estimating (2.9) with Austrian data[10] from 1975 until 2005 yields the results shown in Table 2.1.

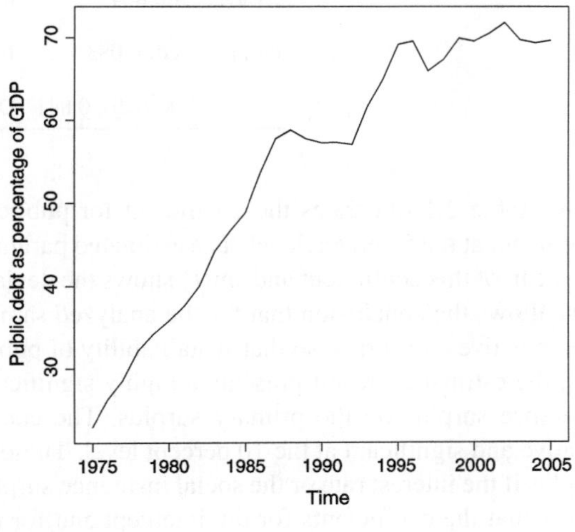

Fig. 2.1 Public debt to GDP ratio for Austria (1975–2005)

[7] All equations are estimated with R (Version 2.5.0) with the package *mgcv* (Version 1.3–28).

[8] For the data source see OECD (2007a).

[9] For a more detailed analysis of Austria see the extensive studies by Neck and Getzner (2001) and Haber and Neck (2006).

[10] See OECD (2007a, 2007b) and International Statistical Yearbook (2006) for the data.

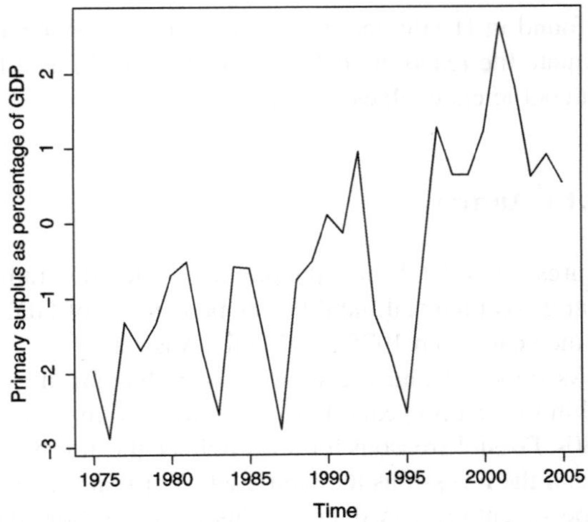

Fig. 2.2 Primary surplus to GDP ratio for Austria (1975–2005)

Table 2.1 Coefficients for (2.9) for Austria

	Coefficient	Stand. error (t-stat)	Pr(> t)
Constant	−0.006	0.024 (−0.241)	0.812
$b(t-1)$	0.115	0.052 (2.208)	0.039
Soc(t)	2.685	0.471 (5.695)	1.44×10^{-5}
int(t)	0.274	0.144 (1.903)	0.072
YVar(t)	−0.804	0.542 (−1.482)	0.154
sm(t)	edf 6.083	F 6.327	p-value 0.00031
	R^2(adj): 0.841	DW: 1.88	

As Table 2.1 illustrates the coefficient for public debt $b(t-1)$ is positive and significant at the 5 percent level. The estimated parameter of interest $\psi(t)$ represents the mean of this coefficient and sm(t) shows the deviation from that mean over time. This allows the conclusion that for the analyzed sample the reaction coefficient has been positive on average so that sustainability of public debt is given. In addition to that, the estimation result presents a highly significant positive effect of the social insurance surplus on the primary surplus. The coefficient for the real interest is positive and significant at the 10 percent level. These effects imply a rise in primary surplus if the interest rate or the social insurance surplus increases. Further Table 2.1 shows that the coefficients for the intercept and for the business cycle variable are not statistically significant. When the estimation is done without the interest rate or without the business cycle variable, the estimated average coefficient for public debt $b(t-1)$ remains positive at the 10 percent significance level.

The estimated degrees of freedom, edf, of sm(t) provide information on possible time-dependencies. Table 2.1 shows for the Austrian data edf = 6.083 and the smooth term sm(t) is significant at the 1 percent level. Hence, we can conclude that

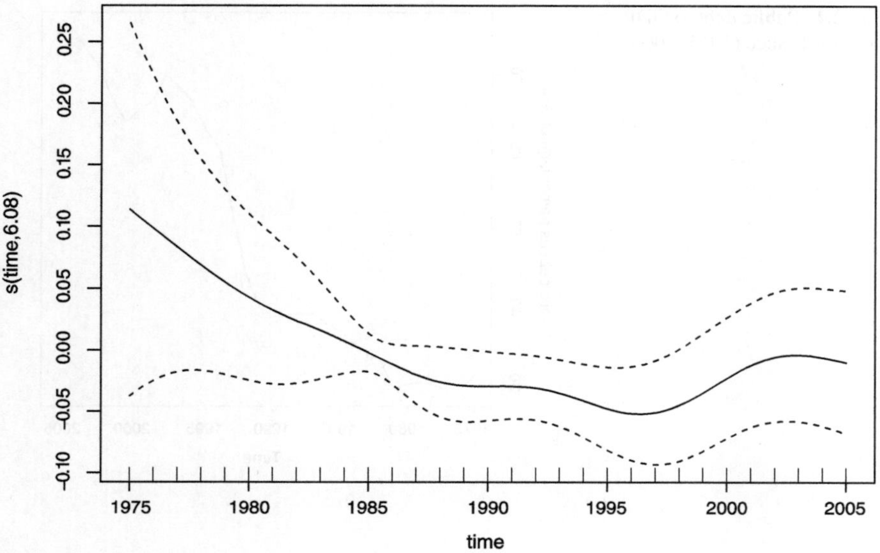

Fig. 2.3 Deviation sm(t) from the average coefficient for $b(t-1)$ for Austria

the reaction coefficient has not stayed constant over time. The goodness of fit of the model is expressed by R^2(adj). For Austria with $R^2(\text{adj}) = 0.841$ a high goodness of fit is given. Applying the Durbin-Watson test, it is possible to check whether the residuals are correlated. For Austria this test statistic does not show any evidence for correlation of the residuals.

The information in Table 2.1 as concerns the smooth term shows that it varies over time and the hypothesis that it is constant can be rejected. Figure 2.3 illustrates the time path of the smooth term, where the two dashed lines represent the 95 percent confidence interval and the solid line shows the point estimate of the smooth term.[11] The curve is drawn such that values larger (smaller) zero indicate that the coefficient was above (below) its average value that is reported in Table 2.1. The actual reaction coefficient in a certain year is the sum of the average coefficient plus the value of the curve, shown in Fig. 2.3, for that year. It can be realized that the reaction of the primary surplus to public debt has declined in the 1970s, before it began to rise again in the late 1990s.

2.2.1.2 France

For France, the evolution of public debt and of the primary surplus relative to GDP are illustrated in Figs. 2.4 and 2.5 for the period from 1975 to 2006.[12]

[11] See also Wood (2001) especially p. 23.

[12] For the data source see OECD (2007a).

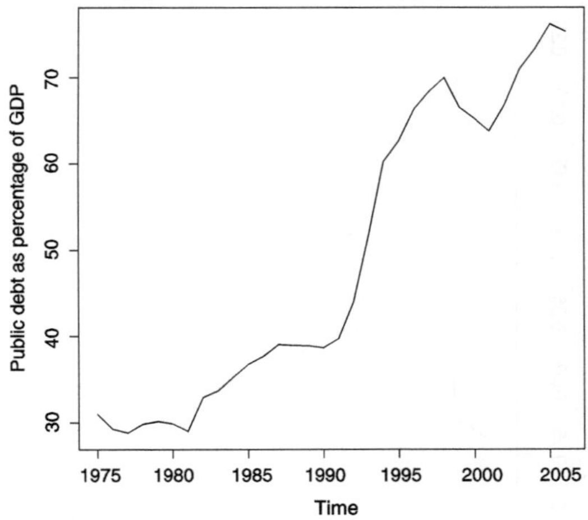

Fig. 2.4 Public debt to GDP ratio for France (1975–2006)

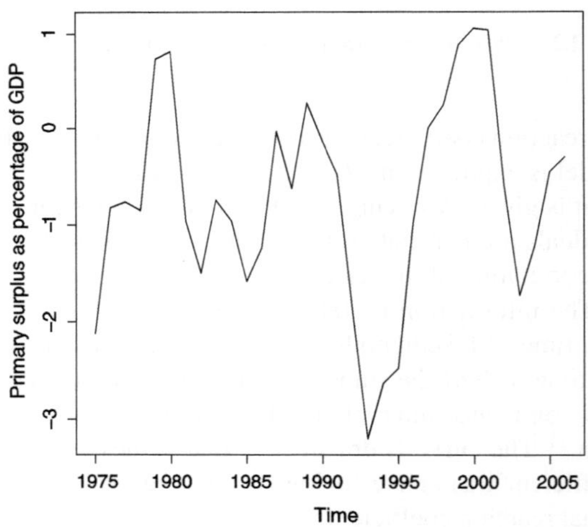

Fig. 2.5 Primary surplus to GDP ratio for France (1975–2006)

Figure 2.4 presents the debt ratio which stays around 30 percent from 1975 until the early eighties. After that three remarkable steps of debt ratio increases are obvious. Firstly, a moderate rise in the 1980s can be observed. Then, during the nineties the debt ratio grows rapidly with a peak in 1998 of about 70 percent, which might be due to the recession at the beginning of the 1990s. After a slight decline, possibly due to fiscal discipline in preparation of the European Monetary Union with the Convergence Criteria, the debt to GDP ratio increased again with the beginning of the new century. Except for the years around the 1980s, 1989 and the period around 2000 Fig. 2.5 shows merely primary deficits.

Table 2.2 Coefficients for (2.9) for France

	Coefficient	Stand. error (t-stat)	Pr($>t$)
Constant	−0.079	0.023 (−3.354)	0.003
$b(t-1)$	0.102	0.054 (1.882)	0.075
Soc(t)	1.171	0.227 (5.166)	4.86×10^{-5}
int(t)	−0.080	0.096 (−0.830)	0.416
YVar(t)	0.601	0.336 (1.789)	0.089
sm(t)	edf 7.215	F 23.02	p-value 1.31×10^{-8}
	R^2(adj): 0.874	DW: 2.48	

With a picture of the French situation in mind the sustainability test is to be applied. We estimate (2.9) with data for France for the period from 1975 to 2006.[13] Table 2.2 presents the results.

Table 2.2 shows a positive average coefficient for public debt that, however, is significant only at the 10 percent level. Estimating the equation without the interest rate or the business cycle variable does neither change the sign of the coefficient nor its significance. The intercept is negative and significant, whereas for the coefficient of the social insurance surplus a highly significant and positive value is obtained. That indicates that a rise in social insurance surplus also goes along with an increase in the primary surplus. Further, the included real interest rate is not statistical significant but the positive coefficient for the business cycle variable is significant at the 10 percent level. This expresses the positive effect of the business cycle parameter on the primary surplus.

The deviation of the reaction coefficient from its mean, given by sm(t), with edf $= 7.215$ indicates a time varying smooth term that is highly significant. As to the goodness of fit of the model, the decision criterion $R^2(\text{adj}) = 0.874$ attests a good fit. The Durbin-Watson test statistic shows no evidence of correlation of the residuals. The results in Table 2.2 reveal that the smooth term changed over time. Figure 2.6 depicts the smooth term sm(t). Again adding together the time varying smooth parameter and the mean of the coefficient for $b(t-1)$ given in Table 2.2 results in a positive $\psi(t)$, which allows the conclusion from the results of the estimation that the primary surplus ratio is raised in response to a growing debt ratio.

2.2.1.3 Germany

Figures 2.7 and 2.8 show the evolution of German public debt and of the primary surplus relative to GDP for the period from 1971 to 2006.[14]

[13] See OECD (2007a, 2007b) for the data.

[14] Please note that until 1990 data for West Germany and starting with 1991 data for entire Germany is used.

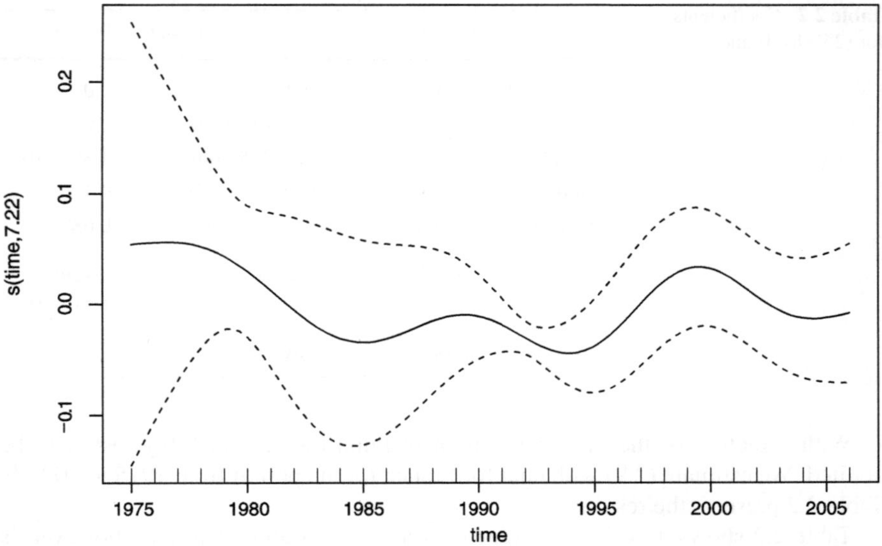

Fig. 2.6 Deviation sm(t) from the average coefficient for $b(t-1)$ for France

Fig. 2.7 Public debt to GDP ratio for Germany (1971–2006)

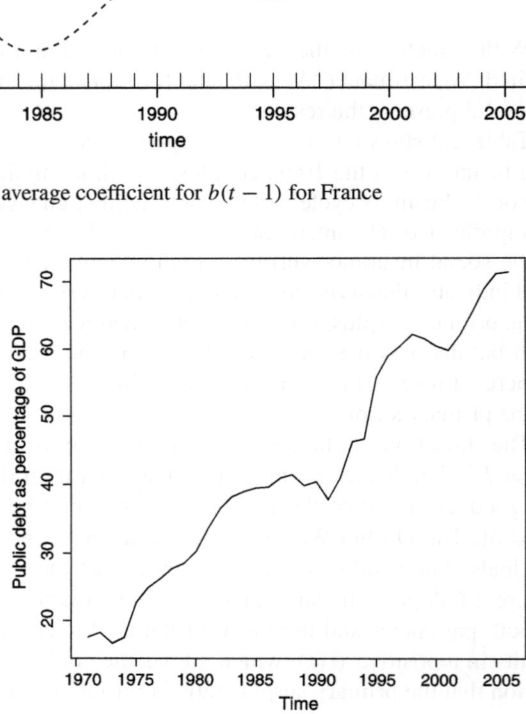

As Fig. 2.7 shows, Germany has suffered from high debt ratios since the middle of the 1970s. There are three major sections of debt ratio growth. First, in the mid-seventies until the late 1980s the debt ratio increased, which might have been due to the oil crisis and its aftermath and the following recession. That period is characterized by persistent primary deficits as picture 2.8 shows. After that the time up to 1990 was characterized by fiscal discipline with a declining debt ratio and primary surpluses. After German unification until the beginning of the new century another rapid increase in the debt ratio can be observed bringing that ratio from around 40

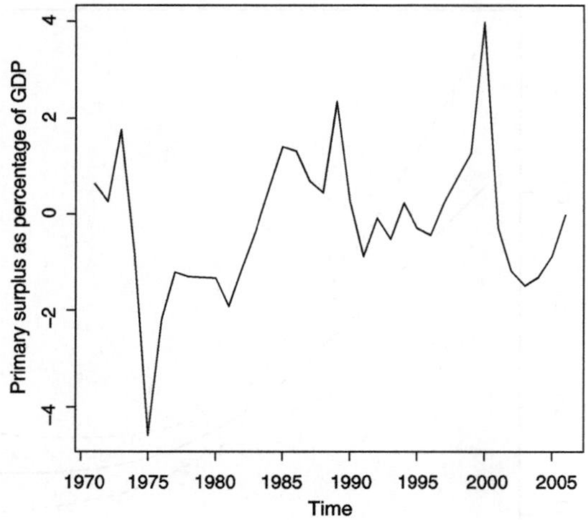

Fig. 2.8 Primary surplus to GDP ratio for Germany (1971–2006)

percent up to more than 60 percent. This comes along with primary deficits. The next increase starts in 2002 with a maximum of 71.3 percent of the debt ratio in 2006. The primary balance shows deficits for this period.

Estimating (2.9) with German data for the years from 1971 to 2006[15] gives results as shown in Table 2.3.

The coefficient of interest for public debt $b(t-1)$ is positive and significant at the 1 percent level. Again, this gives the mean of the coefficient for the time period under consideration so that we can conclude that German fiscal policy has followed a sustainable path. This also holds if the equation is estimated without the interest rate or without the business cycle variable. The intercept shows a negative sign and is highly significant. The business cycle has a negative sign suggesting that the government pursued a pro-cyclical fiscal policy, whereas the coefficient for the social insurance surplus ratio shows a positive sign and is highly significant. For the real interest rate no significant correlation can be noticed.

Table 2.3 Coefficients for (2.9) for Germany

	Coefficient	Stand. error (t-stat)	Pr($>t$)
Constant	−0.061	0.016 (−3.778)	0.0008
$b(t-1)$	0.145	0.049 (2.972)	0.006
Soc(t)	1.995	0.352 (5.674)	4.99×10^{-6}
int(t)	0.192	0.117 (1.694)	0.111
YVar(t)	−0.523	0.243 (−2.154)	0.040
sm(t)	edf 3.977	F 4.28	p-value 0.0020
	R^2(adj): 0.712	DW: 2.11	

[15] See OECD (2007a, 2007b) and International Statistical Yearbook (2007) for the data.

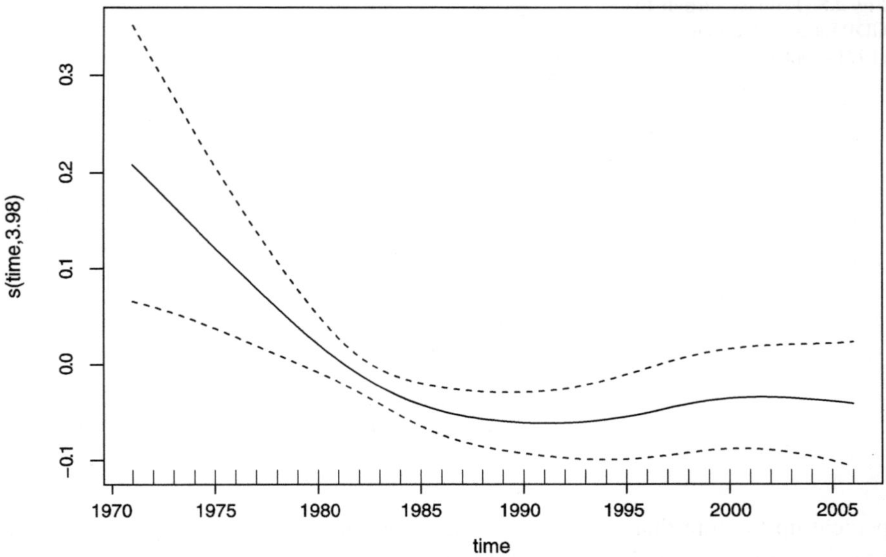

Fig. 2.9 Deviation sm(t) from the average coefficient for $b(t-1)$ for Germany

Again, the variable sm(t) gives the deviation of the coefficient for the debt ratio. Its estimated degrees of freedom are calculated with edf = 3.977. This smooth term with a p-value of 0.0020 is significant at the 1 percent level. Concerning the goodness of fit of the model R^2(adj) = 0.721 shows a high value and the Durbin-Watson test statistic DW = 2.11 shows no evidence for autocorrelation. These results lead to the conclusion that the coefficient for the debt ratio has not been constant for the observed period.

Figure 2.9 displays the path of the deviation from the mean of the reaction coefficient. In combination with the value given in Table 2.3 this picture shows that the time varying coefficient $\psi(t)$, that is given by the mean and the deviation from that mean, has been strictly positive for the years from 1971 until 2006. However, it can also be seen that the coefficient declined over time.

2.2.1.4 Italy

Within Europe the Italian public debt situation is one of the most challenging. As depicted in Fig. 2.10, Italy faces an extraordinary high public debt to GDP ratio. For the estimation, again general government gross financial liabilities as percentage of GDP and the primary surplus relative to GDP for the years 1975 to 2006 are used.[16]

[16]For the data see OECD (2003, 2007a). The debt ratio data is taken from the first source until 1998 and from the second source from 1999 on.

Fig. 2.10 Public debt to GDP ratio for Italy (1975–2006)

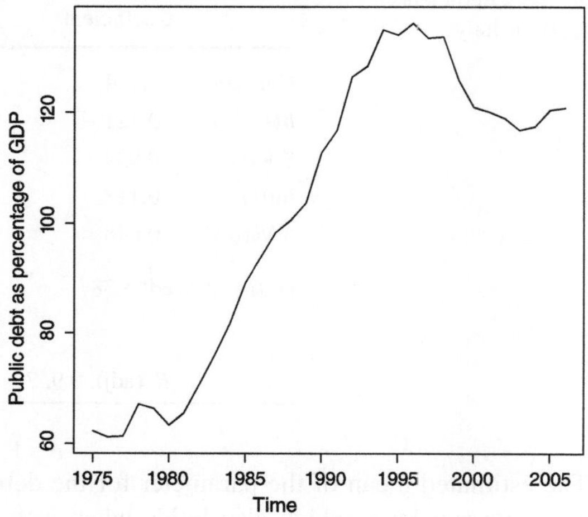

Figure 2.10 shows that starting at an initial value of about 60 percent the Italian debt ratio rapidly grew from the early eighties until the middle of the 1990s. It almost doubled to about 130 percent in the middle of the 1990s. The primary balance ratio in Fig. 2.11 shows permanent deficits until the early nineties. That changed for the years from 1992 until 2004, when surpluses could be realized. With the European Monetary Union ahead and the attained surpluses, a reduction in the debt ratio can be observed from 1997 onwards, although since 2004 the debt ratio started growing again accompanied by primary deficits.

Estimating equation (2.9) for the years from 1975 to 2006[17] gives results as shown in Table 2.4.

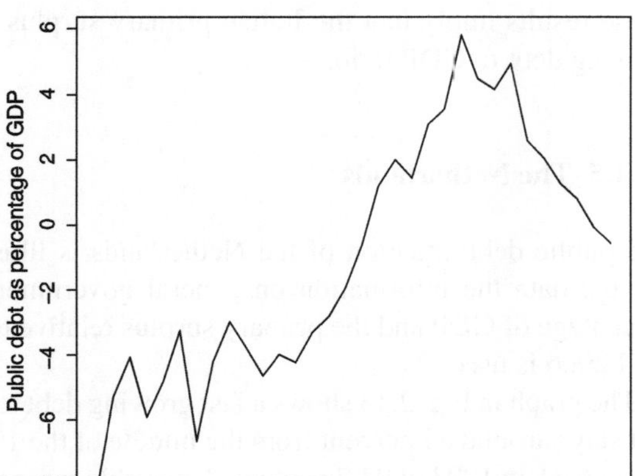

Fig. 2.11 Primary surplus to GDP ratio for Italy (1975–2006)

[17] See OECD (2003, 2007a, 2007b) for the data.

Table 2.4 Coefficients for (2.9) for Italy

	Coefficient	Stand. error (t-stat)	Pr(> t)
Constant	−0.124	0.048 (−2.594)	0.017
$b(t-1)$	0.121	0.051 (2.382)	0.027
Soc(t)	0.934	0.361 (2.591)	0.017
int(t)	0.118	0.126 (0.939)	0.358
YVar(t)	0.648	0.196 (3.306)	0.003
sm(t)	edf 5.387	F 7.67	p-value 5.42×10^{-5}
	R^2(adj): 0.957	DW: 2.16	

The estimated mean of the parameter for the debt ratio is significantly positive at the 5 percent level which also holds when estimated without the interest rate or without the business cycle variable. Hence, in spite of the strongly rising debt ratio in the 1970s and 1980s, Italian fiscal policy would be sustainable. Besides the intercept, the coefficients for the social insurance surplus and for the business cycle variable have a positive sign and are statistically significant while the parameter for the real interest rate is not significant.

Again, sm(t) measures the deviation from the mean of the coefficient for the public debt ratio. The estimated degrees of freedom for the smooth term are given with edf = 5.387 and a high significance is shown for it in Table 2.4. Evidently, the model fits quite good based on $R^2(\text{adj}) = 0.957$. The Durbin-Watson test statistic does not suggest that the residuals are correlated.

The time path sm(t) is shown in Fig. 2.12. The sum of the mean of the coefficient and the deviation from that mean is strictly positive for the entire sample period. These results imply that the Italian primary surplus to GDP ratio increased with a growing debt to GDP ratio.

2.2.1.5 The Netherlands

The public debt situation of the Netherlands is illustrated in Figs. 2.13 and 2.14. For the data the information on general government gross financial liabilities as percentage of GDP and the primary surplus relative to GDP for the years from 1980 until 2006 is used.[18]

The graph in Fig. 2.13 shows a fast growing debt to GDP ratio in the early eighties that stays around 85 percent from the middle of the 1980s to the middle of the 1990s with a peak in 1993 of 93.7 percent. A possible reason for this might be the aftermath of the second oil crisis. The primary balance in Fig. 2.14 shows deficits from 1986 onwards. That trend changed in 1991 to surpluses. A sharp decline in the debt ratio

[18] For the data see OECD (2007a).

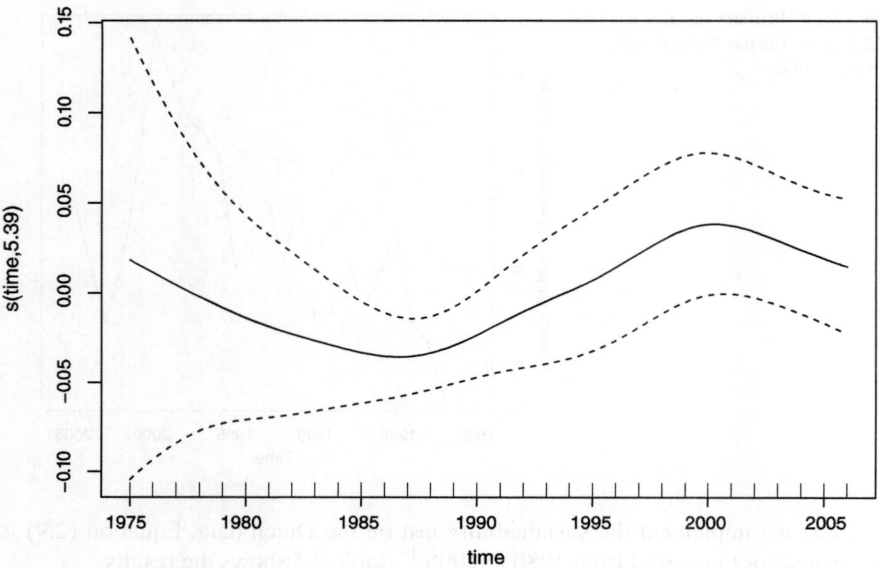

Fig. 2.12 Deviation sm(t) from the average coefficient for $b(t-1)$ for Italy

Fig. 2.13 Public debt to GDP ratio for the Netherlands (1980–2006)

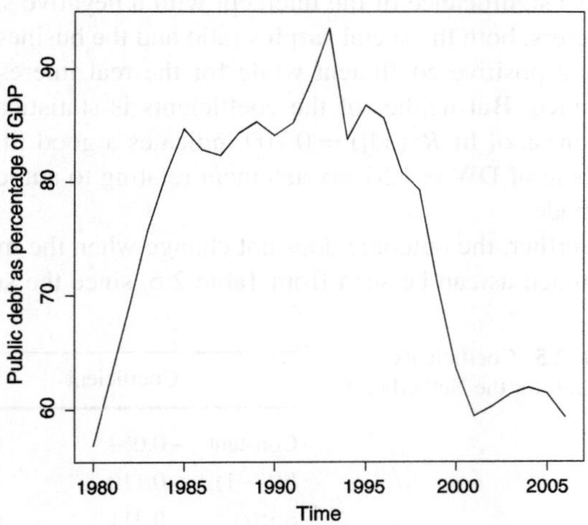

can be observed starting around 1996. The ratio dropped to a level of 59.4 percent. Except for 2003 only primary surpluses can be observed since the mid 1990s that are well above the average value for the total period leading to a sharp decline of the debt to GDP ratio. The evolution of the debt situation in the Netherlands since the early 1990s is basically due to successful macroeconomic reforms undertaken in the early 1980s.

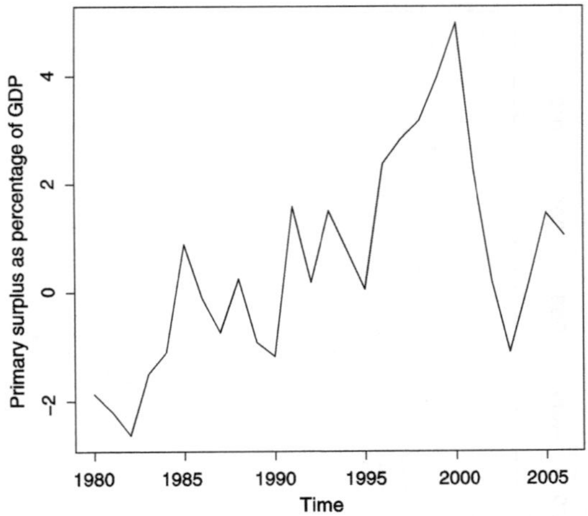

Fig. 2.14 Primary surplus to GDP ratio for the Netherlands (1980–2006)

Next we implement the sustainability test on the Dutch data. Equation (2.9) is estimated for the period from 1980 to 2006.[19] Table 2.5 shows the results.

In Table 2.5 the estimated coefficient for the public debt ratio is positive and significant at the 0.1 percent level. This does not change when the model is estimated without the interest rate or without the business cycle variable. In addition, Table 2.5 shows significance of the intercept with a negative sign. As concerns the other parameters, both the social surplus ratio and the business cycle variable are associated with a positive coefficient while for the real interest rate a negative parameter is obtained. But neither of the coefficients is statistically significant. Regarding the goodness of fit $R^2(\text{adj}) = 0.709$ indicates a good fit. With the Durbin-Watson test statistic of DW $= 1.51$ no statement relating to autocorrelation of the residuals can be made.

Further, the outcome does not change when the model is estimated with a linear approach as can be seen from Table 2.6, since the smooth parameter with edf $= 1$

Table 2.5 Coefficients for (2.9) for the Netherlands

	Coefficient	Stand. error (t-stat)	Pr($> t$)
Constant	−0.064	0.018 (−3.614)	0.002
$b(t-1)$	0.110	0.022 (4.908)	7.45×10^{-5}
Soc(t)	0.311	0.202 (1.544)	0.137
int(t)	−0.403	0.290 (−1.388)	0.180
YVar(t)	0.925	0.741 (1.248)	0.226
sm(t)	edf 1	F 0.188	p-value 0.669
	R^2(adj): 0.709	DW: 1.51	

[19]See OECD (2007a, 2007b) for the data.

Table 2.6 Estimation results for the Netherlands assuming a linear model

	Coefficient	Stand. error (t-stat)	Pr($> t$)
Constant	−0.061	0.016 (−3.822)	0.0009
$b(t-1)$	0.110	0.022 (5.038)	4.81×10^{-5}
Soc(t)	0.350	0.178 (1.967)	0.062
int(t)	−0.500	0.182 (−2.740)	0.012
YVar(t)	0.723	0.564 (1.280)	0.214
	R^2(adj): 0.720	DW: 1.51	

shows no evidence for a change over time.[20] The only difference is that the social surplus and the interest rate are now significantly correlated with the primary surplus, where the coefficient of the interest rate has a negative sign.

2.2.1.6 Portugal

For Portugal Figs. 2.15 and 2.16 show the public debt and primary balance position for the years from 1978 to 2006.[21]

In Fig. 2.15 a sudden rise in the debt to GDP ratio begins with the early 1980s.[22] As shown in Fig. 2.16, until 1986 merely primary deficits relative to GDP were

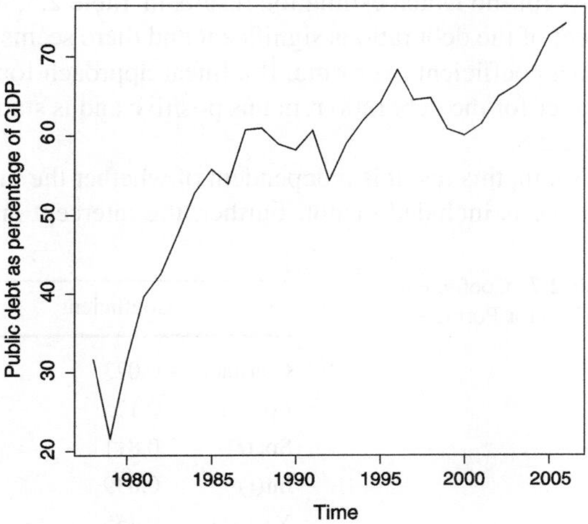

Fig. 2.15 Public debt to GDP ratio for Portugal (1978–2006)

[20]In that case the estimation is performed with lm in R (Version 2.5.0).

[21]See OECD (2003, 2007a) for the data. The debt ratio data is taken from the first source until 1995 and from the second source from 1996 on.

[22]Sustainability of public debt policy in Portugal over long time horizon of 140 years has been performed by Correia et al. (2008).

Fig. 2.16 Primary surplus to GDP ratio for Portugal (1978–2006)

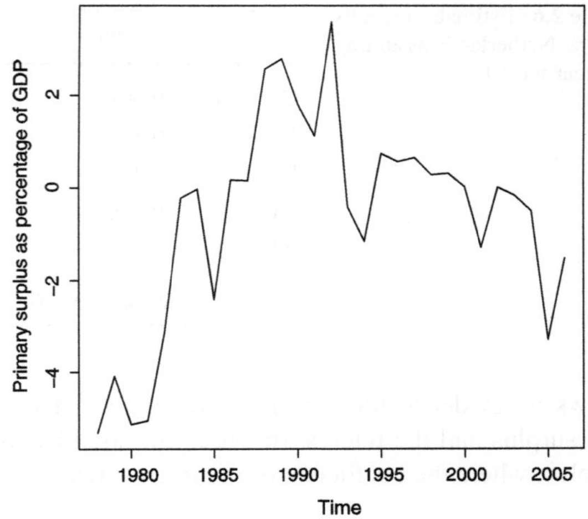

realized. Around 1990, the debt ratio remained around 60 percent. This period is accompanied by positive primary surplus ratios. Another episode of debt ratio increase begins in the middle of the 1990s. After that the debt ratio declines. With the beginning of the new century the public debt to GDP ratio grows again, which comes along with primary deficit ratios.

We estimate (2.9) for Portugal for the years from 1978 to 2006.[23] The results are summarized in Table 2.7.

As for the Dutch estimation results in Table 2.5, for Portugal the estimated coefficient of the debt ratio is significant and there seems to be no evidence for a change in that coefficient over time. If a linear approach for the estimation is used, the parameter for the debt ratio remains positive and is statistically significant as shown in Table 2.8.

Again, this result is independent of whether the interest rate or the business cycle variable is included or not. Further, the intercept and the social insurance surplus

Table 2.7 Coefficients for (2.9) for Portugal

	Coefficient	Stand. error (t-stat)	Pr($> t$)
Constant	−0.073	0.026 (−2.821)	0.0097
$b(t-1)$	0.125	0.047 (2.647)	0.014
Soc(t)	0.811	0.375 (2.162)	0.041
int(t)	0.039	0.118 (0.330)	0.744
YVar(t)	0.455	0.295 (1.544)	0.136
sm(t)	edf 1	F 0.041	p-value 0.842
	R^2(adj): 0.798	DW: 2.01	

[23] See OECD (2003, 2007a, 2007b) for the data.

Table 2.8 Estimation results for Portugal assuming a linear model

	Coefficient	Stand. error (t-stat)	Pr($>t$)
Constant	−0.069	0.017 (−4.135)	0.0004
$b(t-1)$	0.117	0.027 (4.409)	0.0002
Soc(t)	0.826	0.361 (2.288)	0.031
int(t)	0.044	0.112 (0.393)	0.698
YVar(t)	0.482	0.258 (1.872)	0.074
	R^2(adj): 0.807	DW: 2.02	

ratio are statistically significantly correlated with the primary surplus to GDP ratio. This remains valid when a linear approach is estimated as the estimation result given in Table 2.8 demonstrates. The coefficients for the real interest rate and for the business cycle variable are positive but insignificant. With $R^2(\text{adj}) = 0.798$ the fit is relatively good and the Durbin-Watson test statistic shows no evidence for autocorrelation. Based on these empirical results there is evidence that the primary surplus ratio increases as the public debt ratio rises.

2.2.1.7 USA

For the USA Figs. 2.17 and 2.18 show the public debt and primary balance position for the years from 1974 to 2003.[24]

In Fig. 2.17 an increase in the debt to GDP ratio begins with the early 1980s. As shown in Fig. 2.18, the primary surplus relative to GDP has declined from the early

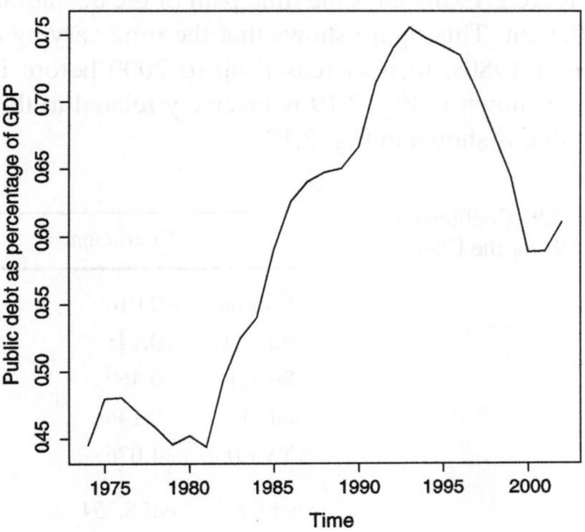

Fig. 2.17 Public debt to GDP ratio for the USA (1974–2003)

[24]See OECD (2003) for the data.

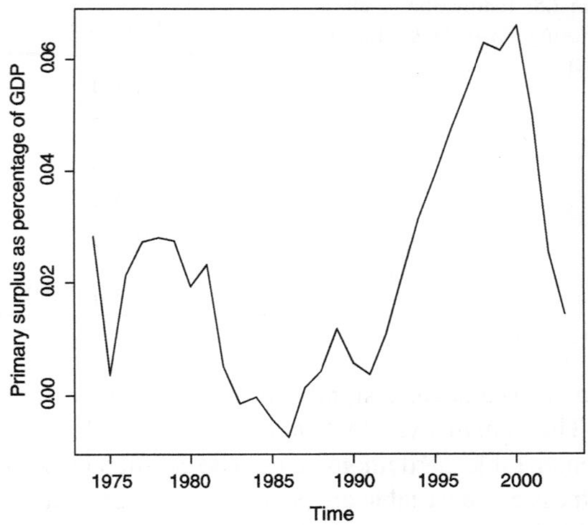

Fig. 2.18 Primary surplus to GDP ratio for the USA (1974–2003)

1980s until the mid 1980s when the first Gulf war took place leading to the rise in the debt ratio. In the 1990s during the Clinton administration the primary surplus rose from about 1 percent of GDP to 6 percent of GDP. As a consequence, the debt to GDP ratio declined from 75 percent in the early 1990s to less than 60 percent by the year 2000.

Estimating (2.9) for the USA for the years from 1974 to 2003 gives the results summarized in Table 2.9.

Table 2.9 shows that the estimated average coefficient of the debt ratio is positive and statistically significant. Further, there is strong evidence for a change in that coefficient over time.

Figure 2.19 displays the time path of the deviation from the mean of the reaction coefficient. This figure shows that the time varying coefficient $\psi(t)$ declined until the mid 1980s, then increased up to 2000 before it began to decline again. The picture shown in Fig. 2.19 is inversely related to the evolution of the debt to GDP ratio that is shown in Fig. 2.17.

Table 2.9 Coefficients for (2.9) for the USA

	Coefficient	Stand. error (t-stat)	Pr($> t$)
Constant	−0.016	0.029 (−0.531)	0.603
$b(t-1)$	0.145	0.05 (2.882)	0.011
Soc(t)	0.467	0.184 (2.544)	0.021
int(t)	0.146	0.066 (2.215)	0.041
YVar(t)	4.076	1.498 (2.720)	0.015
sm(t)	edf 8.354	F 119.2	p-value 2.39×10^{-13}
	R^2(adj): 0.978	DW: 2.55	

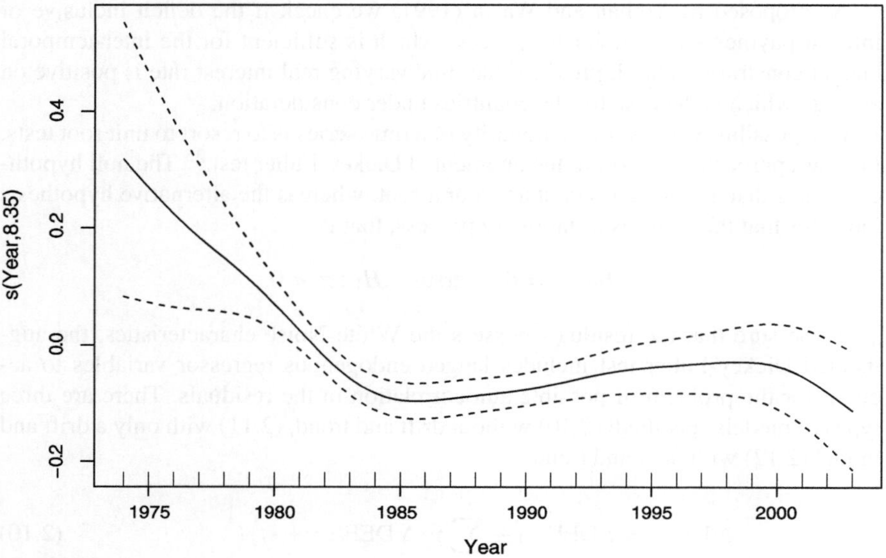

Fig. 2.19 Deviation sm(t) from the average coefficient for $b(t-1)$ for USA

Again, the estimation result is independent of whether the interest rate or the business cycle variable is included or not. Besides the coefficient of the debt ratio, the social insurance surplus ratio, the interest rate and the business cycle ratio are statistically significantly correlated with the primary surplus to GDP ratio. With $R^2(\text{adj}) = 0.978$ the fit is quite good while the Durbin-Watson test statistic is inconclusive. Based on our empirical results there is evidence that the primary surplus ratio increases as the public debt ratio rises in the USA for the period considered in our study.

2.2.2 *Analysis of the Deficit Inclusive of Interest Payments*

In the last section we tested how the primary surplus relative to GDP reacts to variations in the debt ratio. We found that in all countries the primary surplus to GDP ratio is a positive function of the debt to GDP ratio. However, in all countries the debt ratios are clearly increasing over time, except for the Netherlands and, possibly, for the USA.

Therefore, we want to get additional insight into the question of whether debt policies are sustainable by looking at stationarity properties of the deficit inclusive of interest payments. To get the real deficit inclusive of interest payments, we first divide public debt by the GDP deflator, $B_n(t)/P(t) = B(t)$ and, then, we calculate first differences of this series, which gives the real budget deficit or the deficit inclusive of interest payments, $B(t) - B(t-1) = \Delta B(t) = \text{DEF}(t)$. The plots of these series are given in the appendix to this section.

As proposed by Trehan and Walsh (1991) we check if the deficit inclusive of interest payments is a stationary process which is sufficient for the inter-temporal budget constraint to hold, provided the time varying real interest rate is positive on average which is the case for the countries under consideration.

One possibility to test for stationarity of a time series is to resort to unit root tests. For our approach we resort to the augmented Dickey-Fuller test.[25] The null hypothesis states that a time series contains a unit root, whereas the alternative hypothesis indicates that the series is a stationary process, that is:

$$H_0 : \pi = 0 \quad \text{versus} \quad H_1 : \pi < 0.$$

To be sure that the residuals possess the White Noise characteristics, the augmented Dickey-Fuller test includes lagged endogenous regressor variables to account for the problem of possible autocorrelation in the residuals. There are three types of models specified: (2.10) without drift and trend, (2.11) with only a drift and model (2.12) with drift and trend:

$$\Delta \,\mathrm{DEF}_t = \pi \,\mathrm{DEF}_{t-1} + \sum_{j=1}^{k} \gamma_j \Delta \,\mathrm{DEF}_{t-j} + \epsilon_t, \tag{2.10}$$

$$\Delta \,\mathrm{DEF}_t = \beta_0 + \pi \,\mathrm{DEF}_{t-1} + \sum_{j=1}^{k} \gamma_j \Delta \,\mathrm{DEF}_{t-j} + \epsilon_t, \tag{2.11}$$

$$\Delta \,\mathrm{DEF}_t = \beta_0 + \pi \,\mathrm{DEF}_{t-1} + \beta_2 t + \sum_{j=1}^{k} \gamma_j \Delta \,\mathrm{DEF}_{t-j} + \epsilon_t. \tag{2.12}$$

The choice of the type of model depends on the data generating process, which is mostly unknown, but there is a guideline for the model selection, which is described for example in Enders (2005) or in Pfaff (2006).[26]

For the correct estimation the appropriate amount of lags k is to be determined and the suitable model type for the data needs to be specified. Below, this process is assigned to the real budget deficit series and used to analyze the data for the selected countries.

Table 2.10 shows the results of testing for unit roots with the augmented Dickey-Fuller Test.[27]

Concerning the appropriate estimation we first checked how many lags are necessary to obtain a model that shows no autocorrelation in the residuals. For the choice

---

[25] See for example Enders (2005) pp. 221 et seqq.

[26] See especially Enders (2005) pp. 254 to 258 and Pfaff (2006) pp. 27 et seqq.

[27] All tests are performed with the package *urca* in R (Version 2.5.0). See OECD (2003, 2007a), International Statistical Yearbook (2006, 2007) for the data. The time period of the estimations above is retained. Concerning Germany's deficit until 1990 data for West Germany is used. For Italy and Portugal the change of source is after 1998 and 1995. For the critical values see for example Fuller (1976) Table 8.5.2 on p. 373 or Enders (2005) Table A on p. 419.

Table 2.10 Unit root test results for the selected countries

	Aug. Dickey-Fuller	Est. model type
Austria	−4.78***	Trend and Drift, Lags: 1
France	−3.27*	Trend and Drift, Lags: 2
Germany	−3.71**	Trend and Drift, Lags: 3
Italy	−1.07	None, Lags: 1
Netherlands	−4.64***	Trend and Drift, Lags: 0
Portugal	−6.30***	Trend and Drift, Lags: 0
USA	−1.65*	None, Lags: 0
H_0 is rejected at	***(1% level)	**(5% level) *(10% level)

of the lag length, the *general-to-specific* method[28] is used, that is the individual model is estimated with a relatively high number of lags, that is gradually reduced until the t-statistic on the last lag is significant. Further, this lag length is judged based on the autocorrelation and partial autocorrelation function of the residuals as well as on the Box-Ljung test in order to strengthen the decision on the number of lags.

Moreover, staying close to the model type selection guideline mentioned above, we first estimated all models in the least restrictive way, that is inclusive of a trend and a drift. If the computed test statistic value is smaller than the $\hat{\tau}$ critical value[29] it is sufficient to stop the analysis at this point and accept H_1 that there is no unit root indicating that the analyzed time series is a stationary process.[30] This is possible for the deficit series inclusive of interest payments for Austria, France, Germany, the Netherlands, Portugal and the USA.

In case of Italy the H_0 hypothesis $\pi = 0$ cannot be rejected. Hence, it needs to be checked, if a trend is actually at hand. Therefore, it is to test if $\beta_2 = 0$ given $\pi = 0$. This is possible with an F-test related statistic ϕ_3.[31] If the computed test statistic value exceeds the critical value[32] the alternative hypothesis is accepted, that the restriction is binding. Estimating with a trend, an intercept and one lag for Italy, we get $\phi_3 = 1.78$, which is smaller than the critical value at the 10% level (5.61 for 50 observations, 5.91 for a sample size of 25). Consequently, the regression without the trend but only an intercept is estimated. Again, the H_0 Hypothesis $\pi = 0$ cannot be rejected. For that reason it needs to be checked if the intercept term is significant, $\beta_0 = 0$ given $\pi = 0$ with the ϕ_1 statistic. The value for ϕ_1 is $\phi_1 = 1.47$, so that H_0 cannot be rejected for Italy (the critical value at 10% is 3.94 for 50

---

28 See for example Enders (2005), especially pp. 226 et seqq. and Pfaff (2006), especially p. 27.

29 See for example Fuller (1976) Table 8.5.2. on p. 373.

30 See also Enders (2005) Fig. 4.7 on p. 257 and Pfaff (2006) Fig. 2.3 on p. 29.

31 See for example Enders (2005) pp. 222 et seqq.

32 The critical values for the ϕ_1, ϕ_2, ϕ_3 are for example given in Dickey and Fuller (1981) Tables IV, V, VI on p. 1063.

and 4.12 for 25 observations). Finally, the equation with neither an intercept nor a trend variable, (2.10), needs to be estimated. This results in a test statistic of -1.07 compared with the 10% critical value of $\hat{\tau} = -1.61$ (-1.60) for a sample size of 50 (25). Hence, it is possible to conclude that for the Italian budget deficit series the hypothesis of containing a unit root cannot be rejected.

However, looking at the series of the Italian deficit it can be realized that it is extremely oscillating. Figure 2.20 shows a simple p-spline estimation giving Italian public deficit as a function of time, where the average is normalized to zero. The estimation suggests that there is a positive trend in the deficit during the 1980s and a negative trend in the 1990s. Hence, the fact that the Italian budget deficit is not stationary should not be misinterpreted that it is characterized by a positive trend throughout the sample period.

Summarizing the results of this section, Table 2.10 shows that the null hypothesis of containing a unit root is rejected in almost all cases for suitable significance levels. These test results indicate that the series of the budget deficit inclusive of interest payments are stationary processes.[33] These findings are consistent with the results from the estimations above using the regression approach. It implies that for the countries under consideration the inter-temporal budget constraint holds and they act in a sustainable way, although they show high or growing debt ratios and budget deficits.

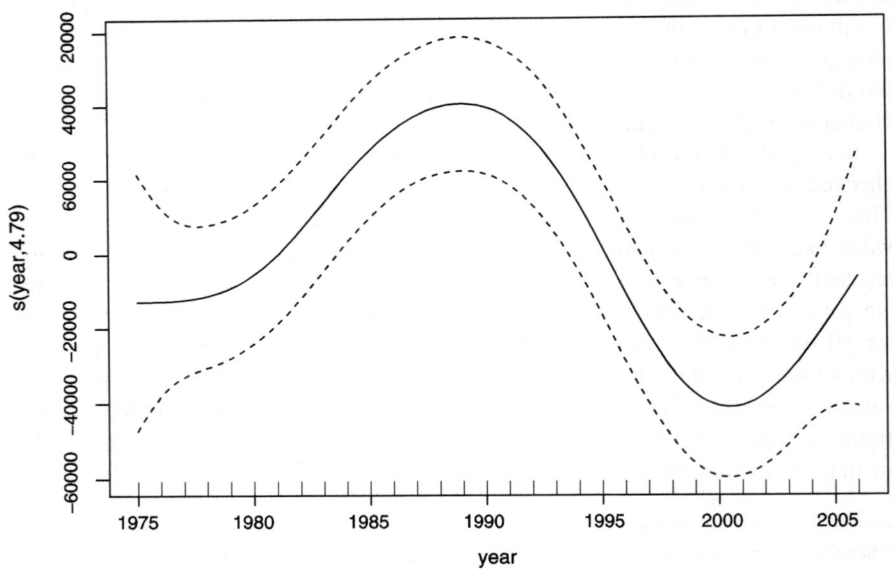

Fig. 2.20 Italian budget deficit as a function of time

[33] Additionally, the Phillips-Perron test can be applied. If the application is possible, it confirms the above stated outcomes for the selected countries.

2.2.3 Conclusion

In this section, we have analyzed whether selected countries of the euro area have followed sustainable debt policies over the last 30 years and we also studied the USA. We did this by analyzing the reaction of the primary surplus to GDP ratio to variations in the debt to GDP ratio which is a powerful test. However, we also argued that a positive reaction does not guarantee that the debt ratio remains bounded which is necessary for a sustainable debt policy in the long-run. Therefore, we also tested for stationarity of the public deficit inclusive of interest payments in order to gain additional insight.

Our results suggest that, for the euro area, three different groups can be distinguished. First, the Netherlands have undergone substantial economic reforms in the 1980s that also stabilized public debt. The Netherlands is the only country with a declining debt ratio and clearly follows a sustainable debt policy. The second group of countries consists of Austria, Germany and Portugal. Although these countries have experienced rising debt ratios over the period under consideration both types of tests suggest that these governments have followed sustainable policies. Finally, France and Italy seem to pursue sustainable debt policies, too. But for France, the statistical significance of the estimation results is clearly smaller than for the countries of the second group. Italy is characterized by strongly oscillating public deficits that first rise and then decline.

Overall, the empirical tests show that there is evidence that the primary surplus increases in reaction to a rise in public debt, both measured relative to GDP, implying sustainability of public debt for the countries of the euro area. However, it was also seen that the debt ratio has risen over time, with the exception of the Netherlands. This shows that the reaction coefficient was not large enough in order to prevent the debt ratio from rising over time. But, in the long-run, the debt ratio must become constant as our theoretical considerations in Sect. 2.1 have shown. Otherwise sustainability cannot be assured.

For the USA, we also found a positive reaction coefficient on average and the public deficit including interest payments is a stationary time series. Hence, public debt has turned out to be sustainable for the time period considered in our study. This is in line with the outcome obtained by Bohn (1998) for a longer time series. In particular, we again found statistical evidence for a positive dependence of the primary surplus relative to GDP on the public debt to GDP ratio. This is somewhat important because this rule will be resorted to in the theoretical models analyzed below.

Comparing our study with other studies in the literature (for a survey see Afonso 2005) one realizes that earlier studies that performed time series analysis with respect to the series of public debt or discounted debt rather favoured the conclusion that debt policies in Europe are not sustainable. More recent studies, in particular those that test how the primary surplus reacts to public debt, tend to conclude that debt policies are sustainable. This may be due to the methodology applied but it may also be the result of stabilization policies in Europe in the late 1990s.

But it should be noted that there are additional aspects that have to be considered. Sustainability of debt policy in the past does not necessarily lead to sustainable future fiscal policies. Due to the decline of the European population, the burden of debt service for future generations can become a severe problem if public debt will not be effectively reduced in the near future. Therefore, primary surpluses are required to reduce the public debt, which needs higher revenues or a cut in spending. For the countries of the euro area, analyzed in this study, a reduction of productive public spending for the time period under consideration can be observed, that is all of them face a decrease in public investment, which is illustrated in the appendix to this section. In some cases now it is less than half of the initial value of the period considered. All in all, although sustainable fiscal policies seem to be given, for politicians this result rather should be a challenge or a chance for the future than an evidence for relief and settling back at the moment.

2.2.4 Appendix

2.2.4.1 Budget Deficits

These graphs show the real public deficit inclusive of interest payments in millions of euro (of the year 2000) of the selected euro area countries (Figs. 2.21–2.27). For the USA, the deficit is in millions of dollar (of the year 1996). Positive values indicate deficits, negative values indicate surpluses. The period as the same as that for which the estimations were performed.[34]

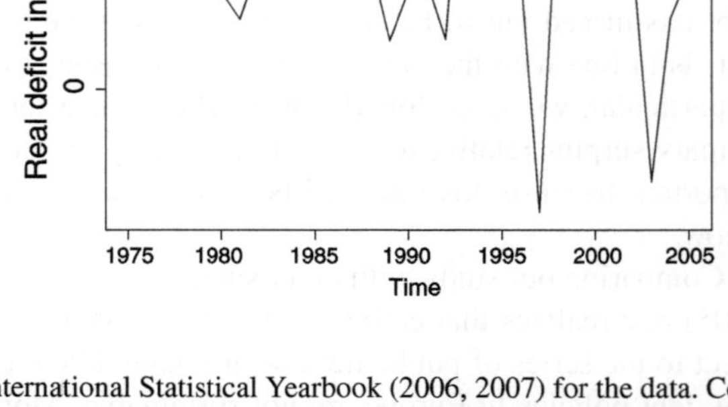

Fig. 2.21 Budget deficit for Austria

[34]See OECD (2003, 2007a) and International Statistical Yearbook (2006, 2007) for the data. Concerning Germany's deficit until 1990 data for West Germany are used. For Italy and Portugal the change of source is after 1998 and 1995. The outlier in the German deficit in 1995 is due to the take-over of the debt of the Treuhandanstalt and of the former East German housing sector by the public sector.

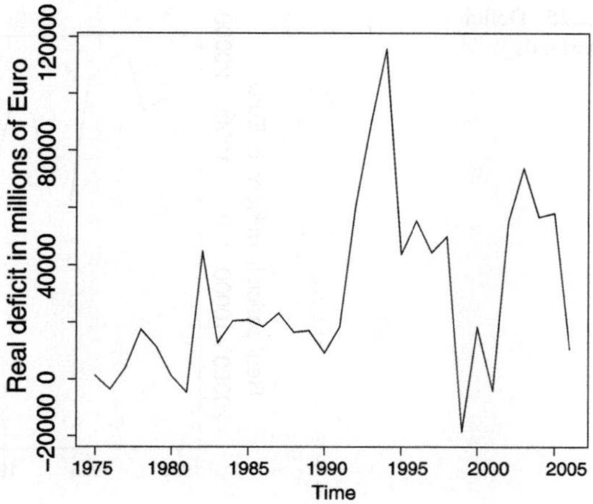

Fig. 2.22 Budget deficit for France

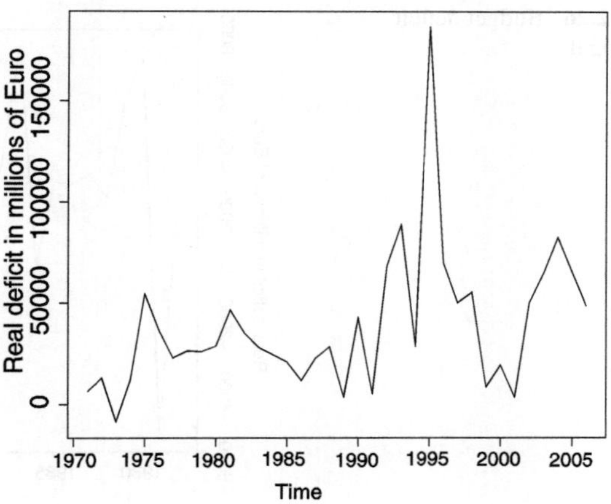

Fig. 2.23 Budget deficit Germany

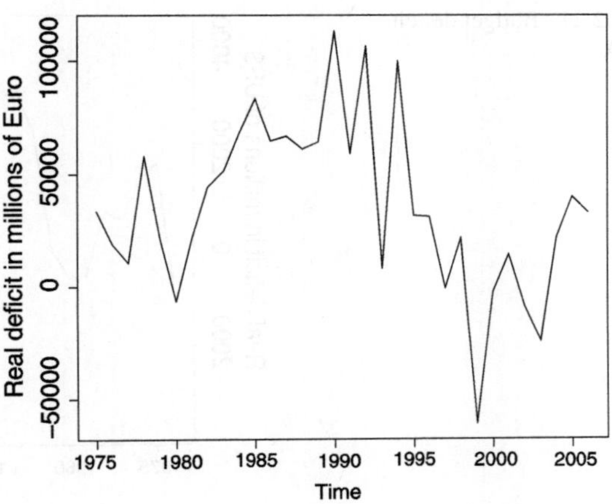

Fig. 2.24 Budget deficit for Italy

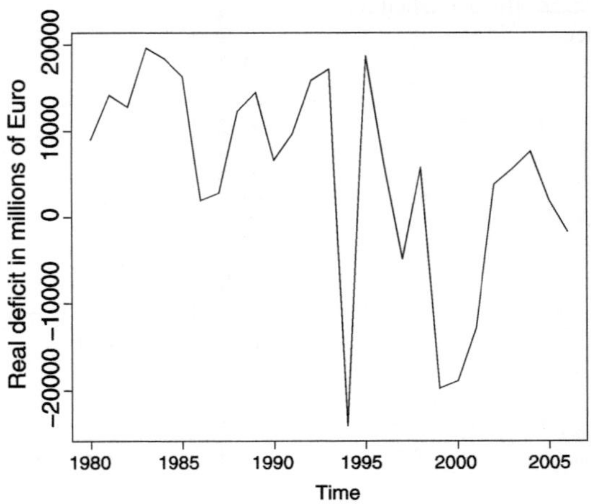

Fig. 2.25 Deficit Netherlands

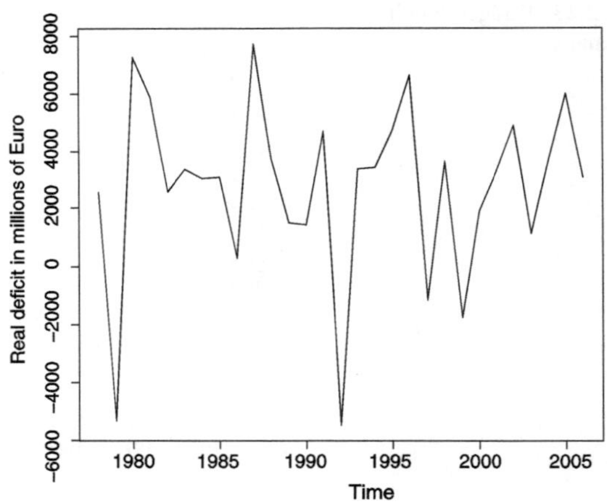

Fig. 2.26 Budget deficit Portugal

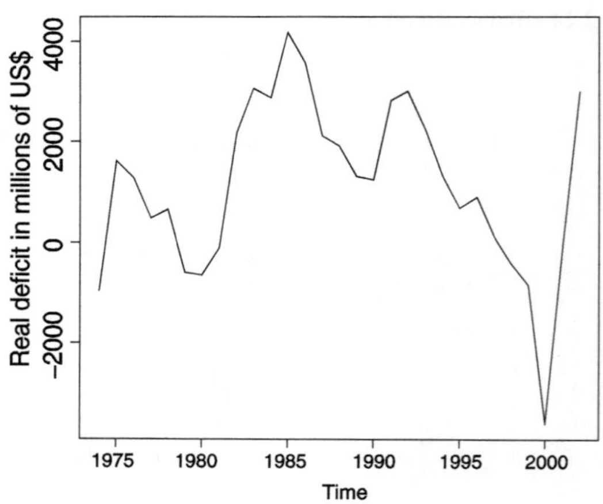

Fig. 2.27 Budget deficit USA

2.2.4.2 Public Investment

The following figures give public investment expenditures relative to GDP for the European countries in our sample (Figs. 2.28–2.33).[35]

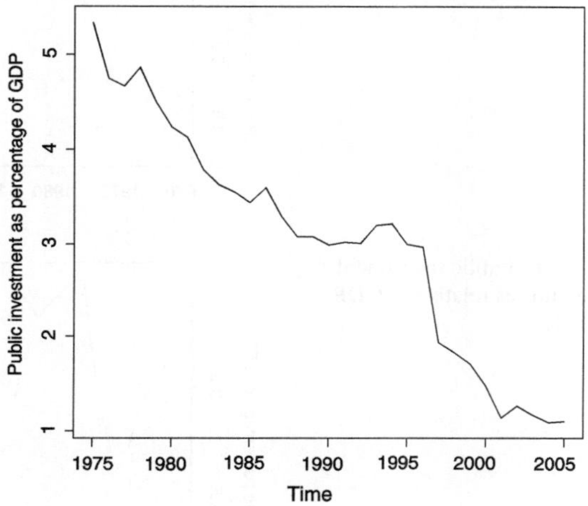

Fig. 2.28 Public investment expenditures relative to GDP for Austria

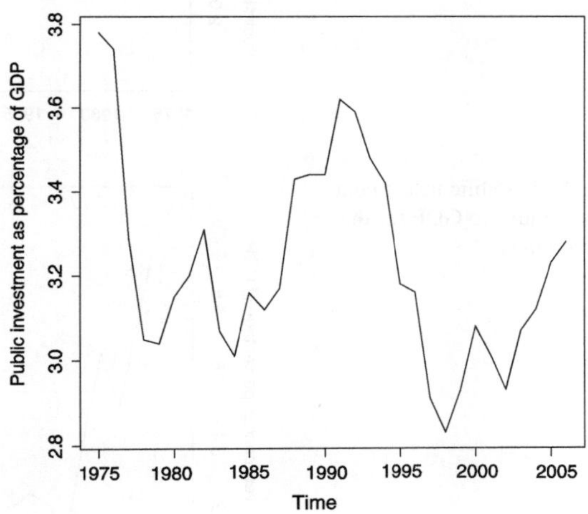

Fig. 2.29 Public investment expenditures relative to GDP for France

[35]See OECD (2007a, 2007b) for the data. Public investment is measured as government fixed capital formation. Concerning Germany's public investment until 1990 data for West Germany and from 1991 on for entire Germany is used.

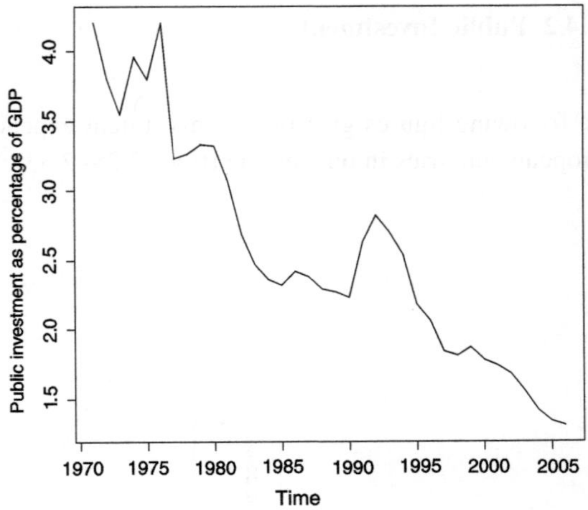

Fig. 2.30 Public investment expenditures relative to GDP for Germany

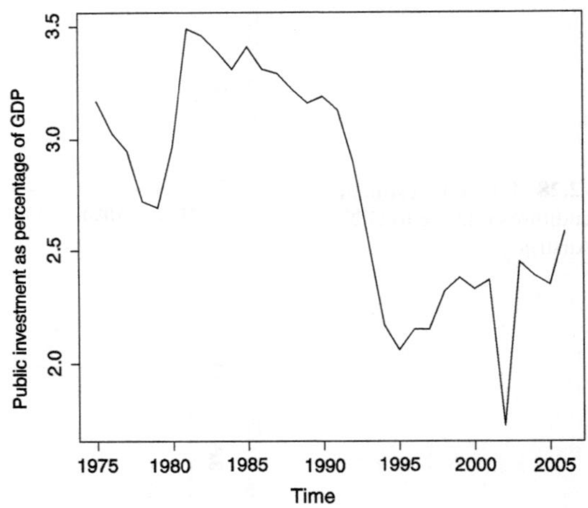

Fig. 2.31 Public investment expenditures relative to GDP for Italy

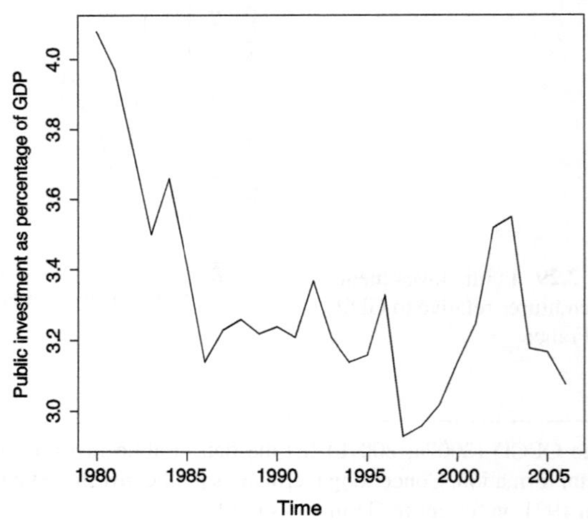

Fig. 2.32 Public investment expenditures to GDP for the Netherlands

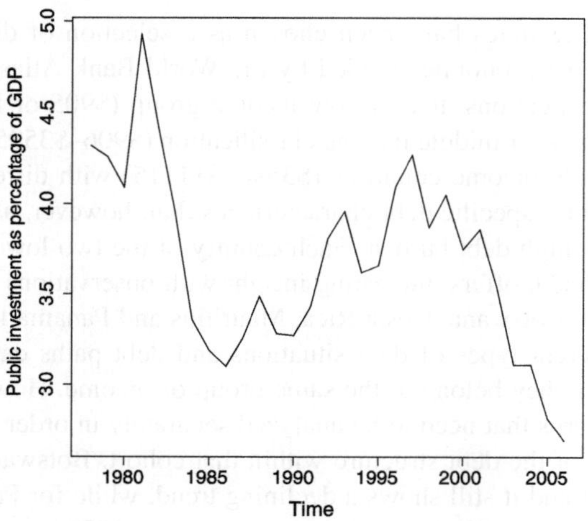

Fig. 2.33 Public investment expenditures relative to GDP for Portugal

2.3 Empirical Evidence for Developing Countries

Prevalent public deficits as well as growing debt levels and debt to GDP ratios have become a severe problem in many parts of the world, as already pointed out in the last section. Especially since the 1970s the unbalanced budgets have put a high burden on the governments of the affected countries. This fact is not only observed in the modern European and North American countries but in part also holds for newly industrializing and developing countries in Asia, Latin America and Africa (cf. Fincke and Greiner 2009). In particular, developing countries are rather vulnerable to debt crises as the 1980s and 1990s have shown. For some countries, this is due to the heavy dependence on raw materials as exporting goods but also to the fact that most of the debt is held by foreign countries in foreign currencies.

From the economic point of view the important question in this context is: are the governments of the developing countries able to react to the persistent budget deficits and growing debt in a sustainable manner? In this section we test whether governments of selected developing countries in Africa and Latin America have pursued sustainable debt policies.

The countries we consider are Botswana, Costa Rica, Mauritius, Panama, Rwanda and Tunisia. Rwanda is classified as low income country, Tunisia belongs to the lower middle income countries and Botswana, Costa Rica, Mauritius and Panama belong to the upper middle income group.[36] Independent of the level of income, they all suffer from high and growing debt to GDP ratios, with the exception of Botswana. In contrast to a similar approach for mainly Asian and South American countries by Sawada (1994) that only considers external debt, we focus on analyzing the overall debt situation, with total debt being calculated by the sum of foreign and domestic debt, in order to reveal the whole particular economic condition of the countries.

---

[36] According to the 'World Bank Atlas Method' classification, see World Bank (2008a).

The states have been chosen as a selection of different nations that represent diverse economies graded by the World Bank Atlas Method within the last three classifications, that is, low income group ($905 or less), Rwanda in this chapter, then lower middle income classification ($906–$3595), Tunisia, and a bale of upper middle income countries ($3596–$11115) with different economic structures and country specific debt characteristics that, however, all face or had been confronted by a high debt burden. Each country of the two lowest classifications, Tunisia and Rwanda, offers interesting insight with observations over quite a long time period. With Botswana, Costa Rica, Mauritius and Panama four countries with completely different types of debt situations and debt paths can be combined as one cohort since they belong to the same group of income. However they show different debt patterns that need to be analyzed separately in order to catch the variety and diversity of the debt structure within that cohort. Botswana has remarkably reduced its debt and it still shows a declining trend, while for Panama the debt ratio shows an almost steadily increasing shape from the 1970s onwards. Concerning Mauritius, a peak during the eighties had been reduced and debt could be successfully stabilized whereas for Costa Rica a low value around 1990 could not have been tightened. Therefore, these selected countries illustrate and cover a variety of different situations of developing countries and show interesting insights and possible useful examples.

Additionally and maybe even more important the relatively long, reliable and incessant time series allow a helpful continuous observance and thus permit a more holistic approach due to the several periods of study.

2.3.1 The Estimation Strategy

Our estimation strategy is the same as the one applied to developed countries in the last subsection. We begin with a description of the fiscal situation for each country. Then, we analyze whether the governments were able to react to higher debt levels by increasing their primary surpluses. Additionally, we test for stationarity of the total deficits in the economies we study. As concerns public debt, we take the sum of foreign and domestic debt.

As regards the empirical estimation of the reaction of the primary surplus relative to GDP we recall that, as for developed countries, we assume that the tax smoothing hypothesis holds, according to that the primary deficit should be used to smooth out variations in expenditures and revenues. Thus, we assume that the primary surplus relative to GDP depends on business cycles, YVar, and on deviations of public spending from its trend, GVar, besides depending on the public debt ratio. The variable YVar gives the deviation of real GDP from its trend and was computed using the Hodrick-Prescott filter. Positive values for YVar indicate booms and negative values indicate recessions. GVar gives the deviation of real public spending from its normal value with positive values indicating expenditures above the normal level and vice versa. The definition is oriented on Bohn's GVar variable.[37] We calculated it as $\text{GVar}_t = (G_t - G_t^*)$ with G_t for real public spending and G_t^* being its trend obtained from the Hodrick-Prescott filter.

Hence, like Bohn (1998) we estimate for the first test the following equation,

$$s(t) = \phi_0 + \psi(t)b(t-1) + \phi_1 \,\text{GVar}(t) + \phi_2 \,\text{YVar}(t) + \epsilon(t), \tag{2.13}$$

with $\epsilon(t)$ an error term, which is assumed to be i.i.d. $N(0, \sigma^2)$. Further, we assume that the lagged debt ratio $b(t-1)$ affects the primary surplus ratio, in order to take account of endogeneity.

For the second test, as supposed by Trehan and Walsh (1991), we estimate the following Augmented Dickey Fuller Test,[38]

$$\begin{aligned} &H_0 : \pi = 0, \quad H_1 : \pi < 0, \\ &\Delta\,\text{DEF}_t = \beta_0 + \pi\,\text{DEF}_{t-1} + \beta_2 t + \sum_{j=1}^{k} \gamma_j \Delta\,\text{DEF}_{t-j} + \epsilon_t. \end{aligned} \tag{2.14}$$

For the estimation the suitable model type for the data needs to be specified. The deficit DEF is the first difference of the level of real total debt, the sum of foreign and domestic debt, divided by the GDP deflator.

The estimations are done with R (Version 2.5.0). The first test is estimated with package mgcv (Version 1.3–23) that uses spline smoothing. Those results are more robust compared to OLS estimation results and it is possible for ψ to vary with time. The Durbin-Watson test statistic is calculated with package car. The second test is estimated with package urca. The Box-Ljung test is implemented in package stats. All data are annual and have been taken from International Financial Statistics of the IMF Database, published in the (International Statistical Yearbook 2007) unless otherwise noted.

2.3.2 Estimation Results

2.3.2.1 Botswana

First, we take a look at the South African country Botswana. In Figs. 2.34 and 2.35 the public debt ratio and the primary surplus relative to GDP for the years from 1978 until 2003 are depicted.[39]

The overall trend of the debt ratio shown in Fig. 2.34 is declining. With an initial value of 30 percent in 1978 and another rise in the early eighties, which might be

[37] For further information see Bohn (1998).

[38] For detailed information see for example Enders (2005), especially Chap. 4, pp. 211–267.

[39] Please notice that due to data availability Botswana's data are taken from International Statistical Yearbook (2006).

Fig. 2.34 Public debt to GDP ratio for Botswana (1978–2003)

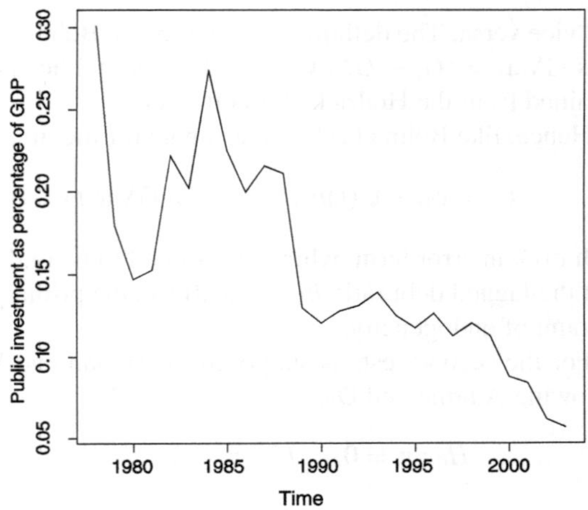

Fig. 2.35 Primary surplus to GDP ratio for Botswana (1978–2003)

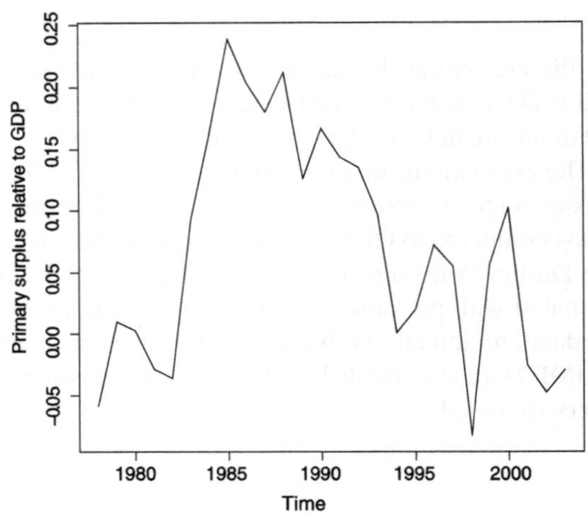

ascribed to bad weather and severe droughts around that time, the public debt relative to GDP continuously declined and in 2003 it amounts to less than 10 percent. The primary balance in Fig. 2.35 shows almost only surpluses with remarkably high values starting at the middle of the 1980s. Hence, these surpluses can explain the steady decrease of the debt to GDP ratio. Thus, for the first test we expect a significantly positive reaction coefficient with this information. The fiscal success can be assigned to the mineral detections and the export strategy that caused large economic growth. The main exporting commodities are diamonds. For example only three mines sum up to more than two thirds of total export revenue and yield almost half of Botswana's GDP.[40]

[40] See Government of Botswana (2008) for further information.

Next, we apply the first test to examine how the primary surplus ratio responds to changes in the public debt ratio. The result is summarized in Table 2.11.

The estimated parameter for the debt ratio reflects the mean of that coefficient. Table 2.11 shows that the average of the debt ratio coefficient $\psi(t)$ is positive and significant at the one percent level. Besides the reaction coefficient only the intercept and the coefficient for the business cycle variable are statistically significant, the latter implying with its positive sign that the primary surplus rises in booms when GDP is above its trend value. Moreover, the coefficient for GVar is not statistically significant. The goodness of fit is given by $R^2(\text{adj}) = 0.704$ and the Durbin-Watson test statistic does not indicate correlation of the residuals.

The deviation from the mean of the reaction coefficient is given by the smooth term sm(t) shown in Fig. 2.36 which is highly significant. The dashed lines give

Table 2.11 Coefficients for (2.13) for Botswana

	Coefficient	Stand. error (t-stat)	Pr(> t)
Constant	−0.122	0.055 (−2.225)	0.038
$b(t-1)$	1.242	0.373 (3.330)	0.003
GVar(t)	0.173	0.138 (1.254)	0.225
YVar(t)	0.427	0.236 (1.812)	0.086
sm(t)	edf 2.551	F 9.111	p-value 8.18×10^{-5}
	R^2(adj): 0.704	DW: 2.05	

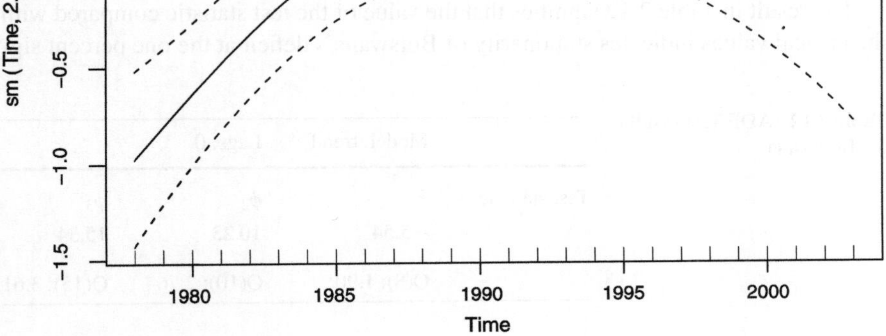

Fig. 2.36 Deviation sm(t) from the average coefficient for $b(t-1)$ for Botswana

the 95 percent confidence interval and the solid line gives the point estimate of the smooth term.

The smooth term in Fig. 2.36 shows that the reaction coefficient $\psi(t)$ is steadily increasing until about 1990. From then on the curve decreases slowly. The rise until 1990 is in accordance with the Figs. 2.34 and 2.35 that the debt was significantly reduced and high primary surpluses were achieved. After that the importance of debt reduction has diminished and a falling trend in primary balances supports that development. The smooth term apparently displays the reversed image of the debt ratio trend. This reflects that the scope of possible reaction in times of a high debt ratio is smaller, thus the value of $\mathrm{sm}(t)$ is low.

With both the smooth term and the positive value of the mean of the coefficient for $b(t-1)$ being significant, it is possible to state that $\psi(t)$ remained positive for the entire period. Therefore we conclude that there is evidence for sustainability of debt policy. If the estimation is implemented with only GVar, only YVar or just $b(t-1)$ the coefficient for the debt ratio remains positive and significant at least at the 5 percent level.

Another informative indicator of the financial situation is the ratio of interest payments relative to GDP. For Botswana it shows 2.0 percent (1986), 1.6 percent (1996) and 0.1 percent (2005).[41] These low values are in accordance with the estimation result. Moreover, if only referred to the external debt, which indicates financial resources going abroad, the ratio of external debt to GDP for Botswana for the same period as the estimation accounts for 15 percent on average and shows clearly an overall decreasing trend. Starting at 27 percent in 1978 it only amounts to 6 percent in 2003. These ratios are additional important figures for developing countries since they supplement the information on the economic situation.

Next, as proposed by Trehan and Walsh (1991), we test for stationarity by applying the Augmented Dickey Fuller test to the budget deficit, which is calculated as the first difference of the real debt value. If the total government deficit is stationary public debt is sustainable unless the interest rate is negative. This holds because the present value of public debt asymptotically converges to zero when public debt rises linearly since it is discounted with an exponential factor. In Table 2.12 the result is given. The time period is the same as for the last test.

The result in Table 2.12 signifies that the value of the test statistic compared with the critical values indicates stationarity of Botswana's deficit at the one percent sig-

Table 2.12 ADF Test results for Botswana

	Model: trend	Lags: 0	
Test statistic	$\hat{\tau}$	ϕ_2	ϕ_3
	−5.54	10.23	15.34
	Q(8): 1.90	Q(10): 2.76	Q(15): 3.61

[41] See World Bank (2008a, 2008b) for the data.

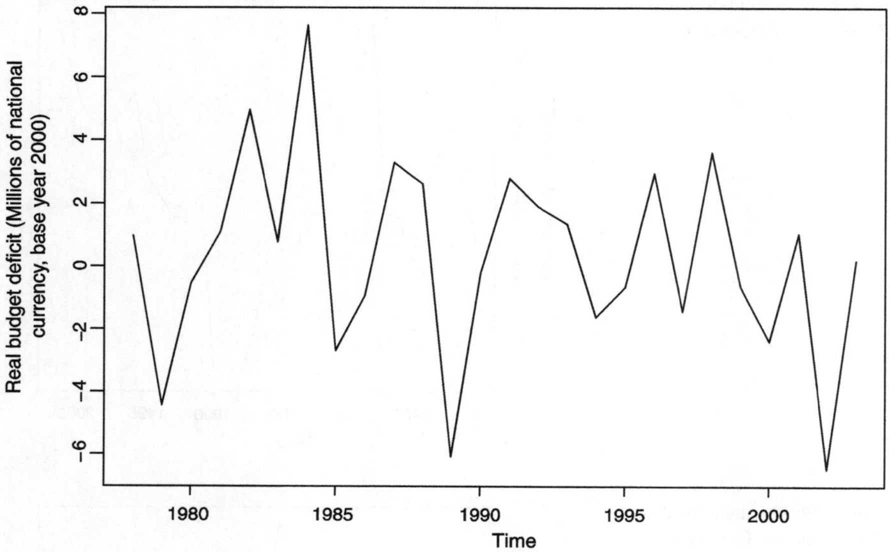

Fig. 2.37 Budget deficit of Botswana (1978–2003)

nificance level.[42] With the F-test related statistic ϕ it is possible to apply additional tests if necessary.[43] For possible autocorrelation of the residuals the ACF and PACF are checked and the Box-Ljung test statistic Q shows no evidence for correlation of the residuals.[44] Therefore, we can conclude that the inter-temporal budget constraint holds and sustainability seems to be given for the period considered. In Fig. 2.37 the deficit is illustrated.

All in all, the results for Botswana support the hypothesis of debt sustainability as expected by the declining debt to GDP ratio over time. Thus, the findings show strong evidence for sustainability of public debt in that country.

2.3.2.2 Costa Rica

The next country we analyze is Costa Rica. Figures 2.38 and 2.39 show the public debt and primary balance relative to GDP, respectively, for Costa Rica from 1970 to 2002.

In Fig. 2.38 the sharp rise of the debt ratio towards 1980 might be due to the crisis in Latin America at the beginning of the 1980s. After that a fall of public debt until

[42]For the critical values see for example Fuller (1976) Table 8.5.2 on p. 373 and Dickey and Fuller (1981) Tables IV, V and VI on p. 1063. Here the critical values of a sample size of 25 are applied.

[43]Here it is not required since the null hypothesis can be rejected.

[44]For information on the Box-Ljung test see for example Enders (2005), especially Chap. 2, Sect. 7, pp. 87 to 88. Critical values can be taken from a χ^2 table.

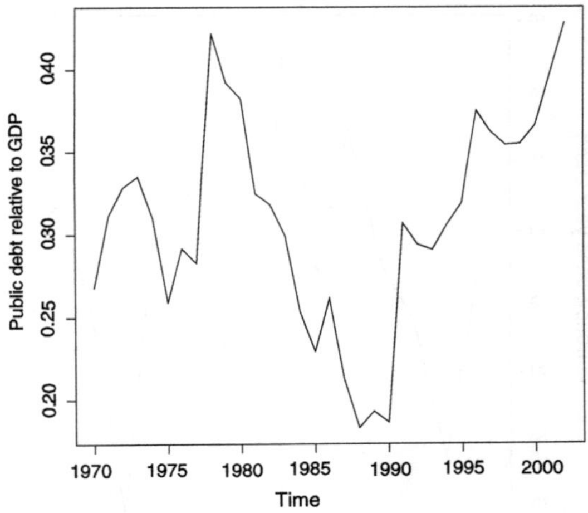

Fig. 2.38 Public debt to GDP ratio for Costa Rica (1970–2002)

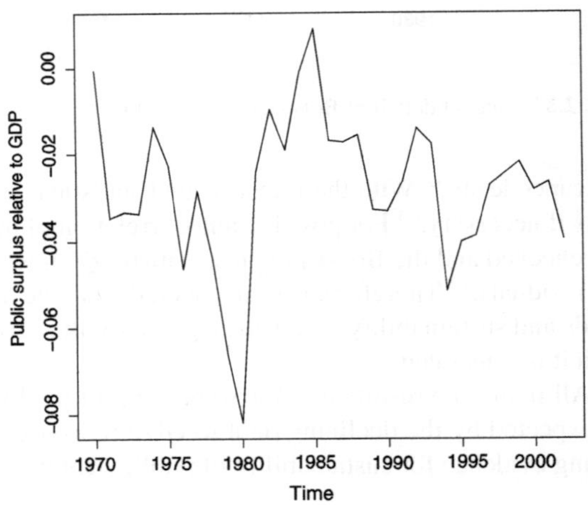

Fig. 2.39 Primary surplus to GDP ratio for Costa Rica (1970–2002)

about 1989 cut the debt by half to less then 20 percent of GDP. This development goes along with a sudden drop of the primary surplus in 1980 as can be observed from Fig. 2.39. Later a rise in primary balances occurs and it shows even surpluses around 1985. Reasons for this decrease in the debt ratio starting in the late eighties might in part be referred to participation in debt rescheduling and refinancing of debt with the Brady-Plan.[45] However, this stage could not be preserved and beginning with the 1990s the debt ratio has again steadily increased with a peak in 1996, which might in part be ascribed to the natural phenomenon *ElNiño* and a following drought.[46] In 2002 public debt to GDP amounts to 43 percent. Parallel to this rise in

[45] See for instance Minkner-Buenjer (1999) especially pp. 170 et seqq.

[46] See for example Minkner-Buenjer (1999) p. 168.

the debt ratio the primary balance ratio tends to diminish from the beginning of the late 1980s until 2002 with persistent and growing primary deficits.

We estimate (2.13) for Costa Rica for the years from 1970 to 2002. The primary surplus and the public debt are measured relative to GDP. The results are presented in Table 2.13.

As Table 2.13 shows the coefficient for public debt $b(t-1)$ is positive, however it is not statistically significant. The estimated parameter $\psi(t)$ gives the mean of that coefficient with $\mathrm{sm}(t)$ again representing the deviation from that mean over time. Further, the estimated coefficient for public expenditures is negative and highly significant, implying that public spending above its normal value reduces the primary surplus ratio. The coefficient for the business cycle variable is positive and significant at the one percent level which expresses that booms (recessions) cause a positive (negative) effect on the primary surplus ratio.

Information on time dependencies of the reaction coefficient is given by the degrees of freedom, edf, of the smooth term $\mathrm{sm}(t)$. For Costa Rica edf $= 7.512$ and it is significant at the one percent level suggesting that the reaction coefficient is characterized by strong variations over time. R^2(adj) describes the goodness of fit. With $R^2(\mathrm{adj}) = 0.882$ a relative high goodness of fit is achieved. To check for correlation of the residuals the Durbin-Watson test statistic is calculated. There is no evidence for correlation of the residuals for Costa Rica.

If the estimation is performed without the business cycle variable or without expenditures or only with the debt ratio, the estimated average coefficient for $b(t-1)$ stays positive in all cases.

The results demonstrate that the reaction coefficient varies over time. The path of the deviation from the mean, $\mathrm{sm}(t)$, is depicted in Fig. 2.40.

First a decline until 1979 can be observed, followed by a steep rise with a peak in the middle of the eighties. Afterwards it dropped again. This can be interpreted as a loss of reaction over time, implying that the response of the primary surplus to GDP ratio with respect to variations in the debt ratio had declined. However, in the recent past $\mathrm{sm}(t)$ has slightly increased.

As for Botswana we calculate some economic figures for Costa Rica to get additional information on the financial situation. First, the interest payments to GDP

Table 2.13 Coefficients for (2.13) for Costa Rica

	Coefficient	Stand. error (t-stat)	Pr($> t$)
Constant	−0.030	0.011 (−2.728)	0.012
$b(t-1)$	0.010	0.037 (0.263)	0.795
GVar(t)	−0.125	0.013 (−9.710)	2.59×10^{-9}
YVar(t)	0.145	0.048 (3.000)	0.007
sm(t)	edf 7.512	F 8.069	p-value 3.82×10^{-5}
	R^2(adj): 0.882	DW: 2.28	

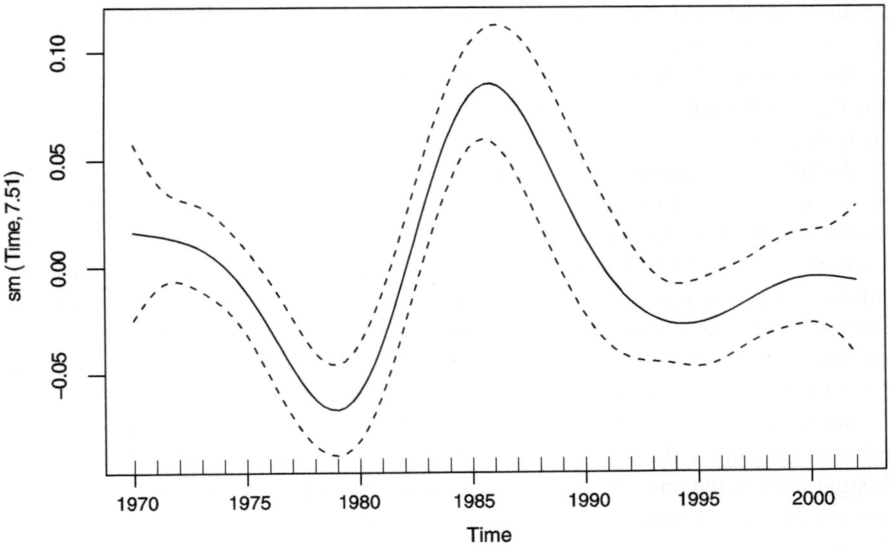

Fig. 2.40 Deviation sm(t) from the average coefficient for $b(t-1)$ for Costa Rica

for Costa Rica are 4.0 percent (1986), 1.6 percent (1996) and 0.6 percent (2005).[47] Although starting with a relatively high value these three ratios show a decreasing trend. Furthermore, the average of the external debt to GDP ratio amounts to 9 percent for the same period as the estimation was performed. However, this ratio is alternating and no explicit trend can be observed. These two indicators are in accordance with the positive but insignificant estimations. The ratios are relatively low but not as unambiguous as those for Botswana.

To get further insight we test the stationarity properties of the deficit inclusive of interest payments. Figure 2.41 shows the evolution of the situation for Costa Rica from 1970 to 2002.

For the test we calculate the first difference of the real debt value of Costa Rica for the years 1969 to 2002. Thus, for the deficit the sample period from above is maintained. Table 2.14 summarizes the results.

As shown in Table 2.14 the deficit is stationary at the one percent level. For possible autocorrelation of the residuals the ACF and PACF are checked and the Box-Ljung test statistic Q shows no evidence for correlation of the residuals. Therefore, it is possible to conclude that the budget deficit of Costa Rica for the considered period is stationary. This indicates that the inter-temporal budget constraint holds, hence the Costa Rican government performs a sustainable debt policy.

All in all, despite a growing debt ratio and a slightly increasing trend of the real budget deficit both tests conclude that there are indications for sustainability,

[47]For the data see World Bank (2008a, 2008b).

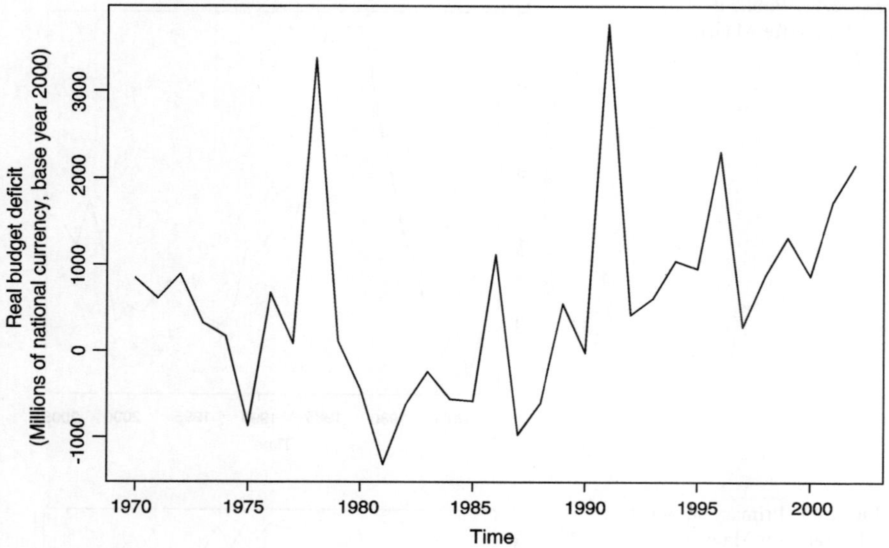

Fig. 2.41 Budget deficit of Costa Rica (1970–2002)

Table 2.14 ADF Test results for Costa Rica

	Model: trend	Lags: 0	
Test statistic	$\hat{\tau}$	ϕ_2	ϕ_3
	−5.02	8.50	12.73
	Q(8): 4.55	Q(10): 9.12	Q(15):15.99

however the significance is smaller than for Botswana and these results only allude to the time period considered.

2.3.2.3 Mauritius

The country we now consider is in South East Africa, namely Mauritius. Figures 2.42 and 2.43 illustrate the total public debt and primary surplus to GDP ratio from 1973 to 2005. The debt ratio in Fig. 2.42 shows a high value in the middle of the eighties. The steep increase since the middle of the seventies might among other things be due to a stagnation of exports and decreasing terms of trade which led to budget deficits.[48] This development then summed up to a growing debt ratio which might at least partly explain the peak around 1985. Later, restrictive guidelines by the IMF and World Bank were imposed to limit imports in order to reduce

[48] See for example Paul (1987), especially p. 24.

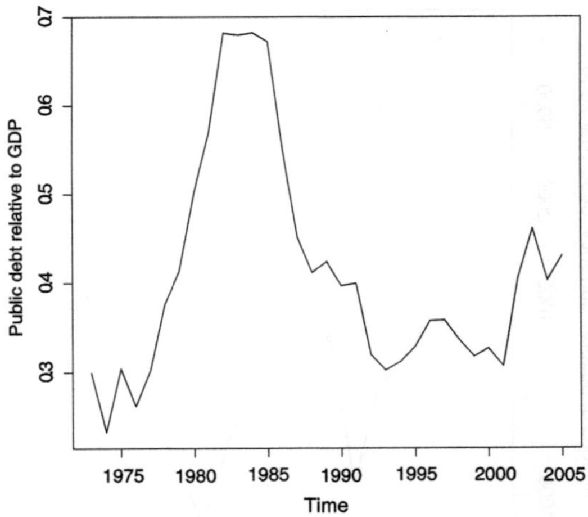

Fig. 2.42 Public debt to GDP ratio for Mauritius (1973–2005)

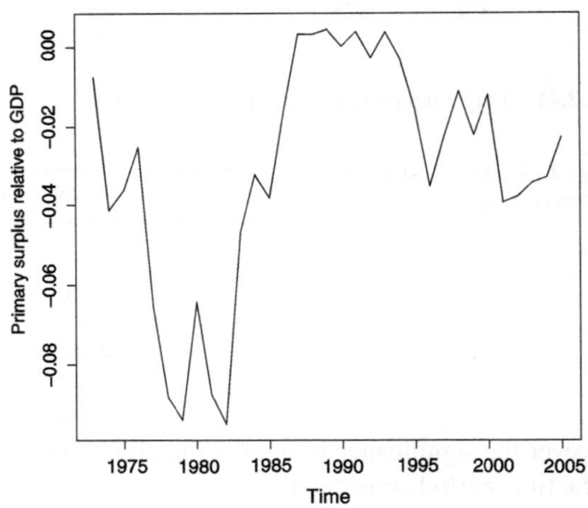

Fig. 2.43 Primary surplus to GDP ratio for Mauritius (1973–2005)

deficits.[49] Then, the debt ratio had been gradually reduced and stabilized around a level of about 35 percent. This decline might be explained by economic reform policies during that time. With a solid industrial base the export commodity has changed from sugar to textile and apparel.[50] But with the beginning of the new century another rise can be observed. Corresponding to that, the primary balance ratio in Fig. 2.43 shows primary deficits for the years characterized by high debt ratios in the middle of the 1980s. However, after that there is a remarkable increase in primary surplus ratios until the late eighties. Nonetheless, its trend has been decreasing recently.

[49] Ibidem.

[50] See for example Embassy of the Republic of Mauritius (2008).

Applying the first test that analyzes the reaction of the primary surplus ratio to variations in the debt to GDP ratio yields results shown in Table 2.15.

As shown in Table 2.15 the average of the coefficient for the debt ratio $\psi(t)$ is positive but not significant at the usual levels. Again, sm(t) reflects the deviation from that mean over time. There is no other significant coefficient but the one for public expenditures has the expected negative sign. The positive sign of $\psi(t)$ remains if the estimation is applied without GVar, YVar or simply with the debt ratio. edf = 5.42 indicates time-dependencies and sm(t) is highly significant. The goodness of fit is relatively high and there seems to be no correlation of the residuals according to the Durbin-Watson test statistic. The time path of the smooth term is depicted in Fig. 2.44.

Table 2.15 Coefficients for (2.13) for Mauritius

	Coefficient	Stand. error (t-stat)	Pr(> t)
Constant	−0.034	0.020 (−1.702)	0.102
$b(t-1)$	0.011	0.052 (0.203)	0.841
GVar(t)	−0.059	0.052 (−1.139)	0.266
YVar(t)	−0.038	0.094 (−0.406)	0.688
sm(t)	edf 5.42	F 10.33	p-value
			2.82×10^{-6}
	R^2(adj): 0.801	DW: 1.94	

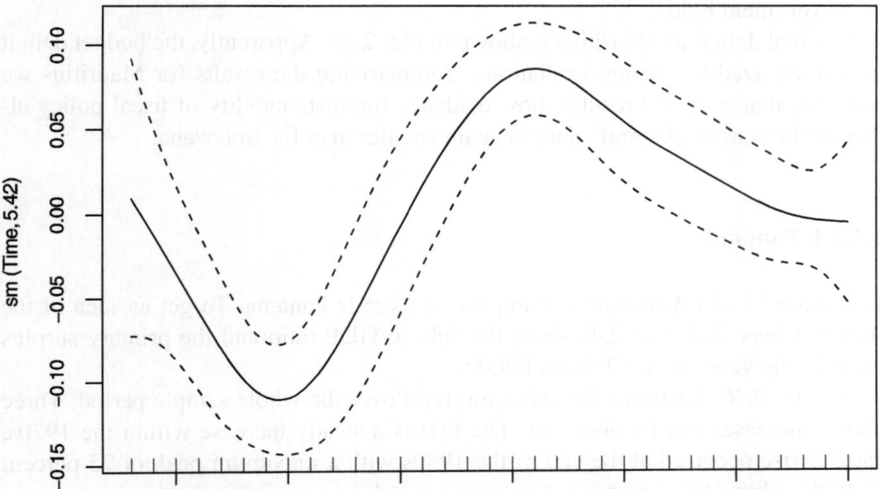

Fig. 2.44 Deviation sm(t) from the average coefficient for $b(t-1)$ for Mauritius

Table 2.16 ADF Test results for Mauritius

	Model: trend	Lags: 0	
Test statistic	$\hat{\tau}$	ϕ_2	ϕ_3
	−5.11	8.73	13.07
	Q(8): 4.35	Q(10): 9.03	Q(15): 11.21

It can be realized that the reaction coefficient had decreased until 1980. Then, it began to rise until the early 1990s before it started to decline again. The decreasing time path again indicates that the government put less importance on the stabilization of public debt. Nevertheless, adding the mean of the coefficient from Table 2.15 and the deviation from that mean gives a positive value, except for the period from the mid 1970s to the middle of the 1980s.

Again we look at the interest payments to GDP ratio and the external debt ratio. For Mauritius the first relation accounts for 2.3 percent (1986), 1.7 percent (1996) and 0.5 percent in 2005.[51] The average of the external debt relative to GDP from 1973 to 2005 is 13 percent, however, for the period around the middle of the eighties the ratio shows high values of more than 20 percent and then decreases steadily to 5 percent in 2005. This seems to be in accordance with the development in Fig. 2.42 though concerning only the external debt contribution.

Next, we apply the stationarity test for Mauritius for the period considered. Again, the real deficit is calculated as the first difference of real public debt. Table 2.16 shows the test result.

With the result from Table 2.16 we can conclude that the real budget deficit of Mauritius is stationary, which suggests that the inter-temporal budget constraint of the government holds.

The real deficit of Mauritius is shown in Fig. 2.45. Apparently, the budget deficit is characterized by strong oscillations. Summarizing the results for Mauritius we conclude that both test results show evidence for sustainability of fiscal policy although the statistical significance is again smaller than for Botswana.

2.3.2.4 Panama

The second Latin American country we analyze is Panama. To get an idea of the situation Figs. 2.46 and 2.47 show the debt to GDP ratio and the primary surplus ratio for the years from 1970 until 2000.

As Fig. 2.46 illustrates the debt ratio rises over the whole sample period. Three abrupt increases can be observed. The first is a steady increase within the 1970s, another rise occurred at the end of the 1980s with a maximum peak of 75 percent in 1989, when Panama endured an economic downturn. After a drop in the early

[51] See World Bank (2008a, 2008b).

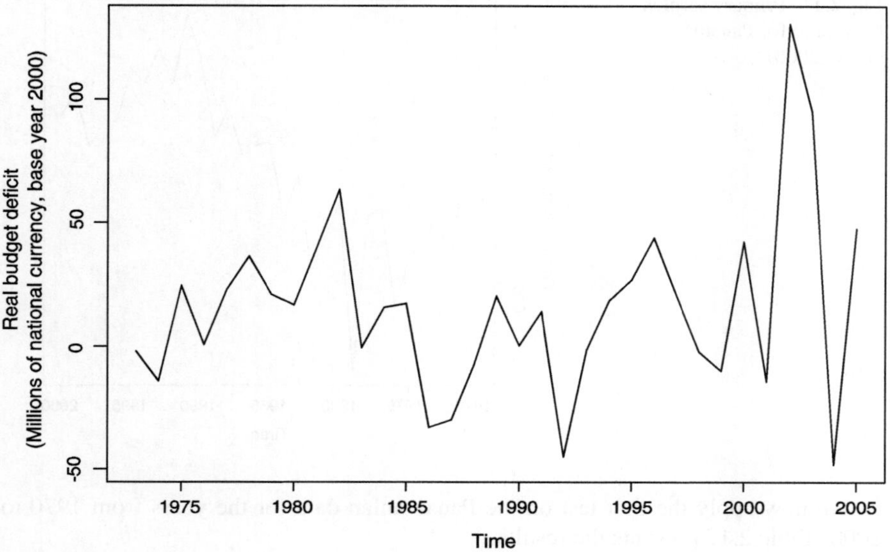

Fig. 2.45 Budget deficit of Mauritius (1973–2005)

Fig. 2.46 Public debt to GDP ratio for Panama (1970–2000)

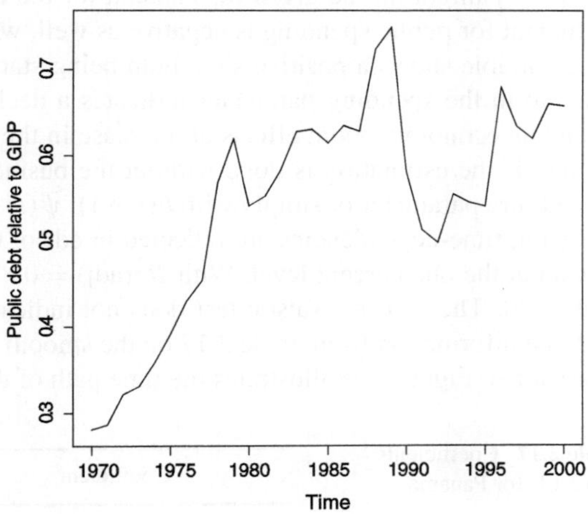

and middle 1990s, that might be explained by economic reforms and later involvements of the IMF for example,[52] the debt ratio has begun to rise again since the late nineties. This evolution of the debt ratio is accompanied by persistent primary deficits until the beginning of the nineties as shown in Fig. 2.47.

[52] See also International Monetary Fund (1995).

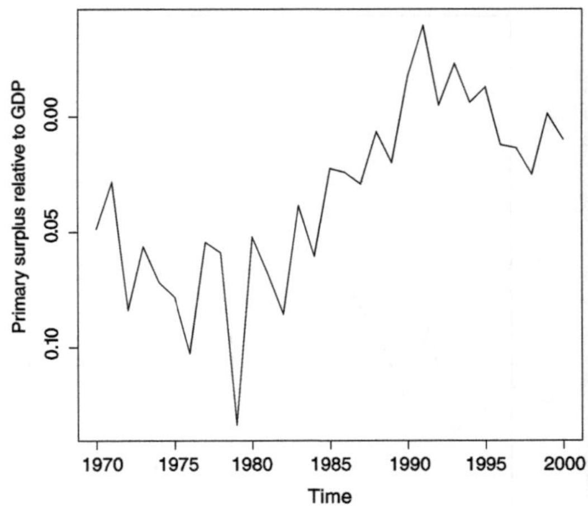

Fig. 2.47 Primary surplus to GDP ratio for Panama (1970–2000)

We now apply the first test on the Panamanian data for the years from 1970 to 2000. Table 2.17 presents the results.

Table 2.17 illustrates that the mean of the parameter of interest $\psi(t)$ is negative and statistically significant at the one percent level. Again, sm(t) shows the deviation from that mean over time. This estimation result indicates that sustainability of debt policy might not be given for Panama for the considered sample period. The coefficient for public spending is negative as well, whereas the one for the business cycle variable shows a positive sign, both being statistically significant. The effect of a rise in the spending parameter indicates a decline in the primary surplus ratio and an economic boom effects an increase in the primary surplus to GDP ratio. Further, if the estimation is done without the business cycle variable, without the expenditure parameter or simply with $b(t-1)$, $\psi(t)$ remains significantly negative.

Again, time-dependencies are reflected in edf of the smooth term, which is significant at the one percent level. With $R^2(\text{adj}) = 0.876$ quite a high goodness of fit is attained. The Durbin-Watson test does not indicate correlation of the residuals. With the information from Table 2.17 on the smooth term, a variation over time can be assumed. Figure 2.48 illustrates the time path of the function.

Table 2.17 Coefficients for (2.13) for Panama

	Coefficient	Stand. error (t-stat)	Pr($> t$)
Constant	0.023	0.020 (1.184)	0.248
$b(t-1)$	−0.131	0.039 (−3.351)	0.003
GVar(t)	−0.229	0.038 (−6.101)	2.53×10^{-6}
YVar(t)	0.243	0.073 (3.314)	0.003
sm(t)	edf 2.706	F 17.43	p-value 1.00×10^{-7}
	R^2(adj): 0.876	DW: 2.26	

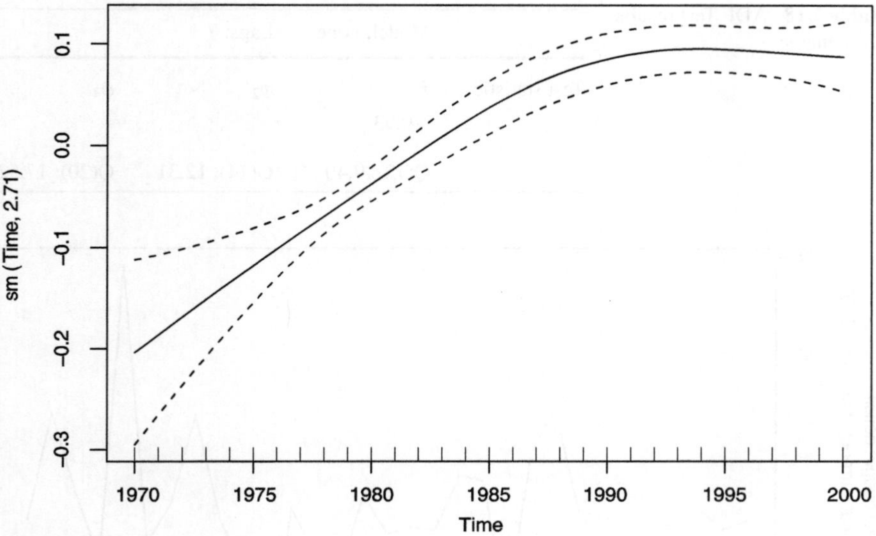

Fig. 2.48 Deviation sm(t) from the average coefficient for $b(t-1)$ for Panama

As shown in Fig. 2.48 the reaction of the primary surplus to public debt steadily increased until around 1990. From then on, the time path remained relatively stable. In spite of this increasing slope, the response has not been increased enough to achieve a positive reaction coefficient on average.

Once more we use the indicators interest payments to GDP and external debt relative to GDP to gain supplementary insight on the financial situation of Panama. The interest payments to GDP ratio accounts for 5.6 percent (1986), 4.1 percent (1996) and 4.2 percent in 2005.[53] Moreover, the external debt ratio for the same period as above shows an average value of 37 percent and a clearly increasing trend starting at 14 percent in 1970 and reaching 48 percent in 2000. These high figures support the estimation result from above.

For additional information we now apply the Augmented Dickey Fuller Test to the budget deficit of Panama. Therefore, the first difference of the real debt from 1969 to 2000 is calculated in order to keep the time period identical. In Table 2.18 the result is presented.

The results from Table 2.18 support the findings from the first test. The deficit is not stationary at any significance level. For possible correlation of the residuals we looked at the ACF and PACF and calculated the Box-Ljung test statistic Q. There are no indications of autocorrelation. Thus, according to both test results, there is doubt whether the inter-temporal budget constraint holds and whether the Panamanian government has pursued a sustainable fiscal policy.

[53] See also World Bank (2008a, 2008b).

Table 2.18 ADF Test results for Panama

	Model: none	Lags: 7	
Test statistic	$\hat{\tau}$	ϕ_2	ϕ_3
	−0.93	–	–
	Q(12): 9.40	Q(14): 12.31	Q(20): 17.52

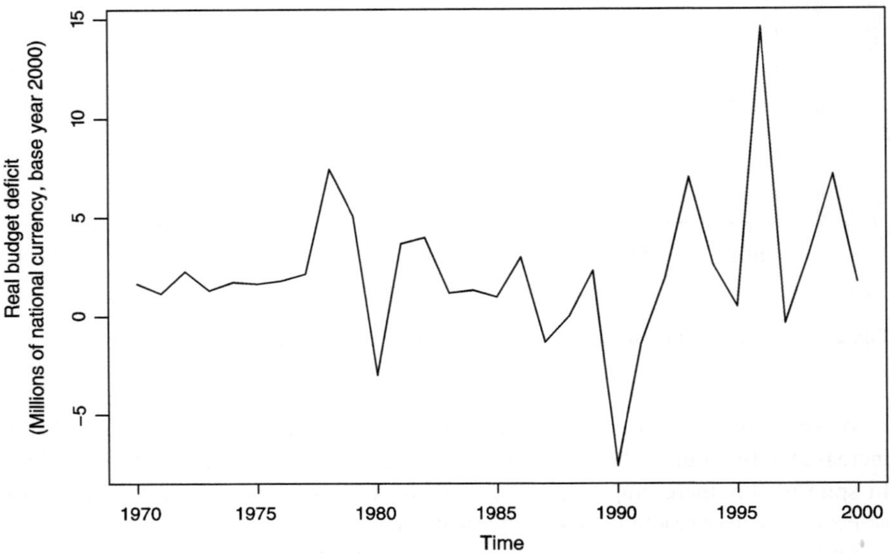

Fig. 2.49 Budget deficit of Panama (1970–2000)

In Fig. 2.49 the real budget deficit of Panama is depicted. As shown in Fig. 2.49 there are three particular outliers, two surpluses in 1980 and 1990 and a high deficit in the middle of the 1990s. The time-path of the deficit had been relatively stable until the middle of the 1970s but began to show strong oscillations from the 1980s onwards.

To summarize the Panamanian situation, both tests suggest that sustainability of public debt for the period considered does not seem to be given.

2.3.2.5 Rwanda

The next state we consider is the East African country Rwanda. In Figs. 2.50 and 2.51 the public debt ratio and the primary balance ratio for the years from 1978 to 2004 are shown. Apparently the debt ratio increases over the whole sample as shown in Fig. 2.50. The two outliers in 1994 and 1995 can be ascribed to the Rwandan Genocide of 1994. The overall trend of the primary surplus ratio is declining, again with the lowest values around the middle of the 1990s as depicted in Fig. 2.51.

Fig. 2.50 Public debt to GDP ratio for Rwanda (1978–2004)

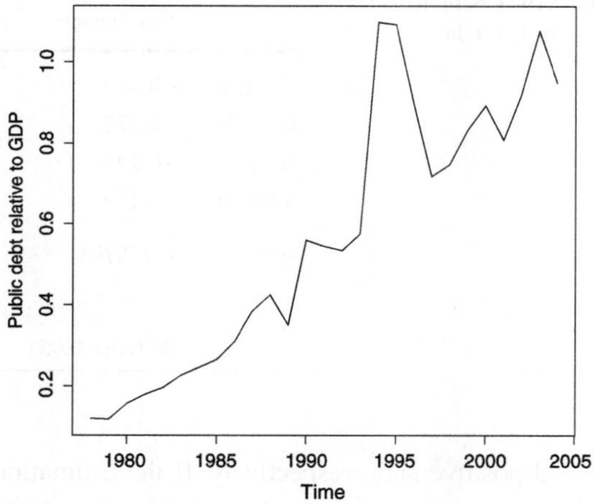

Fig. 2.51 Primary surplus to GDP ratio for Rwanda (1978–2004)

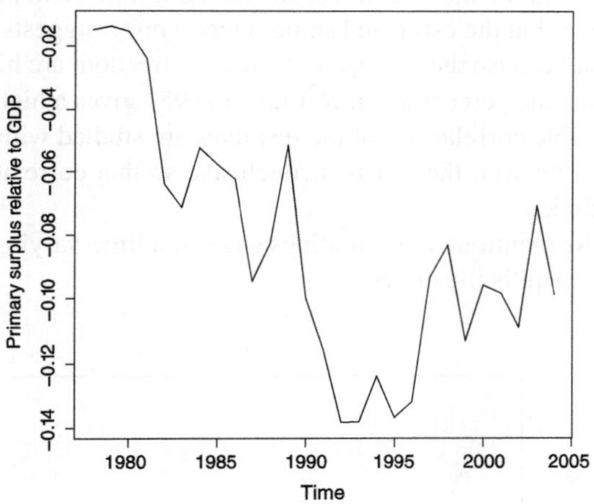

Moreover, Rwanda is one of the countries taking part in the Heavily Indebted Poor Countries (HIPC) Debt Initiative which is a device for debt relief and support of countries facing a high debt burden.[54]

Next, we apply the first test to analyze the response of the primary surplus ratio to changes in the debt to GDP ratio for the sample, where we neglect the year 1994 where the Genocide occurred in order to avoid leverage effects. Table 2.19 summarizes the results.

The average of the coefficient of interest $\psi(t)$ is positive and significant at the one percent level as shown in Table 2.19. The deviation from that mean is again given by the smooth term $sm(t)$. All other coefficients are significant as well. The ones for the expenditure variable and the business cycle show the expected nega-

[54] See also for example International Monetary Fund (2008).

Table 2.19 Coefficients for (2.13) for Rwanda

	Coefficient	Stand. error (t-stat)	Pr(> t)
Constant	−0.110	0.016 (−7.112)	4.66×10^{-6}
$b(t-1)$	0.172	0.051 (3.393)	0.004
GVar(t)	−0.199	0.028 (−7.011)	5.47×10^{-6}
YVar(t)	0.279	0.052 (5.331)	9.88×10^{-5}
sm(t)	edf 7.703	F 21.98	p-value 7.35×10^{-7}
	R^2(adj): 0.951	DW: 2.88	

tive and positive sign, respectively. If the estimation is done for example without the business cycle variable, without the expenditures or with only the debt ratio, the mean of the coefficient for the debt ratio remains positive. Further, Table 2.19 shows that the estimated smooth term sm(t) suggests a time-varying reaction coefficient because the estimated degrees of freedom are high and because it is significant at the one percent level. $R^2(\text{adj}) = 0.951$ gives a high goodness of fit for the model. Possible correlations of the residuals are studied with the Durbin-Watson test statistic. However, the test is inconclusive so that correlation of the residuals cannot be excluded.

As mentioned, our findings suggest a time-varying smooth term. In Fig. 2.52 the time path is illustrated.

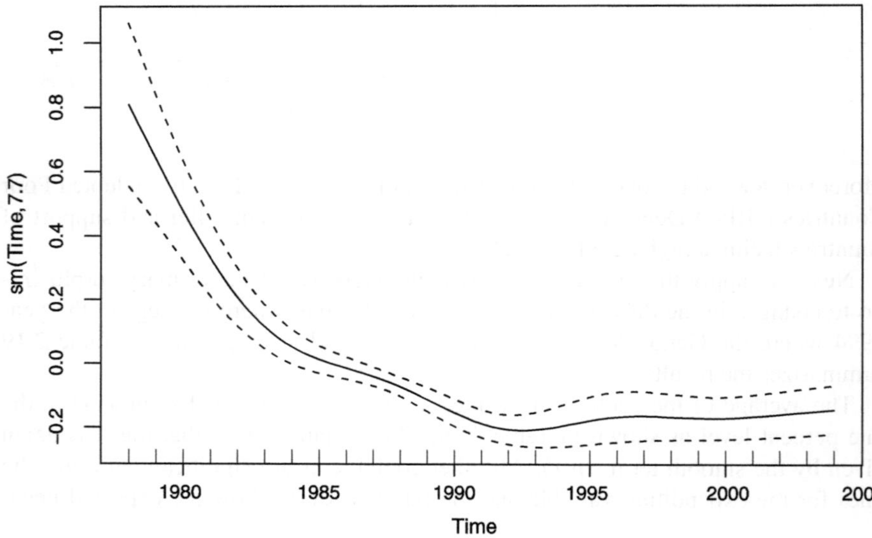

Fig. 2.52 Deviation sm(t) from the average coefficient for $b(t-1)$ for Rwanda

The function is decreasing over time although in conjunction with the estimated average coefficient it stays positive except for the critical years around the Genocide. The negative trend indicates a decreasing reaction of the primary surplus ratio to variations in public debt to GDP. However it had remained relatively stable since the late 1990s.

The indicator interest payments to GDP shows with 0.3 percent (1986), 0.5 percent (1996) and 0.4 percent in 2005 low values.[55] These figures are consistent with the estimation results. However, the external debt relative to GDP accounts for 44 percent on average for the years from 1978 to 2004. Besides that high mean the ratio shows an obviously rising trend with 11 percent in 1978 and 85 percent in 2004. This illustrates the debt structure and the external debt share in combination with Fig. 2.50.

To gain further insight we use the Augmented Dickey Fuller test to analyze stationarity properties of the deficit inclusive of interest payments. For the real budget deficit the first difference of the real public debt is computed. Table 2.20 summarizes the results for the period from 1978 to 2004 for Rwanda.[56]

From Table 2.20 we can conclude that the budget deficit is stationary for the sample considered and, therefore, the test indicates that the inter-temporal budget constraint holds. Hence, it confirms the findings from the first test. The Box-Ljung test statistic suggests that there are no hints for autocorrelation of the residuals.

Figure 2.53 shows the Rwandan real deficit situation, which has been used for the Unit Root test.

After a stable path until the middle of the 1980s, the deficits show a strongly oscillating development from then on. Although not explicitly taken into account in our model, for Rwanda the received grants seem quite important because they amount on average to 4.5 percent of GDP for the years considered. This holds because grants are expected to affect the evolution of public debt even if they are not directly used to reduce the budget deficit. Nevertheless, our analysis demonstrates that the government in Rwanda has performed a responsible debt policy. This is also important for those who give grants to that country.

Figure 2.54 shows Rwanda's received grants measured relative to GDP for the period from 1978 to 2004. Evidently the overall trend is increasing. The two outliers 1994 and 1995 again refer to the Rwandan Genocide.

Table 2.20 ADF Test results for Rwanda

	Model: trend	Lags: 5	
Test statistic	$\hat{\tau}$	ϕ_2	ϕ_3
	−3.30	3.81	5.47
	Q(10): 8.79	Q(15): 12.63	Q(18): 12.77

[55] See also World Bank (2008a, 2008b).

[56] As above without the 1994 observation.

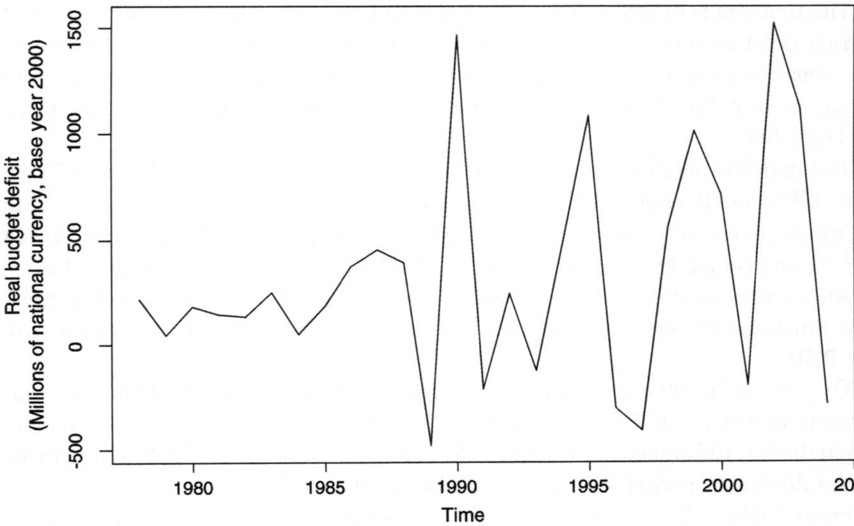

Fig. 2.53 Budget deficit of Rwanda (1978–2004)

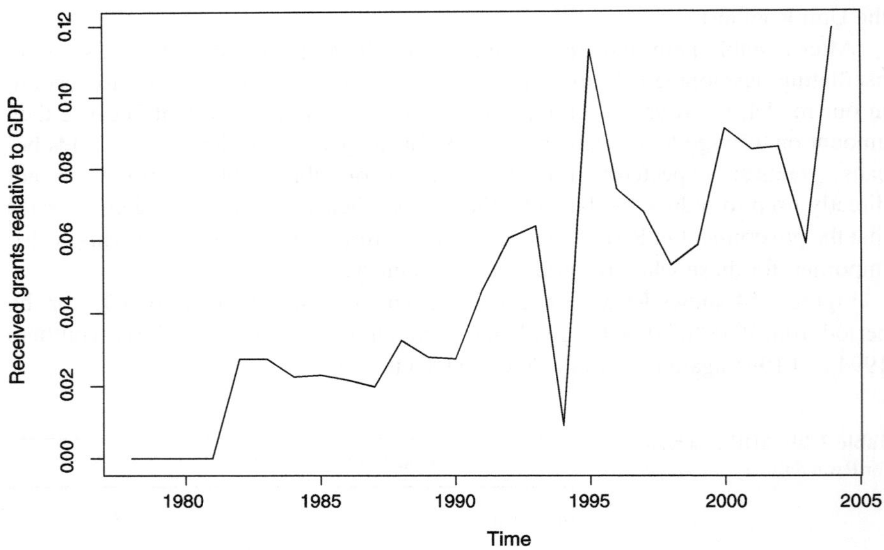

Fig. 2.54 Rwanda's received grants relative to GDP (1978–2004)

Summarizing the analysis of the Rwandan data, both test results indicate that there is evidence for sustainability of debt policy in that country.

2.3.2.6 Tunisia

Finally, we analyze the North African state Tunisia. Figures 2.55 and 2.56 show the public debt and the primary surplus to GDP ratio for the time period from 1972 to 1998. The debt to GDP ratio was increasing as can be seen in Fig. 2.55. There is a remarkable rise starting with the early 1980s until the end of that decade. Reasons for this rapid change might have been bad weather, crops and harvest were destroyed by drought and locusts especially serious in 1988.[57] Moreover structural problems such as an increased role of government and emerging public enterprises intensified the situation. Adjustments by cutting public expenditures and investment were not

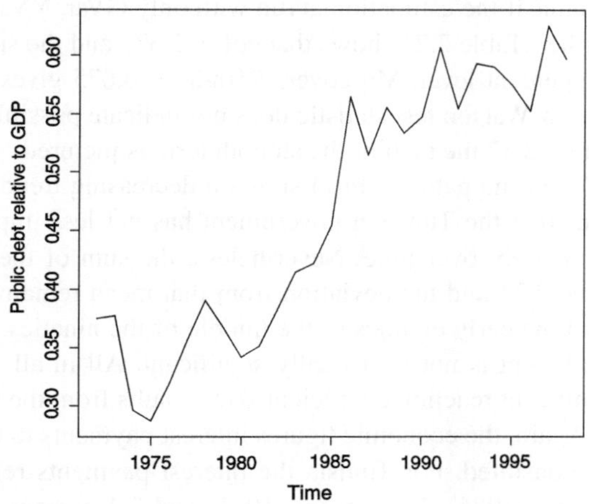

Fig. 2.55 Public debt to GDP ratio for Tunisia (1972–1998)

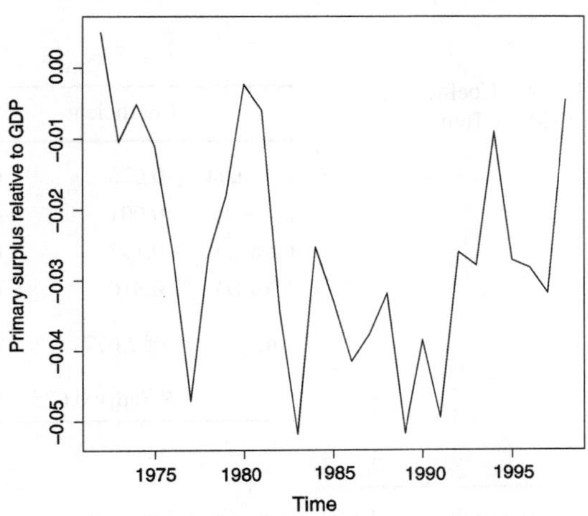

Fig. 2.56 Primary surplus to GDP ratio for Tunisia (1972–1998)

[57] See for example Stork (1990) especially p. 7.

effective immediately to stop the decline of public finances, however reforms decelerated this situation afterwards.[58] From then on, the debt ratio grew rather slowly and fluctuates around a high level of about 55 percent. The primary balance ratio in Fig. 2.56 shows merely primary deficits, except for the first observation in 1972, with an overall decreasing trend.

Now, we apply the first test to study the reaction of the primary surplus ratio to variations in the debt to GDP ratio. In Table 2.21 the results are presented.

As Table 2.21 shows the average of the coefficient for the debt ratio is positive but not significant at the usual levels. As above the deviation from that mean is given by sm(t). The other coefficients, except for the intercept, are statistically significant and they show the expected signs. For the coefficient of interest, ψ, the positive sign remains if the estimation is run with only GVar, YVar or only with the debt ratio.[59] Further, Table 2.21 shows that edf = 2.677 and the smooth term is significant at the one percent level. Moreover, $R^2(\text{adj}) = 0.675$ gives a fair goodness of fit and the Durbin-Watson test statistic does not indicate possible correlations of the residuals. In Fig. 2.57 the path of the smooth term is pictured.

The time path of sm(t) shows a decreasing trend until 1983. This decline indicates that the Tunisian government has put less importance to the stabilization of public debt over time. Nevertheless, the sum of the mean of the coefficient from Table 2.21 and the deviation from that mean remains positive except for the years from the early eighties to the middle of the nineties, but the estimated mean of the coefficient is not statistically significant. All in all, a positive but not statistically significant reaction coefficient $\psi(t)$ results from the test for Tunisia.

Again, the economic figures interest payments to GDP and external debt to GDP are consulted. For Tunisia the interest payments relative to GDP account for 3.4 percent (1986), 2.6 percent (1996) and 2.4 percent in 2005.[60] Compared to those values the average of the external debt to GDP ratio is 33 percent for the years from

Table 2.21 Coefficients for (2.13) for Tunisia

	Coefficient	Stand. error (t-stat)	Pr(> t)
Constant	−0.025	0.022 (−1.122)	0.275
$b(t-1)$	0.001	0.051 (0.016)	0.988
GVar(t)	−0.193	0.059 (−3.279)	0.004
YVar(t)	0.310	0.084 (3.683)	0.001
sm(t)	edf 2.677	F 4.384	p-value 0.005
	R^2(adj): 0.675	DW: 2.28	

[58] See also Nsouli et al. (1993), especially p. 1 et seqq.

[59] For the estimation without GVar ψ is significant at the 10 percent level.

[60] See also World Bank (2008a, 2008b).

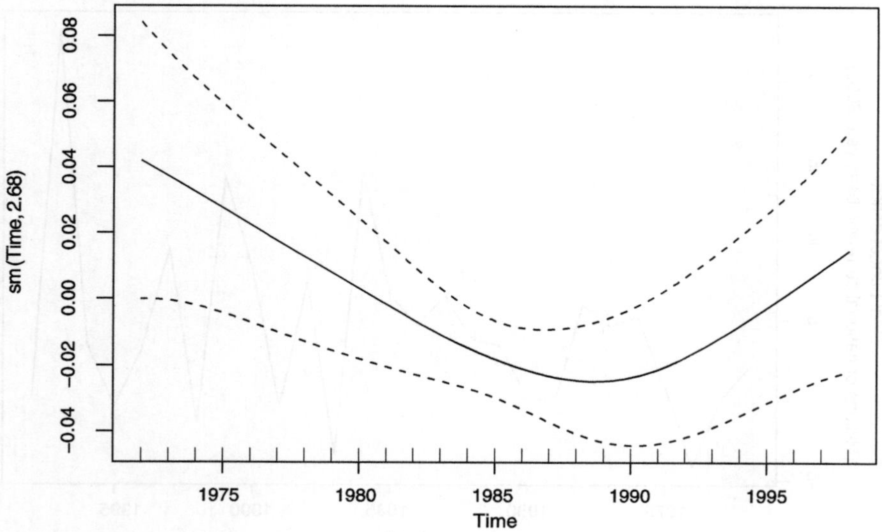

Fig. 2.57 Deviation sm(t) from the average coefficient for $b(t-1)$ for Tunisia

1972 to 1998. These figures yield some extra information on the economic situation of Tunisia since the estimation result is ambiguous.

Additionally, we apply the second test for stationarity to the budget deficit of Tunisia for the same sample period. As above, the deficit is calculated by the first difference of the real public debt. In Table 2.22 the test result is presented.

The result in Table 2.22 indicates that the real budget deficit is stationary. This finding suggests that the inter-temporal budget constraint holds.

In Fig. 2.58 the deficit situation of Tunisia, which is used for the Dickey Fuller test, is depicted with the time period as above. Obviously, the real budget deficit fluctuates over time with higher amplitudes in the recent past. To sum up the outcome for Tunisia, the results of the tests indicate that there seems to be sustainability of fiscal policy despite a growing debt ratio. Nevertheless, it must be pointed out that the estimated coefficient giving the reaction of the primary surplus to variations in public debt is not statistically significant. Therefore, there is some need for the government to put more weight on debt stabilization.

Table 2.22 ADF Test results for Tunisia

	Model: trend	Lags: 0	
Test statistic	$\hat{\tau}$	ϕ_2	ϕ_3
	−6.76	15.30	22.95
	Q(8): 5.31	Q(10): 8.21	Q(15): 11.17

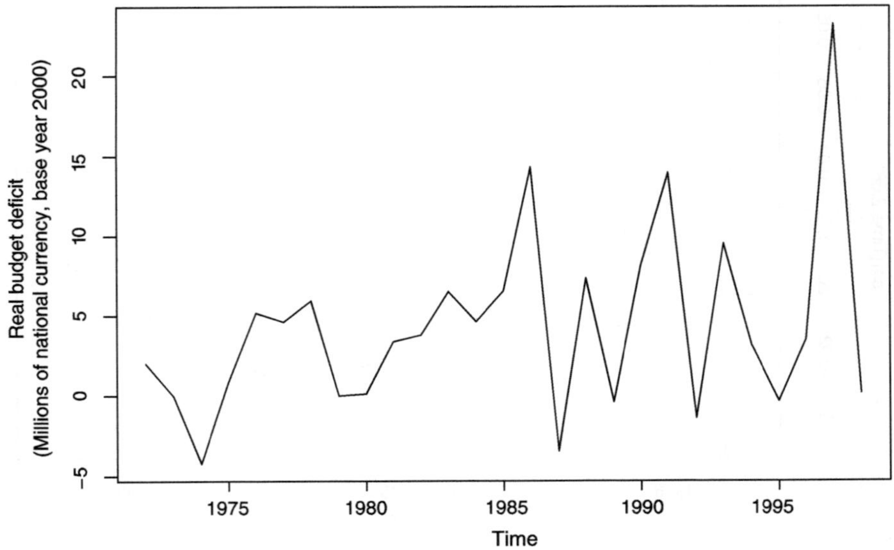

Fig. 2.58 Budget deficit of Tunisia (1972–1998)

2.3.3 Conclusion

This section has studied the development of fiscal variables such as public debt, the primary balance and revenues and public spending (all measured relative to GDP) for selected developing countries. It has empirically analyzed sustainability of debt policies with two different tests in order to study whether the inter-temporal budget constraint holds and solvency is given. The first one aims at estimating the reaction of the primary surplus ratio to changes in public debt relative to GDP. Since a positive response does not necessarily guarantee that the debt ratio remains bounded, stationarity properties of the budget deficit have been analyzed with a second test.

The results of both tests show that Botswana clearly follows a sustainable debt policy and that country can be considered as an ideal as concerns its debt policy. As regards Rwanda, sustainability of fiscal policy seems to be given although the country is characterized by a growing debt ratio. This conclusion is based on a positive and statistically significant reaction of the primary surplus to variations in public debt and on stationary public deficits. By allowing for a time-varying reaction coefficient in the first test it can also be realized that the reaction coefficient has declined over time.

The debt situation in Costa Rica, Mauritius and Tunisia also seems to be stable since the estimated reaction coefficient is positive on average and since the budget deficit is stationary. However, the estimated reaction coefficient is not statistically significant so that this coefficient should be considered with caution. In addition, it suggests that the governments in these countries should put more weight on stabilizing public debt. In contrast to that, for Panama both tests indicate that sustainability might not be given and a debt overhang problem might occur. The debt ratio is rising and although the smooth term of the first test shows an increasing time trend, the reaction coefficient is significantly negative on average. According to the second test stationarity of the deficit does not seem to be given for Panama. Thus, our results should be interpreted as a signal that corrective actions should be taken and the efforts on enforcing a stabilization policy should be intensified in Panama.

But these tests and the results have their limits. They refer only to a partial view and for a detailed analysis of a developing country's situation more aspects should be considered, for example real sector economy attributes such as the total volume of an economy (trade, production, investments) or monetary aspects, for instance those concerning the exchange rate. That, however, is beyond the scope of this analysis. Nevertheless, the tests performed provide meaningful results and offer some insight into the fiscal situations of the countries under consideration.

Chapter 3
Public Debt and Economic Growth: A Theoretical Model

In the last chapter we tested for sustainability of public debt in developed as well as in developing economies. One test we resorted to was to analyze the reaction of the primary surplus, relative to GDP, to variations in the public debt to GDP ratio. We found that there is empirical evidence that the primary surplus is a positive function of public debt for most developed economies and also for some developing countries. In this chapter we will analyze the effect of this outcome for economic growth in endogenous growth models.

Endogenous growth models have become popular in the economics literature with the publication of the papers by Romer (1986, 1990) and Aghion and Howitt (1992). With the emergence of that line of research the long-run growth rate of economies is no longer an exogenous variable but becomes itself an endogenous variable that depends on parameters. Hence, governments cannot only influence the levels of economic variables but also their growth rates through fiscal policies.

Further, it is well known that the government can affect the dynamics of economies by its debt and deficit policy. For example, Schmitt-Grohé and Uribe (1997) demonstrate that a balanced government budget may lead to multiple equilibria if the distortionary income tax rate is used to balance the government budget for given public expenditures. The reason for that outcome is that there is a negative relation between aggregate activity and the income tax rate. If economic agents expect that the after-tax return rises they will increase their supply of production factors leading to a rise in the tax revenue. If public spending is fixed a balanced government budget leads to a lower tax rate such that the initial expectations are fulfilled. As a consequence, there exist multiple equilibria implying that the steady state is indeterminate. The paper by Schmitt-Grohé and Uribe is interesting because it nicely illustrates how self-fulfilling expectations can lead to multiple equilibria. However, neglecting a stock of outstanding public debt raises the question of how relevant their result is for real world economies. This holds because almost all countries are faced with the problem of public debt.

Guo and Harrison (2004) show that the result derived by Schmitt-Grohé and Uribe (1997) does not hold any longer when the tax rate is fixed and public spending is adjusted so that the budget of the government is balanced at each point in

A. Greiner, B. Fincke, *Public Debt and Economic Growth,*
Dynamic Modeling and Econometrics in Economics and Finance 11,
DOI 10.1007/978-3-642-01745-2_3, © Springer-Verlag Berlin Heidelberg 2009

time. Then, the equilibrium is unique and saddle point stable. Thus, it is not the fact that the government budget is balanced but rather the adjustment through variations in the income tax rate that generates the outcome of Schmitt-Grohé and Uribe (1997). The contribution of Guo and Harrison (2004) is remarkable because if one accepts the tax smoothing rule derived by Barro (1979), the question arises why the government should balance its budget through adjustments in the tax rate when a non-constant tax rate leads to an excess burden that can be avoided.

In the present chapter, we want to extend this line of research in several respects as in Greiner (2007a, 2007b). First, we allow for endogenous growth by assuming that there are positive externalities of investment which prevent the marginal product of capital from converging to zero as capital is accumulated. As a consequence, the economy is characterized by ongoing growth, a fact which does not hold for the models by Schmitt-Grohé and Uribe (1997) and Guo and Harrison (2004) where the economy converges to a steady state with zero growth. Taking into account that sustained per-capita growth is an important stylized fact in growth economics this extension is justified. Further, we consider that most industrialized countries are characterized by public debt so that we explicitly take into account a stock of government bonds in our model. The motivation for this lies in the observation that public debt plays an important role in real world economies so that analyzing budget rules without public debt seems to neglect an important aspect.

Within our model we, then, study two policy rules. The first rule is simply the inter-temporal budget constraint stating that the present value of future surpluses must equal the current stock of public debt. To make that constraint operable we posit that the primary surplus of the government is a positive linear function of public debt and a function of GDP. It should be noted that, neglecting seignorage and inflation, this rule leaves three possibilities for a government to react to higher public debt: it can raise taxes, it can reduce public spending or/and public debt is repaid due to a high GDP growth rate leading to large tax revenues. The second rule we consider is the balanced budget rule implying that the level of public debt is constant over time, leading to a zero debt to GDP ratio in the long-run.

The goal of our contribution is to study how the budgetary rule, the deficit rule and the balanced budget rule, affect stability and the growth rate of economies. Since public deficits and public debt play an important role in the euro area, as pointed out in the last chapter, our considerations are not only of theoretical interest but also have consequences for policy makers.

In the next section, we present the structure of our model.

3.1 The Structure of the Growth Model

The structure of our model is basically the same as in Guo and Harrison (2004). Our economy consists of three sectors: A household sector which receives labour income and income from its saving, a productive sector and the government. First, we describe the household sector.

3.1.1 The Household Sector

The household sector is represented by one household which maximizes the discounted stream of utility arising from per-capita consumption, $C(t)$, and from leisure, $L^m - L(t)$, over an infinite time horizon subject to its budget constraint, taking factor prices as given. L^m denotes the maximum available amount of time and $L(t)$ is the actual labor input. The maximization problem of the household can be written as[1]

$$\max_{C,L} \int_0^{\infty} e^{-\rho t} \left(\ln C - L^{1+\gamma}/(1+\gamma)\right) dt, \tag{3.1}$$

subject to

$$(1-\tau)(wL + rK + r_B B + \pi) = \dot{W} + C + \delta K. \tag{3.2}$$

$\rho \in (0, 1)$ is the household's rate of time preference, $\gamma \geq 0$ gives the inter-temporal elasticity of substitution of labour supply and $\delta \in (0, 1)$ is the depreciation rate of capital. w denotes the wage rate and r is the return to capital and r_B is the interest rate on government bonds. $W \equiv B + K$ gives wealth which is equal to public debt, B, and capital, K, and π gives possible profits of the productive sector, the household takes as given in solving its optimization problem. Finally, $\tau \in (0, 1)$ is the constant income tax rate. The dot gives the derivative with respect to time.

A no-arbitrage condition requires that the return to capital equals the return to government bonds yielding $r_B = r - \delta/(1-\tau)$. Thus, the budget constraint of the household can be written as

$$\dot{W} = (1-\tau)(wL + rW + \pi) - \delta W - C. \tag{3.3}$$

The current-value Hamiltonian[2] for this optimization problem is written as

$$\mathcal{H} = \ln C - L^{1+\gamma}/(1+\gamma) + \lambda((1-\tau)(wL + rW + \pi) - \delta W - C), \tag{3.4}$$

where λ is the co-state variable or the shadow price of wealth.

Necessary optimality conditions are given by

$$C = w(1-\tau)L^{-\gamma}, \tag{3.5}$$

$$\dot{C} = C(1-\tau)r - C(\rho + \delta). \tag{3.6}$$

If the transversality condition $\lim_{t\to\infty} e^{-\rho t} W/C = 0$ holds, which is fulfilled for a time path on which assets grow at the same rate as consumption, the necessary conditions are also sufficient.

[1] From now on we omit the time argument t if no ambiguity arises.

[2] For a brief introduction into dynamic optimization see Appendix B of the book.

3.1.2 The Productive Sector

The productive sector is represented by one firm which behaves competitively and which maximizes static profits. The production function of the firm is given by,

$$Y = K^{1-\alpha} \bar{K}^{\xi} L^{\beta}, \tag{3.7}$$

with $(1 - \alpha) \in (0, 1)$ the capital share, $\beta \in (0, 1)$ the labour share and $(1-\alpha) + \beta \leq 1$. Y is output and $\bar{K}$ represents the average economy-wide level of capital and we assume constant returns to capital in the economy, that is $(1-\alpha) + \xi = 1$.

Using $(1-\alpha) + \xi = 1$ and that $K = \bar{K}$ in equilibrium, profit maximization gives

$$r = (1-\alpha) L^{\beta}, \tag{3.8}$$

$$w = \beta L^{\beta-1} K. \tag{3.9}$$

3.1.3 The Government

The government in our economy receives tax revenues from income taxation and has revenues from issuing government bonds. As concerns public spending we follow Guo and Harrison (2004) and assume in this chapter that it is a mere waste of resources that is neither productive nor yields utility for the household. Further, the government sets the primary surplus such that it is a positive linear function of public debt which guarantees that public debt is sustainable, as shown in Sect. 2.1.

The accounting identity describing the accumulation of public debt in continuous time is given by:

$$\dot{B} = r_B B(1-\tau) - S, \tag{3.10}$$

where S is government surplus exclusive of net interest payments.

The inter-temporal budget constraint of the government is fulfilled if

$$\lim_{t\to\infty} e^{-\int_0^t (1-\tau) r_B(\mu) d\mu} B(t) = 0 \tag{3.11}$$

holds, which is the no-Ponzi game condition.

Now, assume that the ratio of the primary surplus to GDP is a positive linear function of the debt to GDP ratio and of a constant. The primary surplus ratio, then, can be written as

$$\frac{S}{Y} = \phi + \psi \frac{B}{Y}, \tag{3.12}$$

where $\phi \in \mathbb{R}$, $\psi \in \mathbb{R}_{++}$ are constants. The parameter ψ determines how strongly the primary surplus reacts to changes in public debt and ϕ determines whether the level of the primary surplus rises or falls with an increase in GDP. Using (3.12) the differential equation describing the evolution of public debt can be written as

$$\dot{B} = (r_B(1-\tau) - \psi)B - \phi Y. \tag{3.13}$$

From the considerations in Sect. 2.1 we know that, given the rule assumed in (3.12), a positive linear dependence of the primary surplus to GDP ratio on the debt ratio, that is $\psi > 0$, is a necessary, and in our model also a sufficient, condition for the inter-temporal budget constraint of the government to be met. Further, Sect. 2.2 has shown that there is empirical evidence that developed countries raise their primary surplus as public debt rises. Therefore, we posit that the government sets the primary surplus according to (3.12) so that the evolution of public debt is given by (3.13). We should also like to point out that, in principle, public debt could be negative implying that the government is creditor. In this chapter, however, we assume throughout that public debt is positive.[3]

Before we go, we briefly discuss the rule given in (3.12). Intuitively, it is clear that economic agents have to run primary surpluses in the future, when they run deficits today, in order to avoid playing a Ponzi game. This also holds true for the government sector as shown above. But assuming that public debt is the only determinant of the primary surplus would be too short-sighted because the government has some discretionary scope and because other variables such as the surplus of social insurances, for example, affect the primary surplus in reality. Therefore, it is reasonable to posit that the primary surplus also depends on the level of GDP in a country that determines the total tax revenue and temporary government spending. But it should be pointed out that sustainability of public debt is independent of how GDP affects the primary surplus as long as the primary surplus is a positive linear function of public debt.

3.2 Analysis of the Model

Before we analyze our model we give the definition of an equilibrium and of a balanced growth path. An equilibrium allocation for our economy is defined as follows.

Definition 1 An equilibrium is a sequence of variables $\{C(t), K(t), B(t)\}_{t=0}^{\infty}$ and a sequence of prices $\{w(t), r(t)\}_{t=0}^{\infty}$ such that, given prices and fiscal rules, the firm maximizes profits, the household solves (3.1) subject to (3.2) and the budget constraint of the government (3.10) is fulfilled with the primary surplus set according to (3.12).

In Definition 2 we define a balanced growth path.

[3]If the government was a creditor there would be no need for the government to stick to the rule defined in (3.12) nor for the balanced budget rule.

Definition 2 A balanced growth path (BGP) is a path such that the economy is in equilibrium and such that consumption and capital grow at the same strictly positive constant growth rate, that is $\dot{C}/C = \dot{K}/K = g$, $g > 0$, $g =$ constant, and either (i) $\dot{B}/B = g$ or (ii) $\dot{B} = 0$.

Definition 2 shows that we consider two different budget rules. Case (i) describes a situation which is characterized by public deficits where government debt grows at the same rate as all other endogenous variables in the long-run. Since the government sets the primary surplus according to (3.12) it does not play a Ponzi game in this case but fulfills the inter-temporal budget constraint. Case (ii) gives the balanced budget rule. This rule guarantees zero public deficits and implies that the debt to GDP ratio converges to zero in the long-run.

To study our model, we note that it is completely described by the following equations,

$$\frac{\dot{C}}{C} = (1-\tau)(1-\alpha)\omega(C/K)^{-\beta/(1-\beta+\gamma)} - (\rho+\delta), \quad C(0) > 0, \tag{3.14}$$

$$\frac{\dot{K}}{K} = \omega(C/K)^{-\beta/(1-\beta+\gamma)}(1-\tau+\phi) - (C/K) - \delta + \psi(B/K),$$
$$K_0 > 0, \tag{3.15}$$

$$\frac{\dot{B}}{B} = (1-\tau)(1-\alpha)\omega(C/K)^{-\beta/(1-\beta+\gamma)} - \phi\omega(C/K)^{-\beta/(1-\beta+\gamma)}(K/B) - \delta - \psi,$$
$$B_0 > 0, \tag{3.16}$$

with $\omega = (\beta(1-\tau))^{\beta/(1-\beta+\gamma)}$ and where we used $r_B = r - \delta/(1-\tau)$. The initial conditions with respect to capital and public debt are assumed to be given while consumption can be chosen by the household at time $t = 0$.

To analyze our economy around a BGP we define the new variables $c \equiv C/K$ and $b \equiv B/K$. Differentiating these variables with respect to time leads to a two dimensional system of differential equations given by

$$\dot{c} = c\big(c - c^{-\beta/(1-\beta+\gamma)}\omega((1-\tau)\alpha+\phi) - \rho - \psi b\big), \tag{3.17}$$

$$\dot{b} = b\big(c - c^{-\beta/(1-\beta+\gamma)}\omega((1-\tau)\alpha+\phi) - \phi\omega c^{-\beta/(1-\beta+\gamma)}b^{-1}\big)$$
$$- b(\psi+\psi b). \tag{3.18}$$

A solution of $\dot{c} = \dot{b} = 0$ with respect to c, b gives a BGP for our model and the corresponding ratios $b^\star, c^\star$ on the BGP.[4]

In the next subsection, we study our model where the government runs permanent deficits but sticks to the rule as defined in (3.12) so that the inter-temporal budget constraint is fulfilled.

[4]The $\star$ denotes BGP values.

3.2.1 Permanent Deficits and the Inter-temporal Budget Constraint

Proposition 4 below gives results as concerns existence, uniqueness and stability of a balanced growth path for our economy where the government runs deficits but sticks to the inter-temporal budget constraint.

Proposition 4 *Assume that the household's time preference and the depreciation rate are sufficiently small. Then, there exists a unique BGP if the government runs permanent deficits but obeys the inter-temporal budget constraint. For $\psi > \rho$ the BGP is saddle point stable, for $\psi < \rho$ the BGP is unstable.*

Proof See the appendix to this section. □

The requirement that the rate of time preference and the depreciation rate must not be too large for a BGP to exist can be seen from (3.14). This is not a strict assumption. From an economic point of view it just states that the after-tax return to capital must be sufficiently large for ongoing growth.

Then, our economy is characterized by a unique BGP which is a saddle point if the reaction of the government to variations in public debt is sufficiently large, that is for $\psi > \rho$. This condition states that the primary surplus must rise sufficiently as public debt increases. In the opposite case, that is for $\psi < \rho$, the economy is unstable. In this case, the reaction of the primary surplus to increases in public debt is not large enough to stabilize the economy. Thus, the debt policy of the government is decisive as to whether the economy is stable or unstable.[5] Proposition 4 also implies that both global and local indeterminacy are excluded.

Global indeterminacy refers to the balanced growth rate that is obtained in the long run and states that the initial value of consumption, which can be chosen freely by society, crucially determines to which BGP the economy converges and, thus, the long-run balanced growth rate. It should be noted that consumption is not a predetermined variable at time $t = 0$ in contrast to the initial stock of physical capital that is given. Local indeterminacy means that the transitional dynamics of two economies, which converge to the same BGP in the long run, crucially depend on the choice of initial consumption, $C(0)$. Thus, the transitional growth rates of those economies are determined by $C(0)$ but not the long-run growth rate, which is the same (see for example Benhabib and Perli 1994, for a more thorough treatment of those two concepts and Buiter 1982, for an exact definition of predetermined and non-predetermined variables).

We should also like to point out that the rule given by (3.12) makes public spending a semi-endogenous variable. This holds because with (3.12) public spending relative to GDP, C_p/Y, is given by

$$C_p/Y = (\tau - \phi) - \psi B/Y. \tag{3.19}$$

[5]It should be noted that $\dot{C}/C = \dot{B}/B$ implies $\rho = \psi + \phi Y/B$. Hence, for the stable case with $\psi > \rho$, $\phi < 0$ must hold when B is positive (see the proof of Proposition 4 in the appendix to this section).

Equation (3.19) shows that, given fiscal parameters τ, ϕ, ψ, public spending relative to GDP is an endogenous variable depending on the public debt ratio. However, the government can control C_p/Y to a certain degree by the choice of ϕ for example. Therefore, it can be called a semi-endogenous variable.

Next, we analyze the balanced budget rule.

3.2.2 The Balanced Budget Rule

To model the balanced budget rule, we set $\phi = 0$ and $\psi = (1 - \tau)r - \delta$. From (3.12) one immediately realizes that this implies $\dot{B} = 0$, that is a balanced budget and, thus, a constant level of public debt. With a balanced government budget the ratio of public spending to GDP, C_p/Y, is again a semi-endogenous variable on the transition path that depends on the interest rate and on the debt ratio. On the BGP, the debt ratio equals zero and the spending ratio equals the income tax rate, that is $C_p/Y = \tau$ holds.[6] Proposition 5 gives results for our economy assuming a balanced government budget.

Proposition 5 *Assume that the household's time preference and the depreciation rate are sufficiently small. Then, there exists a unique saddle point stable BGP if the government runs a balanced budget.*

Proof See the appendix to this section. □

Proposition 5 states that the balanced budget rule yields a unique and saddle point stable BGP, in contrast to the case with permanent public deficits where the economy turned out to be unstable if the reaction of the primary surplus to higher public debt was not sufficiently large. As in the case where the government runs deficits but sticks to the inter-temporal budget constraint, global and local indeterminacy are again excluded. But, in contrast to the former rule, the economy is always saddle point stable with a balanced government budget.

Thus, the overall conclusion we can draw is that stability is the more likely, the more weight the government puts on debt stabilization. This holds because the balanced budget rule always yields a saddle point stable BGP and the model with public deficits is stable if the reaction of the government to higher debt is sufficiently strong.

Next, we compare the long-run growth rate of the inter-temporal budget constraint rule with that of the balanced budget rule. The following proposition gives the result.

Proposition 6 *The long-run growth rate in the economy with the balanced budget rule exceeds the long-run growth rate of the economy with permanent deficits.*

---

[6]Note that in case of permanent deficits a positive value for C_p/Y is not guaranteed on the BGP unless the tax rate is sufficiently large.

Proof See the appendix to this section. □

The result stated in Proposition 6 is far-reaching. It says that an economy where the government runs a balanced budget gives a higher growth rate in the long-run than an economy where the government runs deficits. The economic reason for that outcome is that a positive public debt ratio leads to a crowding out of investment which does not occur with the balanced budget rule where the debt ratio asymptotically equals zero. The crowding out results from the fact that the shadow price of wealth is smaller if the government runs deficits because it implies that less of the household's savings is used for the formation of productive private capital. That leads to a lower return to capital, r, in case the government runs deficits compared to the situation with a balanced government budget. Consequently, the share of consumption relative to GDP is larger and the investment share is smaller leading to a lower balanced growth rate in the long-run.

3.3 Conclusion

In this chapter we have analyzed the basic endogenous growth model with externalities of capital and elastic labour supply and studied how governments can affect stability of the economy and its growth rate through their debt policies. Assuming constant tax rates, we could demonstrate that the model is the more likely to be stable the more weight the government puts on stabilizing public debt.

Thus, the balanced budget rule turned out to generate a unique BGP that is always saddle point stable. If the government runs permanent deficits, what is more realistic, and sticks to the inter-temporal budget constraint, the BGP is also unique, independent of the governmental reaction to higher public debt. However, in this case convergence to the BGP and, thus stability, is only given if the reaction of the primary surplus to higher public debt is sufficiently large. If the government does not react enough to higher public debt, that is if the increase in the primary surplus is relatively small as debt rises, the economy is unstable. Finally, we could demonstrate that the balanced budget rule implies a higher growth rate compared to the economy with permanent deficits.

In the next section, we study an endogenous growth model where the government invests in a productive public capital stock.

Appendix

Proof of Proposition 4 To prove this proposition we set $\dot{C}/C = \dot{B}/B$, which must hold on a BGP, giving

$$\phi \omega c^{-\beta/(1-\beta+\gamma)} b^{-1} = \rho - \psi \tag{A3.1}$$

Substituting this relation in $\dot{b}/b$ gives,

$$\dot{b}/b = c - \omega c^{-\beta/(1-\beta+\gamma)}((1-\tau)\alpha + \rho\phi/(\rho-\psi))$$

From (A3.1) we know that $b > 0$ implies that ϕ and $\rho - \psi$ have the same sign so that $\phi/(\rho-\psi) > 0$ holds. With this, it is easily seen that the following relations hold,

$$\lim_{c\to 0}(\dot{b}/b) = -\infty, \qquad \lim_{c\to\infty}(\dot{b}/b) = +\infty, \qquad \partial(\dot{b}/b)/\partial c > 0.$$

This proves the existence of a unique $c^\star$ which solves $\dot{b}/b = 0$ and, thus, of a unique BGP for a sufficiently small value of $(\rho+\delta)$.

To study stability, we compute the Jacobian matrix evaluated at the rest point of (3.17)–(3.18). The Jacobian is given by

$$J = \begin{bmatrix} a_{11} & -\psi c \\ a_{21} & \phi\omega c^{-\beta/(1-\beta+\gamma)} b^{-1} - \psi b \end{bmatrix},$$

with c and b evaluated at the rest point $\{c^\star, b^\star\}$ and a_{11} and a_{21} given by

$$a_{11} = c\big(1 + (\beta/(1-\beta+\gamma))\omega c^{-1-\beta/(1-\beta+\gamma)}(\phi + (1-\tau)\alpha)\big),$$
$$a_{21} = b\big(1 + (\beta/(1-\beta+\gamma))\omega c^{-1-\beta/(1-\beta+\gamma)}(\phi(1+b^{-1}) + (1-\tau)\alpha)\big).$$

The determinant of the Jacobian matrix can be computed as

$$\det J = (\rho-\psi)\big(c + (\beta/(1-\beta+\gamma))\omega c^{-\beta/(1-\beta+\gamma)}(1-\tau)\alpha\big) + \rho\big(\beta/(1-\beta+\gamma)\big)\phi\omega c^{-\beta/(1-\beta+\gamma)}$$

Using (A3.1) we can rewrite the determinant as follows,

$$\det J = (\rho-\psi)\big(c + (\beta/(1-\beta+\gamma))\omega c^{-\beta/(1-\beta+\gamma)}(1-\tau)\alpha\big) + \rho\big(\beta/(1-\beta+\gamma)\big)(\rho-\psi)b$$

For $\psi > \rho$ the determinant is negative since $b > 0$ holds.

For $\psi < \rho$ the determinant is positive. To show that the BGP is unstable we have to compute the trace of the Jacobian, $\operatorname{tr} J$, which is given by,

$$\operatorname{tr} J = c - \psi b + (\beta/(1-\beta+\gamma))\omega c^{-\beta/(1-\beta+\gamma)}(\phi + (1-\tau)\alpha) + \phi\omega b^{-1} c^{-\beta/(1-\beta+\gamma)}.$$

To see that $\operatorname{tr} J$ is positive we first note that a positive value of b implies $\phi > 0$ for $\psi < \rho$. Further, from $\dot{c}/c = 0$ we get $c - \psi b = \rho + c^{-\beta/(1-\beta+\gamma)}(\phi + (1-\tau)\alpha) > 0$, so that the trace of the Jacobian is positive, too. Since the trace and the determinant are both positive, the BGP is unstable for $\psi < \rho$. Thus, Proposition 4 is proven. □

Proof of Proposition 5 To prove Proposition 5, we first note that the balanced budget rule implies $b^\star = 0$ since public debt is constant while the capital stock grows over time. Further, $\phi = 0$ and $\psi = (1-\tau)r - \delta$ hold in this case. Using this, the equation $\dot{c}/c$ can be written as

$$\dot{c}/c = \left(c - c^{-\beta/(1-\beta+\gamma)}(1-\tau)\alpha - \rho\right)$$

It is easily seen that the following relations hold,

$$\lim_{c\to 0}(\dot{c}/c) = -\infty, \qquad \lim_{c\to\infty}(\dot{c}/c) = +\infty, \qquad \partial(\dot{c}/c)/\partial c > 0.$$

This proves the existence of a unique $c^\star$ which solves $\dot{c}/c = 0$ and, thus, of a unique BGP for a sufficiently small value of $(\rho+\delta)$.

The Jacobian is given by

$$\mathrm{J} = \begin{bmatrix} a_{11} & -c(1-\tau)(1-\alpha)\omega c^{-\beta/(1-\beta+\gamma)} \\ 0 & -g \end{bmatrix},$$

with c and b evaluated at the rest point $\{c^\star, 0\}$ and a_{11} given by

$$a_{11} = c + (1-\tau)\alpha\omega(\beta/(1-\beta+\gamma))c^{-\beta/(1-\beta+\gamma)}.$$

One eigenvalue is $a_{11} > 0$, and the second is $-g < 0$ so that the BGP is saddle point stable. Thus, the proposition is proven. □

Proof of Proposition 6 To prove this proposition we note that $\dot{C}/C = \dot{K}/K$ holds on the BGP. With a balanced government budget this is equivalent to,

$$(1-\tau)(1-\alpha)\omega c^{-\beta/(1-\beta+\gamma)} - (\rho+\delta) = (1-\tau)\omega c^{-\beta/(1-\beta+\gamma)} - c - \delta \quad \text{(A3.2)}$$

With permanent public deficits $\dot{C}/C = \dot{K}/K$ is equivalent to,

$$\begin{aligned}(1-\tau)(1-\alpha)\omega c^{-\beta/(1-\beta+\gamma)} - (\rho+\delta) \\ = (1-\tau)\omega c^{-\beta/(1-\beta+\gamma)} - c - \delta + \psi b + \phi\omega c^{-\beta/(1-\beta+\gamma)}\end{aligned} \quad \text{(A3.3)}$$

Further, with permanent public deficits we get from $\dot{C}/C = \dot{B}/B$,

$$\psi b = -\phi\omega c^{-\beta/(1-\beta+\gamma)} + \rho b$$

Inserting this in (A3.3) leads to

$$\begin{aligned}(1-\tau)(1-\alpha)\omega c^{-\beta/(1-\beta+\gamma)} - (\rho+\delta) \\ = (1-\tau)\omega c^{-\beta/(1-\beta+\gamma)} - c - \delta + \rho b\end{aligned} \quad \text{(A3.4)}$$

which holds on a BGP in the economy with permanent budget deficits.

The graph of the left hand side of (A3.2) is the same as the graph of the left hand side of (A3.4). The graph of the right hand side of (A3.2) is below the graph of the right hand side of (A3.4) for $b > 0$. Consequently, the intersection point of the left hand side with the right hand side of (A3.2) is to the left of that of (A3.4) implying that $c^{\star}$ in the economy with the balanced budget rule is smaller than $c^{\star}$ in the economy with permanent budget deficits. Therefore, the balanced budget rule yields a higher long-run growth rate. □

Chapter 4
Public Debt, Productive Public Spending and Economic Growth with Full Employment

In the last chapter it was demonstrated that an economy with a balanced government budget always generates a higher long-run growth rate than an economy where the government runs permanent deficits. In addition, it could be shown that, in case of permanent public deficits, stability of the economy is only given if the reaction of the primary surplus to public debt is sufficiently high. The underlying model was an endogenous growth model with public spending being a pure waste of resources. Now, it could be argued that the results may change when government spending is productive, like investment in public infrastructure for example, in particular the outcome as regards growth effects might be different. Therefore, we study in this chapter an endogenous growth model with productive public spending.

One strand in the endogenous growth literature assumes that the government invests in a productive public capital stock which raises the incentive to invest (see for example Futagami et al. 1993). This approach goes back to Arrow and Kurz (1970) who, however, do not analyze models leading to sustained growth endogenously.

Most of the endogenous growth models with productive public spending are characterized by the assumption of a balanced government budget. Exemptions of this are the approaches by Greiner and Semmler (2000) and by Ghosh and Mourmouras (2004). In these contributions it is assumed that the government may finance public expenditures by deficits but the government has to stick to some well-defined budgetary regimes.[1] Greiner and Semmler (2000) study growth effects of fiscal policy and find that more strict regimes generate a higher balanced growth rate because the debt ratio in these regimes is smaller compared to that in less strict budgetary regimes, where the government may run deficits not only to finance public investment. Ghosh and Mourmouras (2004) analyze welfare effects of these regimes and demonstrate that the choice of the budgetary regime does not only affect the long-run growth rate but is also crucial as concerns welfare. An interesting contribution along this line of research is provided by Futagami et al. (2008) who study an endogenous growth model with productive public spending and public debt but assume

[1]For a survey of budgetary regimes resorted to in the economics literature, see van Ewijk (1991).

A. Greiner, B. Fincke, *Public Debt and Economic Growth*,
Dynamic Modeling and Econometrics in Economics and Finance 11,
DOI 10.1007/978-3-642-01745-2_4, © Springer-Verlag Berlin Heidelberg 2009

that government debt must converge to a certain exogenously given debt ratio asymptotically. They demonstrate that there exist two balanced growth paths to which the economy can converge in the long-run, with one being saddle point stable and the other being saddle point stable or asymptotically stable. Further, these authors show that a deficit financed increase in productive public spending raises the low balanced growth rate while it reduces the high balanced growth rate.

While the assumption of budgetary regimes or of a debt ratio to which an economy must converge in the long-run is plausible and can be found in the real world, it may nevertheless be considered as ad hoc. However, this does not hold for the inter-temporal budget constraint of the government. This constraint is in a way a natural constraint any government must obey. It should also be pointed out that, given a fixed tax rate and fixed unproductive public spending, a rise in the primary surplus ratio, as a result of a higher debt ratio, can lead to a decline in productive public spending. And there is indeed empirical evidence that public investment is reduced as the debt service rises, instead of other unproductive public spending. Examples of such studies are the ones by Oxley and Martin (1991), Gong et al. (2001) or Heinemann (2002).[2]

It should also be recalled that the fact that an increase in the primary surplus, as debt grows, guarantees sustainability of public debt, is more general than the Ricardo equivalence theorem and contains the latter as a special case. This holds because there are three ways for the government to raise the primary surplus: First, it can raise taxes, second it can reduce spending and, third, the surplus can increase due to a higher GDP leading to more tax revenues.

In this chapter we take up the approach by Futagami et al. (1993) and allow for public debt and public deficits as in Greiner (2008b). In addition, we posit as in the preceding chapter that the primary surplus relative to GDP is a positive function of the debt to GDP ratio as this guarantees sustainability of public debt. To start with, we present the structure of our growth model in the next section.

4.1 The Endogenous Growth Model

Our economy consists of three sectors: A household sector which receives labour income and income from its saving, a productive sector and the government. First, we describe the household sector.

4.1.1 Households

The household sector is represented by one household which maximizes the discounted stream of utility arising from per-capita consumption, $C(t)$, over an infinite

[2]See also the conclusion of Chap. 2.2.

time horizon subject to its budget constraint, taking factor prices as given. The utility function is assumed to be logarithmic, $U(C) = \ln C$, and the household has one unit of labour, L, which it supplies inelastically, in contrast to the model of the last chapter.[3] The maximization problem can be written as

$$\max_{C} \int_{0}^{\infty} e^{-\rho t} \ln C dt, \tag{4.1}$$

subject to

$$(1-\tau)(w + rW + \pi) = \dot{W} + C. \tag{4.2}$$

ρ is the subjective discount rate, w is the wage rate and r is the interest rate. $W \equiv B + K$ gives wealth which is equal to public debt, B, and private capital, K, and π gives possible profits of the productive sector, the household takes as given in solving its optimization problem. Finally, $\tau \in (0, 1)$ is the constant income tax rate. The dot gives the derivative with respect to time and we neglect depreciation of private capital in this section.

To solve this problem we formulate the current-value Hamiltonian which is written as

$$\mathcal{H} = \ln C + \lambda((1-\tau)(w + rW + \pi) - C). \tag{4.3}$$

Necessary optimality conditions are given by

$$C^{-1} = \lambda, \tag{4.4}$$

$$\dot{\lambda} = \rho\lambda - \lambda(1-\tau)r. \tag{4.5}$$

If the transversality condition $\lim_{t\to\infty} e^{-\rho t} W/C = 0$ holds, which is fulfilled for a time path on which assets grow at the same rate as consumption, the necessary conditions are also sufficient.

4.1.2 Firms

The productive sector is represented by one firm which behaves competitively and which maximizes static profits. The production function of the firm is given by

$$Y = K^{1-\alpha} G^{\alpha} L^{\beta}, \tag{4.6}$$

with $(1-\alpha) + \beta \leq 1$. $(1-\alpha)$ again denotes the private capital share and β gives the labour share. Y is output, G denotes public capital and α gives the elasticity of output with respect to public capital. Using that labour is set to one, $L = 1$, profit maximization gives

$$w = \beta K^{1-\alpha} G^{\alpha}, \tag{4.7}$$

$$r = (1-\alpha) K^{-\alpha} G^{\alpha}. \tag{4.8}$$

---

[3] From now on we again omit the time argument t if no ambiguity arises.

4.1.3 The Government

The government in our economy receives tax revenues from income taxation and has revenues from issuing government bonds it then uses for public investment, I_p, and for public consumption, C_p. As concerns public consumption we assume that this type of spending does neither yield utility nor raise productivity but is only a waste of resources. Further, the government sets the primary surplus such that it is a positive linear function of public debt which guarantees that public debt is sustainable. We note that the accounting identity describing the accumulation of public debt in continuous time is given by:

$$\dot{B} = rB(1-\tau) - S, \tag{4.9}$$

where S is government surplus exclusive of net interest payments.

The inter-temporal budget constraint of the government is fulfilled if

$$B(0) = \int_0^\infty e^{-\int_0^\mu (1-\tau)r(\nu)d\nu} S(\mu)d\mu \leftrightarrow \lim_{t\to\infty} e^{-\int_0^t (1-\tau)r(\mu)d\mu} B(t) = 0 \tag{4.10}$$

holds. Equation (4.10) is the present-value borrowing constraint which states that public debt at time zero must equal the future present-value surpluses.

Again, we assume that the ratio of the primary surplus to GDP ratio is a positive linear function of the debt to GDP ratio and of a constant. The primary surplus ratio, then, can be written as

$$\frac{S}{Y} = \phi + \psi\frac{B}{Y} = \frac{\tau Y - I_p - C_p}{Y}, \tag{4.11}$$

where $\phi \in \mathbb{R}$, $\psi \in \mathbb{R}_{++}$ are constants. The parameter ψ determines how strong the primary surplus reacts to changes in public debt and ϕ determines whether the level of the primary surplus rises or falls with an increase in GDP.

Using (4.11) the differential equation describing the evolution of public debt can be written as

$$\dot{B} = (r(1-\tau) - \psi)B - \phi Y. \tag{4.12}$$

From Sect. 2.1 we know that a positive linear dependence of the primary surplus to GDP ratio on the debt ratio, that is $\psi > 0$, is a necessary condition for the inter-temporal budget constraint of the government to be met. Therefore, we posit that the government sets the primary surplus according to (4.11) so that the evolution of public debt is given by (4.12).

Defining $C_p/I_p = \kappa$ as public consumption relative to public investment, that is constant, and using that the evolution of public debt is given by $\dot{B} = rB(1-\tau) + I_p(1+\kappa) - \tau Y = rB(1-\tau) - \psi B - \phi Y$ public investment can be written as

$$I_p = \omega(\tau - \phi)Y - \omega\psi B, \tag{4.13}$$

where $\omega = 1/(1+\kappa)$. Neglecting depreciation, the differential equation describing the evolution of public capital, then, is written as

$$\dot{G} = I_p = \omega(\tau - \phi)Y - \omega\psi B. \tag{4.14}$$

4.1.4 Equilibrium Conditions and the Balanced Growth Path

Before we analyze our model we give the definition of an equilibrium and of a balanced growth path. An equilibrium allocation for our economy is defined as follows.

Definition 3 An equilibrium is a sequence of variables $\{C(t), K(t), G(t), B(t)\}_{t=0}^{\infty}$ and a sequence of prices $\{w(t), r(t)\}_{t=0}^{\infty}$ such that, given prices and fiscal parameters, the firm maximizes profits, the household solves (4.1) subject to (4.2) and the budget constraint of the government (4.9) is fulfilled with the primary surplus set according to (4.11).

Resorting to (4.4), (4.5) and (4.8), the growth rate of consumption is derived as

$$\frac{\dot{C}}{C} = -\rho + (1-\tau)(1-\alpha)K^{-\alpha}G^{\alpha}. \tag{4.15}$$

The economy-wide resource constraint is obtained by combining (4.12) and (4.2) as

$$\frac{\dot{K}}{K} = -\frac{C}{K} + \frac{K^{1-\alpha}G^{\alpha}}{K} + \psi\frac{B}{K} + (\phi - \tau)\frac{K^{1-\alpha}G^{\alpha}}{K}. \tag{4.16}$$

Thus, in equilibrium the economy is completely described by (4.15), (4.16), (4.12) and (4.14) plus the limiting transversality condition of the household.

In Definition 4 we give the definition of a balanced growth path for this section.

Definition 4 A balanced growth path (BGP) is a path such that the economy is in equilibrium and such that consumption, private capital and public capital grow at the same strictly positive constant growth rate, that is $\dot{C}/C = \dot{K}/K = \dot{G}/G = g$, $g > 0$, $g =$ constant, and either

(i) $\dot{B} = 0$ or
(ii) $\dot{B}/B = g_B$, with $0 < g_B < g$, $g_B =$ constant, or
(iii) $\dot{B}/B = \dot{C}/C = \dot{K}/K = \dot{G}/G = g$.

Definition 4 shows that we now consider three different scenarios. Scenario (i) is the balanced budget scenario where the government has at each point in time a balanced budget. But this does not necessarily imply that public debt equals zero. If the level of initial debt is positive, the debt to capital ratio and also the debt to GDP ratio are positive but decline over time and converge to zero in the long-run. Scenario (ii) describes a situation where the government always runs a deficit so that the growth rate of public debt is positive in the long-run. But public debt grows at a smaller rate than capital, consumption and output.[4] This implies that the debt ratio also converges to zero in the long-run since public debt grows at a smaller rate than capital and output. The last scenario, scenario (iii) finally, describes the case which is characterized by public deficits where government debt grows at the same rate as all other endogenous variables in the long-run.

To analyze our economy around a BGP we define the new variables $x \equiv G/K$, $b \equiv B/K$ and $c \equiv C/K$. Differentiating these variables with respect to time leads to a three dimensional system of differential equations given by

$$\dot{x} = x((\tau - \phi)x^{\alpha-1}\omega - \omega\psi b/x + c - x^{\alpha} - \psi b + (\tau - \phi)x^{\alpha}), \tag{4.17}$$

$$\dot{b} = b((1-\alpha)x^{\alpha}(1-\tau) - \psi - \phi x^{\alpha}/b + c - x^{\alpha} - \psi b + (\tau - \phi)x^{\alpha}), \tag{4.18}$$

$$\dot{c} = c((1-\alpha)x^{\alpha}(1-\tau) - \rho + c - x^{\alpha} - \psi b + (\tau - \phi)x^{\alpha}). \tag{4.19}$$

A solution of $\dot{x} = \dot{b} = \dot{c} = 0$ with respect to x, b, c gives a BGP for our model and the corresponding ratios $x^{\star}, b^{\star}, c^{\star}$ on the BGP.[5] In the next section we analyze growth and welfare effects of our scenarios as given in Definition 4.

4.2 Analyzing the Model

In this section we study the structure of our model as well as growth and welfare effects of the different scenarios. Further, we analyze how a transition from scenario (iii), where the debt ratio is strictly positive in the long-run, to scenario (i) and to scenario (ii), and vice versa, affects growth and welfare.

4.2.1 The Asymptotic Behaviour of the Model

First, we analyze scenario (i) and scenario (ii). Scenario (i) is obtained by setting the reaction coefficient ψ equal to the net return on capital, $(1-\tau)r$, making ψ an endogenous variable. Further, ϕ is set equal to zero for all times, that is $\phi = 0$, for $t \in [0, \infty)$. Scenario (ii) is obtained by setting $\phi = 0$ and by letting ψ be an exogenous parameter which can take arbitrary but strictly positive values. Proposition 7 gives results as concerns existence, uniqueness and stability of a balanced growth path for these two scenarios.

Proposition 7 *There exists a unique saddle point stable balanced growth path for scenario* (i). *For $\rho < \psi < r(1-\tau)$, scenario* (ii) *is also characterized by a unique saddle point stable balanced growth path.*

---

[4]Needless to say that GDP grows at the same rate as capital and consumption on a BGP.

[5]The $\star$ denotes BGP values and we exclude the economically meaningless BGP $x^{\star} = c^{\star} = 0$.

Proof See the appendix to this section. □

This proposition demonstrates that both the balanced budget scenario and the scenario with public deficits but an asymptotically zero debt ratio are characterized by unique BGPs which are saddle point stable, where a certain parameter restriction must be fulfilled for scenario (ii). The restriction $\rho < \psi < r(1-\tau)$ states that, on the one hand, ψ must not be too small, $\psi > \rho$, so that sustained growth is possible. This holds because otherwise public debt would become too large requiring too many resources for the debt service so that ongoing growth would not be possible. The positive effect of ψ on the growth rate can be seen from (4.16). On the other hand, ψ must not be too large, $\psi < r(1-\tau)$, because otherwise the government would not invest enough in public capital so that sustained growth would not be possible either, which can be seen from (4.14).

Saddle point stability means that there exists a unique value $c(0)$ such that the economy converges to the balanced growth path in the long-run. If one takes both $x(0)$ and $b(0)$ as given, since both x and b are state variables, this implies that the economy is determinate. However, from an economic point of view, it seems plausible to make a difference between capital stocks and public debt. This holds because capital stocks need a longer time period to be built up whereas public debt can be changed faster since it is a financial variable. Therefore, from an economic point of view the assumption that $b(0)$ can be controlled could also be justified.

As concerns scenario (iii), where public debt grows at the same rate as consumption and capital in the long-run, the analytical model turns out to be quite complicated and no unambiguous results can be derived. But it is possible to derive a result as concerns the public debt to private capital ratio for the analytical model. This is the contents of Proposition 8.

Proposition 8 *Assume that there exists a balanced growth path in scenario* (iii). *Then, the ratio of public debt to private capital is given by*

$$b^{\star} = \frac{\omega(\tau-\phi)(x^{\star})^{\alpha} - gx^{\star}}{\psi\omega}.$$

$\phi < \tau$ is necessary for $b^{\star}$ to be positive and $\phi \geq \tau$ is sufficient for $b^{\star}$ to be negative.

Proof See the appendix to this section. □

Proposition 8 shows that the reaction of the primary surplus to variations of GDP is crucial as concerns the question of whether sustained growth is feasible in the long-run together with a positive value of public debt. It should be recalled that the parameter ϕ determines whether, and if so how strongly, the level of the primary surplus rises as GDP increases. Proposition 8 states that for relatively large values of ϕ, that is for $\phi \geq \tau$, sustained growth is only feasible if public debt is negative, that is if the government is a creditor. At first sight, this result may seem counter intuitive. However, if the government puts too high a weight on controlling public debt, by setting ϕ to a high value, it spends too little for public investment so that in this case sustained growth is only feasible if the government has built up a stock of wealth out of which it finances productive public spending. From a technical point of view, this is seen from the differential equation for $\dot{G}$, (4.14), which shows that public investment would be negative for $\phi \geq \tau$, unless B was negative, too.

In the next subsection we analyze growth effects of the different scenarios.

4.2.2 Growth Effects of the Different Scenarios

Our first concern is to answer the question of which scenario brings about a higher growth rate of consumption and of capital in the long-run. Proposition 9 gives the answer to this question.

Proposition 9 *Assume that the government does not dispose of a stock of wealth and that there exists a balanced growth path with a strictly positive public debt ratio in scenario* (iii). *Then, the balanced growth rate in scenario* (iii) *is lower than the balanced growth rate in scenario* (i). *Further, the balanced growth rate in scenario* (i) *is equal to the balanced growth rate in scenario* (ii).

Proof See the appendix to this section. □

The outcome that the balanced growth rate in scenario (i), the balanced budget scenario, is equal to that obtained in scenario (ii), where public debt grows less than capital and output in the long-run, is not too surprising. This holds because asymptotically the debt ratio equals zero in both scenarios, so that both scenarios are described by the same equations.

A more interesting result is the outcome that a balanced budget always leads to a higher growth rate in the long-run compared to a scenario where public debt grows at the same rate as consumption and capital. This is indeed a strong result because it states that, starting from a balanced budget, a deficit financed public investment can never raise the long-run growth rate if it leads to a positive debt ratio in the long-run. The economic intuition behind this result is that a positive debt ratio in the long-run requires resources for the debt service which cannot be used for productive public spending, leading to a lower balanced growth rate. Hence, starting from a balanced government budget, a deficit financed increase in public investment raises the transitional growth rates of private and public capital but brings about a lower growth rate in the long-run, unless the government balances its budget again or lets public debt grow at a smaller rate than GDP in the long-run, so that the debt to GDP ratio converges to zero.

The only possibility to achieve a balanced growth rate exceeding the one of the balanced budget scenario is given if the government has built up a stock of wealth it uses to finance its expenditures and to lend to the household sector. In this case, the government is a creditor implying that b is negative.[6] In a corollary to proposition 9 we treat this case.

Corollary 2 *Assume that the government has built up a stock of wealth. Then, the balanced growth rate in scenario* (iii) *exceeds the balanced growth rate of scenario* (i).

Proof See the appendix to this section. □

It must be pointed out that the result in proposition 9 only states that a balanced government budget, or a scenario where public debt grows at a smaller rate than capital and output in the long-run, gives a higher balanced growth path compared to a scenario where public debt grows at the same rate as capital and output. It does not say anything about long-run growth effects of deficit financed public investment given the scenario where public debt grows at the balanced growth rate in the long-run. Thus, a deficit financed increase in public investment may yield a higher balanced growth rate in the latter scenario and reduce the long-run debt ratio.

In order to see this we resort to a numerical example. As to the parameter values we set the elasticity of output with respect to public capital to 20 percent, that is $\alpha = 0.2$. The income tax rate is set to 10 percent, $\tau = 0.1$, and the rate of time preference is 15 percent, $\rho = 0.15$. Assuming that one time period comprises several years such a high rate can be justified. The reaction coefficient ψ is set to $\psi = 0.05$ and $\omega = 0.1$.

Table 4.1 gives the balanced growth rate, g, and the debt to private capital ratio on the BGP, $b^\star$, for different values of ϕ.

To interpret the outcome shown in Table 4.1, it should be noted that a deficit financed increase in public investment is modelled by a decline in ϕ which can be seen from (4.13). Thus, Table 4.1 demonstrates that a deficit financed increase in public investment raises the balanced growth rate. One can also realize that for negative values of ϕ, implying that the primary surplus declines as GDP rises, sustained growth is only feasible with a negative public debt with this parameter constellation. In this case, the government has built up a stock of wealth out of which it finances productive public spending.

It should also be mentioned that the Jacobian matrix of (4.17)–(4.19), with the parameter values underlying Table 4.1, is characterized by one negative eigenvalue

Table 4.1 Balanced growth rate and the debt to private capital ratio for different ϕ with $\psi = 0.05$

	$\phi = 0.005$	$\phi = 0.0025$	$\phi = -0.0025$	$\phi = -0.005$
g	0.189	0.191	0.196	0.198
$b^\star$	0.024	0.012	−0.012	−0.024

[6]It should be noted that there would be no need for the government to stick to the rule defined in (4.11) nor for the balanced budget rule if the government was a creditor. However, the result stated in Corollary 2 also holds without rule (4.11), which is shown in the appendix to this section.

and two positive eigenvalues. Thus, the government must be able to control initial public debt, for example by levying a lump-sum tax at $t = 0$, and set $b(0)$ such that the economy starts on the one-dimensional stable manifold leading the economy to the BGP in the long-run.

The economy becomes stable if the reaction coefficient ψ is set to a higher value. Then, the Jacobian matrix is characterized by two negative eigenvalues and one positive eigenvalue. In that case, taking $x(0)$ and $b(0)$ as given, there exists a unique value for initial consumption relative to capital, $c(0)$, such that the economy converges to the BGP in the long-run.

However, with a higher value for ψ that stabilizes the economy, a deficit financed increase in public investment reduces the balanced growth rate. In this case, more public investments financed through deficits lead to a temporary increase in the growth rate of public capital but to a smaller growth rate in the long-run. The reason is that with a high reaction coefficient, the negative feedback effect of higher debt is larger, because more resources are used for the debt service that cannot be invested in productive public capital. Table 4.2 shows the results of deficit financed increases in public investment that are again modelled by a decrease in ϕ.

Summarizing our results obtained from the simulations up to now, we can state that the higher ψ, that is the stronger the primary surplus and, thus public spending, react to increases in public debt, the sooner the model is stable. But in this case, a deficit financed increase in public investment reduces the balanced growth rate because of the strong feedback effects associated with public debt. Hence, there exists a trade-off between stabilizing the economy and getting positive growth effects of deficit financed public investment.

We should also like to point out the possibility of conjugate complex eigenvalues. For example, with $\psi = -0.025$ there is one positive real eigenvalue and two complex conjugate eigenvalues with negative real parts for $\psi \in (0.1912, 0.25)$. For $\psi = 0.191275$ there are two purely imaginary eigenvalues and for smaller values of ψ the two complex conjugate eigenvalues have positive real parts. Finally, for ψ smaller than about 0.187 the BGP does not exist any longer. This suggests that the system undergoes a Hopf bifurcation that can lead to stable limit cycles.[7]

Before we study welfare effects, we next illustrate the effect resulting from a transition from scenario (iii), where public debt grows at the balanced growth rate in the long-run, to the balanced budget scenario, scenario (i). To do so, we assume that the economy is originally on the BGP when the government decides to balance

Table 4.2 Balanced growth rate and the debt to private capital ratio for different ϕ with $\psi = 0.25$

	$\phi = 0.005$	$\phi = 0.0025$	$\phi = -0.0025$	$\phi = -0.005$
g	0.198	0.196	0.191	0.189
$b^\star$	−0.024	−0.012	0.012	0.024

[7]More examples, illustrating the results in Tables 4.1 and 4.2 as well as the proof that limit cycles may emerge, are given in Greiner (2007a, 2007b). The emergence of a Hopf bifurcation leading to stable limit cycles is also shown in Chap. 5.2.

its budget from $t = 0$ onwards. To do so, we choose the parameter values underlying Table 4.2 with $\phi = -0.005$, so that $b^\star$ is positive and the Jacobian matrix of (4.17)–(4.19) has two negative eigenvalues.

To analyze the effects of a change from scenario (iii) to scenario (i) we study the solution of the linearized system of (4.17)–(4.19) which is given by

$$x(t) = x^\star + C_1 v_{11} e^{\lambda_1 t} + C_2 v_{21} e^{\lambda_2 t}, \tag{4.20}$$

$$b(t) = b^\star + C_1 v_{12} e^{\lambda_1 t} + C_2 v_{22} e^{\lambda_2 t}, \tag{4.21}$$

$$c(t) = c^\star + C_1 v_{13} e^{\lambda_1 t} + C_2 v_{23} e^{\lambda_2 t}, \tag{4.22}$$

with v_{jl} the l-th element of the eigenvector belonging to the negative real eigenvalue λ_j, $j = 1, 2$. C_j, $j = 1, 2$, are constants determined by the initial conditions $x(0)$ and $b(0)$. Setting $t = 0$ gives C_j, $j = 1, 2$, as a function of $x(0)$ and $b(0)$. Inserting these C_j, $j = 1, 2$, in (4.22) gives the unique $c(0)$ on the stable manifold leading to the BGP in the long-run. Given $x(t)$, $b(t)$ and $c(t)$ from (4.20)–(4.22) one can compute the growth rates of C, B, G and K according to (4.15), (4.12), (4.14) and (4.16).

Figure 4.1 shows the transitional growth rates of C, G and K after the government balances its budget at time $t = 0$.

The constant line left of the $t = 0$ axis gives the balanced growth rate of the economy in scenario (iii) which is $g = 0.189$. Switching to a balanced government budget at $t = 0$, by setting $\phi = 0$ and $\psi = (1 - \tau)r$, leads to a downward jump of the growth rate of public capital at $t = 0$ because ϕ is increased from $\phi = -0.005$ to $\phi = 0$ and ψ also rises at $t = 0$ which has a negative effect on public investment, which can be seen from (4.14). Hence, balancing the government budget at $t = 0$ brings about an immediate reduction in public investment, which was to be

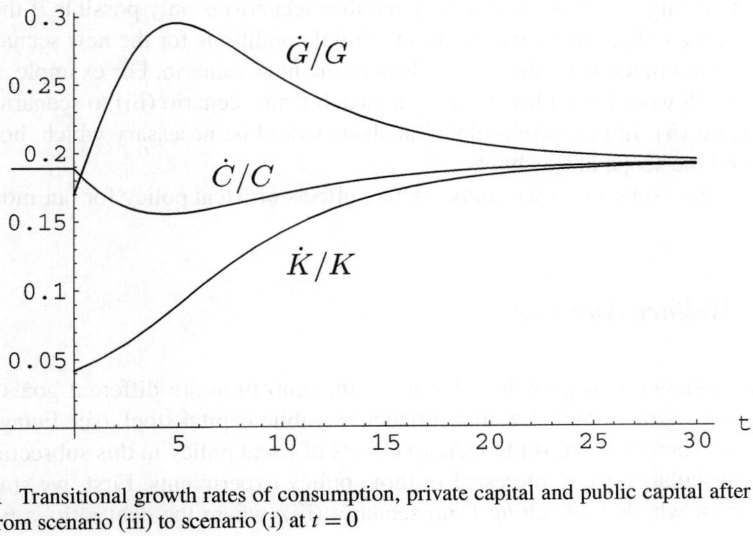

Fig. 4.1 Transitional growth rates of consumption, private capital and public capital after a transition from scenario (iii) to scenario (i) at $t = 0$

expected. Since x is fixed at $t = 0$ the growth rate of consumption does not react at $t = 0$. The growth rate of private capital jumps downward at $t = 0$ because the ratio of consumption to private capital rises and compensates the increase in ϕ and ψ. The growth rate of public debt, of course, equals zero from $t = 0$ onward. Over time, the growth rates of consumption, of private capital and of public capital converge to the balanced growth rate of scenario (i) given by $g = 0.193$.

For sake of completeness we want to mention that a change from scenario (iii) to scenario (ii), where public debt grows at a smaller rate than capital in the long-run, gives the same picture as shown in Fig. 4.1 from a qualitative point of view. That is, the growth rate of public capital first jumps down, then rises and overshoots its long-run value before it converges to the balanced growth rate. The growth rate of private consumption declines and then rises again. The private capital stock first jumps down and then rises again and converges to the BGP. But there is a difference in the adjustment path of public debt. Since ϕ rises from $\phi = -0.005$ to $\phi = 0$ the growth rate of public debt jumps down at $t = 0$, but since ψ remains unchanged it is not immediately equal to zero as it is the case when the government switches to the balanced budget scenario. The growth rate of public debt continues to decline for a certain time period and, then, rises again and converges to its new long-run value which is smaller than the growth rates of consumption and capital.

We also want to state that a change from the balanced budget scenario, scenario (i), to scenario (iii), where public debt grows at the same rate as all other variables in the long-run, is just reverse to Fig. 4.1. Thus, both private and public investment jump upwards at $t = 0$ and then converge to the BGP, where the growth rate of public capital overshoots, or better undershoots, its long-run value. The growth rate of consumption rises and then declines again and converges to the balanced growth rate. The growth rate of public debt, which equals zero for $t < 0$, jumps upward at $t = 0$ and then declines again and also approaches the balanced growth rate.

Finally, it should be pointed out that, if one performs a linear analysis around the BGP, the change from one scenario to another scenario is only possible if the BGP values in the old scenario, which are the initial conditions for the new scenario, do not differ too much from the BGP values of the new scenario. For example, setting $\phi = -0.015$ would not allow to study a switch from scenario (iii) to scenario (i) or to scenario (ii). In that case a global analysis would be necessary which, however, is beyond the scope of this book.

In the next subsection we study welfare effects of fiscal policy for our model.

4.2.3 Welfare Analysis

It is well known that growth and welfare maximization are different goals in the endogenous growth model with a productive public capital stock (see Futagami et al. 1993). Therefore, we study welfare effects of fiscal policy in this subsection.

In particular, we are interested in three policy experiments. First, we study the question of whether switching from scenario (iii), where the debt ratio is positive

Table 4.3 Welfare in scenario (iii) and welfare resulting from a transition to scenario (ii) and to scenario (i), respectively

	Scenario (iii)	From scenario (iii) to (ii)	From scenario (iii) to (i)
F	−1.174	1.350	1.209

in the long-run, to scenario (i) and to scenario (ii) raises welfare. Second, we analyze welfare effects of switching from a balanced budget scenario, scenario (i), to scenario (iii), where the government runs into debt. Third, we calculate welfare for the three scenarios for given initial conditions with respect to the capital stocks and with respect to public debt.

To compute welfare effects we numerically calculate the expression

$$F = \arg\max_{C(t)} \int_0^\infty e^{-\rho t} \ln C(t) dt, \tag{4.23}$$

where we set $K(0) = 1$. The value for consumption is obtained by numerically solving (4.15), with $x(t)$ again given by (4.20)–(4.22).

In Table 4.3 we report the outcome of our first policy experiment. As to the parameter values we use those of the last section with $\psi = 0.25$, in scenario (ii) and (iii), and $\phi = -0.005$ in scenario (iii).

Table 4.3 shows that scenario (iii), where debt grows at the balanced growth rate, leads to smaller welfare than a transition from scenario (iii) to scenario (ii), where debt grows in the long-run but at a lower rate than capital and output, and to smaller welfare than a transition to scenario (i), the balanced budget scenario. Comparing scenarios (ii) and (i), one can realize that scenario (i), the balanced budget scenario, yields lower welfare than scenario (ii), where public debt grows in the long-run but less than output.

The reason for this outcome is that the level of consumption at $t = 0$ in scenario (i) rises less than in scenario (ii). On the other hand, the growth rate of consumption temporarily declines and the decline in scenario (ii) is stronger than that in scenario (i). But this transitionally higher growth rate of consumption in scenario (i), compared to scenario (ii), is not sufficient to compensate for the stronger increase of consumption at $t = 0$ in scenario (ii). Therefore, scenario (ii) yields higher welfare than scenario (i) as reported in the table above.

In Table 4.4 we present the outcome of our second policy experiment where the government switches from a balanced budget scenario, scenario (i), to scenario (iii) with a positive government debt. Technically, this is achieved by setting $\phi = -0.005$ giving $b^\star = 0.0235$.

Table 4.4 Welfare in scenario (i) and welfare resulting from a transition to scenario (iii) with $b^\star > 0$

	Scenario (i)	From scenario (i) to (iii)
F	−1.037	−8.293

Table 4.5 Welfare in scenario (i), in scenario (ii) and in scenario (iii) for given initial conditions $x(0) = 0.03$ and $b(0) = 0.02$

	Scenario (i)	Scenario (ii)	Scenario (iii)
F	1.202	1.317	−1.921

Table 4.4 shows that switching from a balanced budget scenario to a scenario where the government runs deficits and accumulates a stock of debt reduces welfare. The reason for this outcome is that the government deficit at $t = 0$ leads to an upward jump of public and private investment and to a decline in the level of consumption at $t = 0$. The growth rate of consumption rises temporarily but the increase is compensated by the decrease in consumption at $t = 0$ and by the lower balanced growth rate so that welfare declines.

In the last experiment, finally, we set the initial conditions with respect to x and b to arbitrary values and, then, compute welfare for the three scenarios. Table 4.5 gives the result of this exercise with $x(0) = 0.03$ and $b(0) = 0.02$.

Table 4.5 confirms the outcome of Table 4.3. It demonstrates that scenario (iii), where public debt grows at the balanced growth rate in the long-run, performs worse than scenario (i) and worse than scenario (ii). Comparing the balanced budget scenario, scenario (i), with scenario (ii), where public debt grows less than capital and consumption in the long-run, shows that scenario (ii) leads to higher welfare than scenario (i).

Hence, the main conclusion we can draw from this subsection is that scenario (iii), where public debt grows at the balanced growth rate in the long-run, performs worse than scenario (i) and worse than scenario (ii) as concerns welfare. Comparing scenario (i) with scenario (ii) shows that scenario (ii) seems to perform better. The reason for this result is that initial private consumption in the balanced budget scenario, scenario (i), is smaller than in scenario (ii), where debt grows but less than output. However, since the difference in welfare is only small, care must be taken in generalizing this result. This holds because it cannot be excluded that the initial conditions of the capital stocks and of government debt may be decisive as to whether scenario (i) or scenario (ii) performs better.

4.3 Excursus: Human Capital Accumulation

In this section, we study an endogenous growth model with human capital accumulation that is the result of public spending. The government hires teachers and finances additional expenditures for human capital formation. As in the last section, it may run deficits but sets the primary surplus again such that it is a positive function of public debt.

The seminal papers in the field of endogenous growth with human capital are the contributions by Uzawa (1965) and by Lucas (1998). There, the representative individual decides how much of his available time is spent for producing physical output and how much is used for the formation of human capital. Rebelo (1991) extended this class of models by assuming that both physical capital and human capital enter the production process of human capital, in contrast to the model by Uzawa and Lucas who posit that human capital formation is the result of human capital input alone.

However, neither of theses models allows for public spending in the process of human capital formation. Contributions, which take into account that the public sector can stimulate the formation of human capital by devoting public resources to schooling, are for example Glomm and Ravikumar (1992), Ni and Wang (1994), Beauchemin (2001), Blankenau and Simpson (2004) and Greiner (2008c). In those contributions, human capital accumulation results either from both private and public services, as in Glomm and Ravikumar and in Blankenau, or from public spending alone, as in Ni and Wang, in Beauchemin and in Greiner.

As concerns the empirical relevance of human capital, there is evidence that education is positively correlated with income growth. At the microeconomic level the positive correlation seems to be quite robust. On the macroeconomic level the findings are more fragile (see Krueger and Lindahl 2001) which, however, may be due to measurement errors. Thus, Krueger and Lindahl demonstrate that cross-country regressions indicate that the change in education is positively correlated with economic growth if measurement errors are accounted for. Further, Levine and Renelt (1992) have shown that human capital, measured by the secondary enrollment rate, is a robust variable in growth regressions. Therefore, building endogenous growth models with human capital as the engine of growth seems to be justified.

4.3.1 The Structure of the Growth Model

Our economy consists of three sectors: A household sector which receives labour income and income from its saving, a productive sector and the government. First, we describe the household and the productive sector.

4.3.1.1 The Household and the Productive Sector

Overall population in the economy is assumed to be constant and the household sector is represented by one household which maximizes the discounted stream of utility resulting from consumption, C, over an infinite time horizon subject to its budget constraint.[8] The utility function is assumed to be given by $U(C) = (C^{1-\sigma} - 1)/(1-\sigma)$ and labour, L, is supplied inelastically. The maximization problem, then, can be written as

$$\max_{C} \int_{0}^{\infty} e^{-\rho t}(C^{1-\sigma} - 1)/(1-\sigma)dt, \tag{4.24}$$

[8] Note that we again omit the time argument t if no ambiguity arises.

subject to

$$(1-\tau)(wuL + rW) = \dot{W} + C. \tag{4.25}$$

We denote by ρ the subjective discount rate, $1/\sigma$ is the inter-temporal elasticity of substitution of consumption between two points in time, w is the wage rate and r is the interest rate. Assets are denoted by $W \equiv B + K$ which are equal to public debt, B, and physical capital, K, and $\tau \in (0, 1)$ is the income tax rate. The dot gives the derivative with respect to time and we neglect depreciation of private capital.

Further, u gives that part of available time used of production and $1-u$ is that part of time used for education, which builds up a human capital stock. We assume that the part of time used for human capital formation is determined by the government through mandatory attendance laws so that the household takes u as exogenously given.

To solve this problem we formulate the current-value Hamiltonian which is written as

$$\mathcal{H} = (C^{1-\sigma} - 1)/(1-\sigma) + \lambda((1-\tau)(wuL + rW) - C). \tag{4.26}$$

Necessary optimality conditions are given by

$$\lambda = C^{-\sigma}, \tag{4.27}$$

$$\dot{\lambda} = \rho\lambda - \lambda(1-\tau)r. \tag{4.28}$$

If the transversality condition $\lim_{t\to\infty} e^{-\rho t}\lambda W = 0$ holds the necessary conditions are also sufficient.

The productive sector is represented by one firm which behaves competitively and which maximizes static profits. The production function of the firm is given by

$$Y = K^{1-\alpha}(uh_c L)^{\alpha}, \tag{4.29}$$

with $0 < \alpha < 1$. $(1-\alpha)$ is the private capital share and α gives the labour share. Human per capita capital is denoted by h_c, which is labour augmenting, and u is that part of the labour force employed in the final goods sector. Profit maximization yields

$$w = \alpha(uL)^{-1}Y, \tag{4.30}$$

$$r = (1-\alpha)K^{-1}Y. \tag{4.31}$$

Using (4.27), (4.28), (4.29) and (4.31), which must hold in equilibrium, the growth rate of consumption is derived as

$$\frac{\dot{C}}{C} = -\frac{\rho}{\sigma} + \frac{(1-\tau)(1-\alpha)K^{-\alpha}(uh_c L)^{\alpha}}{\sigma}. \tag{4.32}$$

4.3.1.2 Human Capital Formation

Human capital in our economy is produced in the schooling sector where we assume that the government decides about the time the household has to spend for education. Additionally, the government uses public resources for education in the schooling sector, like expenditures for books and other teaching material, which is an input in the process of human capital formation, too. Thus, the input in the schooling sector is composed of time spent for education by the household and of schooling expenditures by the government. We assume decreasing returns to scale in each input alone and constant returns to scale in both inputs together.

As concerns the production function for human capital formation we assume a Cobb-Douglas specification. Normalizing labour to one, $L \equiv 1$, which holds from now on, the differential equation describing the change in human per capita capital can be written as

$$\dot{h}_c = \epsilon((1-u)h_c)^{\gamma} E^{1-\gamma}, \tag{4.33}$$

with E public resources used in the schooling sector, $\epsilon > 0$ a technology parameter and $\gamma \in (0, 1)$ is the elasticity of human capital formation with respect to the time spent for education.

4.3.1.3 The Government

The government in our economy receives tax revenues from income taxation and has revenues from issuing government bonds it then uses for public spending in the schooling sector and for interest payments on public debt. Thus, the period budget constraint of the government is given by

$$\dot{B} = rB + E - T, \tag{4.34}$$

with T denoting tax revenue.

Further, as in the preceding sections the government fixes the primary surplus to GDP ratio such that it is a positive linear function of the debt to GDP ratio. The primary surplus ratio, then, can be written as

$$\frac{S}{Y} = \phi + \psi \frac{B}{Y}, \tag{4.35}$$

where $\phi, \psi \in \mathbb{R}$ are constants and $\psi > 0$ holds.

Using (4.35), the differential equation describing the evolution of public debt, equation (4.34), can be rewritten as

$$\dot{B} = (r - \psi)B - \phi Y. \tag{4.36}$$

It should be recalled that, as in the model of the last section, this assumption brings a feedback effect of higher government debt into the model. If the government increases public debt, for whatever reasons, it must raise the primary surplus so that fiscal policy remains sustainable. This, however, means that more resources must be used for the debt service implying that the government has less scope for other types of spending, for example for the formation of human capital as in this model. In the next subsection we define equilibrium conditions and the balanced growth path.

4.3.1.4 Equilibrium Conditions and the Balanced Growth Path

An equilibrium allocation is defined as an allocation such that the firm maximizes profits implying that factor prices equal their marginal products ((4.30) and (4.31)), the household solves (4.24) subject to (4.25) and the budget constraint of the government (4.34) is fulfilled and the government sticks to the rule defined in (4.35).

Using (4.34) and (4.36) we get E in equilibrium. Inserting the resulting value in (4.33), the growth rate of human capital is described by the following differential equation,

$$\frac{\dot{h}_c}{h_c} = \epsilon \frac{((1-u)h_c)^{\gamma}}{h_c} \left(\left(\frac{uh_c}{K} \right)^{\alpha} K(\tau - \phi) - B(\psi - \tau r) \right)^{1-\gamma}, \tag{4.37}$$

with r given by (4.31).

The economy-wide resource constraint is obtained by combining equations (4.25) and (4.36) as

$$\frac{\dot{K}}{K} = \frac{Y}{K}(1 + \phi - \tau) - \frac{C}{K} - \frac{B}{K}(r\tau - \psi). \tag{4.38}$$

Thus, the economy is completely described by (4.32), (4.36), (4.37) and (4.38) plus the limiting transversality condition of the household.

A balanced growth path (BGP) is defined as a path on which all endogenous variables grow at the same rate, that is $\dot{K}/K = \dot{B}/B = \dot{C}/C = \dot{h}_c/h_c$ holds, and the inter-temporal budget constraint of the government is fulfilled. Assuming that $\sigma > (1-\tau) - \rho/r$ holds, so that the difference between the interest rate and the growth rate on the BGP is strictly positive, and positing that the government sets the primary surplus according to (4.35) with $\psi > 0$, any path which satisfies $\dot{K}/K = \dot{B}/B = \dot{C}/C = \dot{h}_c/h_c$ is associated with a sustainable public debt.

It should be noted that, in this section, we do not consider a balanced government budget nor a growth rate of public debt that is positive but smaller than the balanced growth rate. Instead, we are interested in how fiscal policy affects growth and stability on a path where public debt grows at the same rate as all other variables. Hence, in contrast to our earlier analyses, we only consider the situation where the long-run growth rate of public debt is positive and equal to that of the GDP so that the debt to GDP ratio remains constant.

To analyze our economy around a BGP we define the new variables $h \equiv h_c/K$, $b \equiv B/K$ and $c \equiv C/K$. Differentiating these variables with respect to time yields a three dimensional system of differential equations given by

$$\begin{aligned} \dot{h} &= h\epsilon(1-u)^{\gamma}(u^{\alpha}h^{\alpha-1}(\tau - \phi) + (b/h)(\tau(1-\alpha)h^{\alpha}u^{\alpha} - \psi))^{1-\gamma} \\ &\quad + h(c + b(\tau(1-\alpha)h^{\alpha}u^{\alpha} - \psi) - u^{\alpha}h^{\alpha}(1 + \phi - \tau)), \end{aligned} \tag{4.39}$$

$$\begin{aligned}\dot{b} &= b(c + b(\tau(1-\alpha)h^{\alpha}u^{\alpha} - \psi) - u^{\alpha}h^{\alpha}(1+\phi-\tau)) - \phi u^{\alpha}h^{\alpha} \\ &\quad + (1-\alpha)u^{\alpha}h^{\alpha}b - b\psi, \qquad (4.40)\\ \dot{c} &= c((1-\tau)(1-\alpha)u^{\alpha}h^{\alpha}/\sigma - \rho/\sigma - u^{\alpha}h^{\alpha}(1+\phi-\tau) + c) \\ &\quad + cb(\tau(1-\alpha)h^{\alpha}u^{\alpha} - \psi). \qquad (4.41)\end{aligned}$$

A solution of $\dot{h} = \dot{b} = \dot{c} = 0$ with respect to h, b, c gives a BGP for our model and the corresponding ratios $h^{\star}$, $b^{\star}$, $c^{\star}$ on the BGP.[9] In the next section we derive some economic implications of our model and numerically study its dynamics.

4.3.2 Analysis of the Model

To get insight into our model we first solve (4.41) with respect to c, insert that value in (4.40) and set (4.40) equal to zero giving

$$b^{\star} = \frac{\phi u^{\alpha}(h^{\star})^{\alpha}}{(r-g)-\psi}, \qquad (4.42)$$

with $r = (1-\alpha)(uh^{\star})^{\alpha}$ and g given by (4.32). From (4.42) we can derive a first result.

Since $b^{\star}$ is an endogenous variable, it can be positive or negative, with the latter implying that the government is a creditor. However, a positive value of government debt is more realistic since most real world economies are characterized by public debt and we limit our analysis to this case.

Assume that $\phi < 0$ holds. This implies that the primary surplus declines as GDP rises and the government raises its spending for education with higher GDP. In this case, ψ must be sufficiently large, more concretely $\psi > r - g$ must hold, so that the debt-capital ratio is positive on the BGP, which can be seen from (4.42). This means that the reaction of the government to increases in public debt must be sufficiently strong such that a BGP with public debt is feasible. If this does not hold, that is if the reaction of the government to higher public debt is relatively small, the government must be a creditor for the economy to achieve sustained growth.

If $\phi > 0$, that is if the primary surplus rises as GDP increases, the contrary holds. In this case, ψ must not be too large, that is $\psi < r - g$ must hold, so that sustained growth with positive public debt is feasible. This holds because a positive ϕ and a high ψ imply that the government does not invest sufficiently in the formation of human capital, which is the source of economic growth in our model. Consequently, if $\phi > 0$ and if ψ is relatively large, the government must be a creditor in order finance its investment in the schooling sector in order to achieve sustained growth. This can be seen from (4.37) which shows that for a positive ϕ and for a sufficiently

[9]The $\star$ denotes BGP values and we exclude the economically meaningless BGP $h^{\star} = b^{\star} = c^{\star} = 0$.

large ψ, a negative government debt has a positive effect on the growth rate of human capital.

These considerations have shown that neither a too severe nor a too loose budgetary policy are compatible with sustained growth if the government is a debtor. On the one hand, if the government does not control public debt sufficiently, public debt becomes too high leading to a crowding-out of private investment, making sustained growth impossible. In this case, sustained growth is only possible if the government is a creditor.

On the other hand, the government must not conduct a too strict budgetary policy. This holds because with a too strict budgetary policy the government does not invest enough in the formation of human capital, which is the source of economic growth. In this case, sustained growth is not feasible either and the government again must be a creditor, so that it can finance necessary investment in the schooling sector to build up human capital.

Next, we resort to numerical examples in order to gain additional insight into our growth model.

4.3.2.1 Results for the Model on the BGP

To analyze our model further, we resort to simulations. We do so because the analytical model turns out to become too complex to derive further results.

As a benchmark for our simulations we set the income tax rate to twenty percent, $\tau = 0.2$, and the elasticity of production with respect to physical capital is set to 30 percent, $1-\alpha = 0.3$. The rate of time preference is set to 5 percent, $\rho = 0.05$, and we assume a logarithmic utility function, $\sigma = 1$. Further, 90 percent of the available time is assumed to be used in the final goods sector, $u = 0.9$, and 10 percent for human capital formation. As concerns the elasticity of human capital formation with respect to time we consider two values, $\gamma = 0.75$ and $\gamma = 0.5$. This implies that a marginal increase in time used for human capital formation raises human capital by 75 percent and by 50 percent, respectively. It also implies that time spent for education is more important compared to educational spending of the government. Finally, we set $\epsilon = 0.15$.

In Tables 4.6 and 4.7 we report results of our simulations for different values of ϕ and for values of ψ which are smaller than the subjective discount rate ρ. For $\sigma = 1$,

Table 4.6 Long-run growth rate and endogenous variables on the BGP for different ϕ and small values of ψ with $\gamma = 0.75$

ϕ	$\psi = 0.015$				$\psi = 0.035$			
	$b^\star$	$h^\star$	g	$E^\star/Y^\star$	$b^\star$	$h^\star$	g	$E^\star/Y^\star$
$\phi = 0.05$	0.27	0.19	1.86%	0.15	0.44	0.18	1.76%	0.11
$\phi = 0.01$	0.06	0.19	1.96%	0.2	0.09	0.19	1.94%	0.2
$\phi = -0.01$	−0.06	0.19	2.01%	0.23	−0.09	0.19	2.02%	0.24
$\phi = -0.05$	−0.28	0.19	2.09%	0.28	−0.45	0.2	2.14%	0.32

Table 4.7 Long-run growth rate and endogenous variables on the BGP for different ϕ and small values of ψ with $\gamma = 0.5$

ϕ	$\psi = 0.015$				$\psi = 0.035$			
	$b^\star$	$h^\star$	g	$E^\star/Y^\star$	$b^\star$	$h^\star$	g	$E^\star/Y^\star$
$\phi = 0.05$	0.28	0.2	2.27%	0.15	0.45	0.19	2.06%	0.11
$\phi = 0.01$	0.06	0.21	2.52%	0.21	0.09	0.21	2.49%	0.2
$\phi = -0.01$	−0.06	0.22	2.63%	0.23	−0.09	0.22	2.66%	0.24
$\phi = -0.05$	−0.3	0.22	2.84%	0.28	−0.48	0.23	2.97%	0.32

the latter implies that $(r - g) - \psi > 0$ holds on the BGP. The balanced growth rate g is given in percent and $E^\star/Y^\star$ gives education expenditures relative to GDP.

Tables 4.6 and 4.7 confirm the result derived for the analytical model that for small values of the reaction coefficient ψ, ϕ must be positive so that sustained growth with positive public debt is feasible. In this case, the primary surplus must rise as GDP rises, otherwise endogenous growth with a positive government debt is not possible. If this does not hold, that is if ϕ is negative, the government must be a creditor and the level of public debt is negative.

If ϕ is negative and ψ is small and if the government was a debtor, public debt would become extremely large and the government would require too large a fraction of the resources in the economy for interest payments on public debt. This would lead to a crowding-out of private investment, which can be seen from the economy wide resource constraint (4.38). From (4.38), one realizes that private investment relative to capital, $I/K = \dot{K}/K$, will be low if ϕ is negative and if ψ is smaller $r\tau$ (in case B is positive). Therefore, sustained growth is not feasible with a negative ϕ and a small ψ unless the government is a creditor.

Further, one realizes that for a given value of ψ the growth rate rises as ϕ is decreased. This means that a decrease in ϕ, which reflects a deficit financed increase in public spending for education since it implies that the government reduces its primary surplus at the expense of government spending for human capital formation, leads to higher growth. Thus, higher spending for human capital enhances long-run growth even if financed through public deficits in this case.

The reason for this outcome is to be seen in the fact that ψ, giving the reaction of the primary surplus to higher public debt, is small. A small ψ implies small negative feedback effects of higher debt and, consequently, a deficit financed increase in public spending for human capital formation raises the balanced growth rate. However, it must be pointed out that, if the government is a debtor, this policy is only feasible as long as the government raises its primary surplus with increases in GDP, that is as long as $\phi > 0$ holds. If ϕ is negative the government must be a creditor so that sustained growth is possible at all and so that this fiscal policy leads to higher long-run growth.

These qualitative results hold for both $\gamma = 0.75$ and $\gamma = 0.5$. Further, the smaller the value of γ the more important is educational spending of the government relative to time as input. Therefore, the balanced growth rate g is the higher the smaller γ

for a given value of educational spending to GDP, $E^\star/Y^\star$, which can be clearly seen from Table 4.6 and from Table 4.7.

As to stability, the BGP is unstable in all cases, because the Jacobian has two positive eigenvalues and one negative. This means that the economy can converge to the BGP in the long-run only if the government levies a lump-sum tax at time zero which is used to control initial public debt, $B(0)$. Then, initial debt and initial consumption, $B(0)$ and $C(0)$, must be chosen such that the economy converges to the BGP in the long-run and these values are uniquely determined.

To gain further insight into our model we next set $\psi > \rho$ implying that $(r-g)-\psi < 0$ holds on the BGP. The results of the simulations are shown in Tables 4.8 and 4.9.

Tables 4.8 and 4.9 demonstrate that for relatively large values of ψ the situation changes. In this case, the government must be a creditor if ϕ is positive. A large value of ψ implies that the government raises the primary surplus to a great extent as public debt rises. Thus, a deficit financed increase in public spending for schooling, modelled by a decrease in ϕ, goes along with strong feedback effects of the higher public debt, so that in the end the economy ends up with less education spending per GDP and, consequently, with a lower long-run growth rate. In this case, one can state that the government policy is too strict, in the sense that it pays too much attention to the control of public debt, instead of fostering economic growth by investing into education. Therefore, sustained growth with a positive government debt for large values of ψ is only possible if ϕ is negative, that is if the government does not raise the primary surplus as GDP rises but invests in education. If this does not hold, the

Table 4.8 Long-run growth rate and endogenous variables on the BGP for different ϕ and large values of ψ with $\gamma = 0.75$

ϕ	$\psi = 0.075$				$\psi = 0.1$			
	$b^\star$	$h^\star$	g	$E^\star/Y^\star$	$b^\star$	$h^\star$	g	$E^\star/Y^\star$
$\phi = 0.05$	−2.65	0.22	2.61%	0.8	−0.46	0.2	2.15%	0.32
$\phi = 0.01$	−0.41	0.2	2.13%	0.31	−0.09	0.19	2.02%	0.24
$\phi = -0.01$	0.36	0.18	1.81%	0.13	0.09	0.19	1.95%	0.2
$\phi = -0.05$	No BGP				0.43	0.18	1.77%	0.12

Table 4.9 Long-run growth rate and endogenous variables on the BGP for different ϕ and large values of ψ with $\gamma = 0.5$

ϕ	$\psi = 0.075$				$\psi = 0.1$			
	$b^\star$	$h^\star$	g	$E^\star/Y^\star$	$b^\star$	$h^\star$	g	$E^\star/Y^\star$
$\phi = 0.05$	No BGP				−0.56	0.23	3.03%	0.34
$\phi = 0.01$	−0.73	0.24	3.15%	0.37	−0.1	0.22	2.67%	0.24
$\phi = -0.01$	0.41	0.2	2.11%	0.12	0.1	0.21	2.48%	0.2
$\phi = -0.05$	No BGP				0.45	0.19	2.05%	0.11

government must be a creditor with a certain stock of wealth out of which it finances necessary investment in the schooling sector.

As for Tables 4.6 and 4.7 we get a higher balanced growth rate in Tables 4.8 and 4.9 for a smaller value of γ. Again, the reason is that with a higher elasticity of human capital production with respect to educational spending, reflected by a lower γ, a given level of educational spending leads to a higher balanced growth rate.

As concerns stability, the economy is stable for all situations considered in Tables 4.8 and 4.9, with two eigenvalues of the Jacobian being negative or having negative real parts, in case they are complex conjugate, and one eigenvalue being positive. This means that, for any given value of public debt at time zero, $B(0)$, there exists a unique value of consumption at time zero, $C(0)$, which can be chosen freely, such that the economy converges to the BGP in the long-run. Thus, the long-run equilibrium is determinate. In this case, the government does not have to control public debt at time zero so that convergence to the BGP is assured.

Hence, from Tables 4.6 and 4.7 and Tables 4.8 and 4.9 we can conclude that a strong reaction of the primary surplus to higher public debt, expressed by a large ψ, tends to stabilize the economy. On the other hand, high values of ψ imply that the feedback effect of public debt is large so that deficit financed expenditures for human capital formation, modelled by decreases in ϕ, lead to lower growth, whereas for small values of ψ the reverse holds. Thus, there is a monotonic relationship between growth and deficit financed spending for human capital formation which is negative for large values of ψ and positive for small values of ψ.

These considerations show that there is again a trade-off between stabilizing the economy, by choosing a high value for ψ, and getting positive growth effects of deficit financed spending for human capital, which is achieved by setting ψ to a low value.

4.3.2.2 Sensitivity Analysis of the Dynamics

The dynamic system in the last subsection was characterized by a unique economic reasonable BGP which is either stable or unstable. In the latter case, the government must intervene at time zero and control public debt such that the economy converges to the BGP in the long-run. Now, we look at the dynamics of our growth model in more detail. It turns out that for $\psi < \rho$, existence of a BGP implies that it is unique. For $\psi > \rho$ and for a sufficiently large difference $\psi - \rho$, the BGP is also unique.

If the difference $\psi - \rho$ is small, we can observe a situation which is characterized by two BGPs, where one is unstable, while the other is stable. In this case, the economy converges to the second BGP unless the government intervenes at $t = 0$ by levying a lump-sum tax, which is used to control $B(0)$ such that the economy converges to the first BGP.

In addition, if we continuously vary the parameter ψ, the second BGP may undergo a Hopf bifurcation leading to persistent cycles.[10] In this case, the BGP is

[10] For a statement of the Hopf bifurcation theorem see for example Hassard et al. (1981).

stable for certain values of ψ. If we decrease ψ the system becomes unstable and for a certain range of the parameter ψ in between stability and instability, sustained cycles occur. This implies that the economy is characterized by endogenously oscillating growth rates and does not converge to a constant long-run BGP.

We should like to point out that, as in the last subsection, higher values of ψ tend to stabilize the economy, which seems to be intuitively clear. Thus, the stronger the reaction of the government to higher public debt, more concretely, the stronger the increase in the primary surplus as public debt rises, the more likely it is that the dynamic system describing the economy is stable. Thus, we can state that the economy is locally stable for relatively large values of ψ. As ψ is continuously decreased, the BGP looses stability and, before becoming unstable, persistent cycles can emerge.

4.4 Conclusion

In this chapter we have presented an endogenous growth model with productive public spending and public debt where the government can run deficits in order to finance public investment. In addition, we have posited that the primary surplus to GDP ratio is a positive function of the debt to GDP ratio because this guarantees that public debt remains sustainable. The main results of analyzing our model can be summarized as follows.

1. It turned out that a balanced budget scenario brings about a higher long-run growth rate than a scenario where public debt grows at the balanced growth rate, that is at the same rate as all other variables. Further, a scenario where public debt grows in the long-run, but at a lower rate than the balanced growth rate, yields the same long-run growth rate as the balanced budget scenario. A balanced growth rate exceeding the one of the balanced budget scenario can only be obtained when the government is a creditor. This means that the government must have built up a stock of wealth it uses to finance its expenditures and to lend to the private sector.

2. Starting from a balanced budget, a deficit financed public investment raises transitional growth rates but leads to a smaller long-run growth rate if this fiscal policy leads to a positive debt ratio in the long-run. Only if the government switches back to the balanced budget scenario or to the scenario where public debt grows slower than capital and output, a temporarily deficit financed public investment raises transitional growth without leading to smaller growth in the long-run.

3. The fact that a balanced budget gives the highest possible growth rate in the long-run, unless the government is a creditor, does not imply that a deficit financed increase in public investment always reduces long-run growth. Thus, if the economy is on a balanced growth path where public debt grows at the balanced growth rate, a deficit financed increase in public investment may lead to a higher balanced growth rate and to a smaller debt ratio in the long-run. However, this occurs only when the response of the primary surplus to public debt is small so that the model is unstable, implying that the government must impose an additional lump-sum tax to control public debt. In general, it can be said that the stronger the response of the primary

surplus to public debt the sooner the model is stable. But, then, a deficit financed increase in public debt leads to a smaller balanced growth rate. Hence, there is a trade-off between stabilizing the economy and getting positive growth effects of deficit financed public investment.

4. As concerns welfare, numerical examples have shown that the scenario where public debt grows at the balanced growth rate yields smaller welfare than the balanced budget scenario and smaller welfare than the scenario where public debt grows at a smaller rate than capital and output in the long-run. Further, evidence was found that the latter scenario leads to higher welfare than the balanced budget scenario. However, it cannot be excluded that this result depends on the initial conditions with respect to the capital stocks and with respect to public debt. Here, additional research is necessary in order to find how robust this outcome is.

Overall, it can be stated that a scenario where public debt grows at the same rate as capital and output yields smaller growth and welfare in the long-run, compared to the balanced budget scenario and compared to the scenario where debt grows, but less than capital and output. Comparing the latter two scenarios, a balanced budget scenario may perform worse so that the scenario where debt grows, but less than output and capital, makes the economy better off compared to the balanced budget scenario. But even that scenario would require in part drastic changes for countries of the euro area where many economies have difficulties in sticking to the 60% debt criterion. In any case, changing policies such that debt ratios decline over time instead of remaining constant would benefit economies.

In an extension to that model we studied an economy where human capital formation is the source of ongoing growth and where human capital formation is the result of public spending. Qualitatively, the results are the same as those obtained for productive public investment in infrastructure.

Hence, the analysis of that model has demonstrated that a loose fiscal policy, where the government does not pay great attention to stabilizing debt, does not permit sustained growth in the long-run, unless the government is a creditor. In this case, there is a crowding-out of private investment and sustained growth is not feasible, unless the government is a creditor and lends to the private sector, so that the latter can finance necessary investment in physical capital. On the other hand, if the government puts a large weight on debt stabilization and does not invest sufficiently in the formation of human capital, sustained growth is not possible either, unless the government is again a creditor. In this case, the government must use its wealth in order to finance necessary investment in the formation of human capital.

As concerns stability, our analysis has shown that a strong rise in the primary surplus as a reaction to higher public debt stabilizes the economy. In addition, we have seen that for certain values of the reaction coefficient, cyclical growth can occur. If the reaction coefficient is set to a larger value, the economy stabilizes and converges to the constant balanced growth rate, if the reaction coefficient is set to a lower value, the economy becomes unstable.

Appendix

Proof of Proposition 7 To prove this proposition with scenario (i), we set $\phi = 0$, $\psi = (1-\tau)(1-\alpha)x^{\alpha}$ and $b = 0$. Setting $\dot{x} = 0$ and solving this equation with respect to c gives c as a function of x and of parameters. Substituting this function for c in $\dot{c}$ gives $q(x,\cdot) = (1-\alpha)x^{\alpha}(1-\tau) - \rho - \omega\tau x^{\alpha-1}$. It is easily seen that $\lim_{x\to 0} q(x,\cdot) = -\infty$, $\lim_{x\to\infty} q(x,\cdot) = +\infty$ and $\partial q(\cdot)/\partial x > 0$. Thus, existence of a unique BGP is shown.

To show saddle point stability, we compute the Jacobian matrix evaluated at the rest point of (4.17)–(4.19). The Jacobian is given by

$$\mathrm{J} = \begin{bmatrix} \partial\dot{x}/\partial x & \partial\dot{x}/\partial b & \partial\dot{x}/\partial c \\ 0 & \partial\dot{b}/\partial b & 0 \\ \partial\dot{c}/\partial x & \partial\dot{c}/\partial b & \partial\dot{c}/\partial c \end{bmatrix}.$$

One eigenvalue of this matrix is given by $\lambda_1 = \partial\dot{b}/\partial b = -\dot{K}/K = -g$. Thus, we know that one eigenvalue, λ_1, is negative. Further, it is easily shown that $(\partial\dot{x}/\partial x)(\partial\dot{c}/\partial c) - (\partial\dot{x}/\partial c)(\partial\dot{c}/\partial x) < 0$ holds, so that complex conjugate eigenvalues are excluded. The determinant of J is given by $\det \mathrm{J} = \partial\dot{b}/\partial b(\tau(\alpha-1)x^{\alpha-2}\omega - (1-\tau)(1-\alpha)\alpha x^{\alpha-1})c^{\star}x^{\star} > 0$. Since the product of the eigenvalues equals the determinant, $\lambda_1 \cdot \lambda_2 \cdot \lambda_3 = \det \mathrm{J} > 0$, and because of $\lambda_1 < 0$, we know that two eigenvalues are negative and one is positive.

For scenario (ii) we set $\phi = 0$ and $b = 0$. Then, we proceed analogously so that existence and uniqueness is readily shown. For $\dot{B}/B < \dot{C}/C$ to hold we must have $\rho < \psi$ and $\psi < (1-\tau)r$ must hold for $\dot{B}/B > 0$. Because of $b^{\star} = 0$ the Jacobian matrix is the same as for scenario (i) except for $\partial\dot{b}/\partial b$. $\partial\dot{b}/\partial b$ now is given by $\partial\dot{b}/\partial b = \lambda_1 = \dot{B}/B - \dot{K}/K < 0$, because of $\dot{B}/B < \dot{K}/K$ at the BGP. In particular, the determinant is again positive implying that two eigenvalues are negative and one is positive. □

Proof of Proposition 8 To prove Proposition 8, $\dot{c} = 0$ is solved with respect to c giving $c = c(x, b, \cdot)$. Inserting $c = c(x, b, \cdot)$ in $\dot{x}$ and solving $\dot{x} = 0$ with respect to b gives $b^{\star}$ as shown in proposition 8. It is immediately seen that $\phi < \tau$ is a necessary condition for $b^{\star}$ to be positive while $\phi \geq \tau$ is a sufficient condition for $b^{\star}$ to be negative. □

Proof of Proposition 9 To prove this proposition we note that we set $\phi = 0$, $\psi = (1-\tau)(1-\alpha)x^{\alpha}$ and $b = 0$ to get scenario (i). Further, the balanced growth rate is given by $\dot{C}/C = -\rho + (1-\tau)(1-\alpha)x^{\alpha}$. Along a BGP we have $\dot{C}/C = \dot{G}/G$ which implies

$$-\rho + (1-\tau)(1-\alpha)x^{\alpha} = \tau\omega x^{\alpha-1}. \tag{A4.1}$$

The left hand side in (A4.1) is monotonically increasing in x and the right hand side is monotonically declining in x. A value $x_i^{\star}$ such that the left hand side in (A4.1) equals the right hand side gives a BGP for scenario (i).

For scenario (ii), $\dot{C}/C = \dot{G}/G$ implies

$$-\rho + (1-\tau)(1-\alpha)x^{\alpha} = \tau\omega x^{\alpha-1} - \phi\omega x^{\alpha-1} - \omega\psi b/x. \qquad \text{(A4.2)}$$

Again, a value $x^{\star}_{ii}$ such that the left hand side in (A4.2) equals the right hand side gives a BGP for scenario (ii).

The function on the left hand side of equation (A4.1) and of equation (A4.2) are identical. The graph of the function on the right hand side of (A4.1), however, is above the graph of the function on the right hand side of (A4.2) for all $x \in [0, \infty)$ for $b \geq 0$ and for $\phi > 0$. Therefore, the left hand side and the right hand side in (A4.1) intersect at a larger value of x than the left hand side and the right hand side in (A4.2), giving a higher balanced growth rate for scenario (i). To show this for $\phi < 0$, we note that on the BGP $b^{\star}$ is given by $b^{\star} = \phi(x^{\star})^{\alpha-1}/(\rho - \psi)$ which follows from $\dot{C}/C = \dot{B}/B$. Inserting this in the right hand side of (A4.2) and deleting the * gives

$$-\rho + (1-\tau)(1-\alpha)x^{\alpha} = \tau\omega x^{\alpha-1} - \phi\omega x^{\alpha-1}\rho/(\rho - \psi). \qquad \text{(A4.3)}$$

If $-\phi\omega x^{\alpha-1}\rho/(\rho-\psi) < 0$, the point of intersection of the left hand side and the right hand side in (A4.1) occurs at a larger value of x than in (A4.3). For $\psi > \rho$ it is immediately seen that $-\phi\omega x^{\alpha-1}\rho/(\rho-\psi) < 0$ holds (recall that $\phi < 0$). For $\psi < \rho$ the reverse holds, but public debt becomes negative because of $b^{\star}/x^{\star} = \phi(x^{\star})^{\alpha-1}/(\rho-\psi)$. In this case, $x^{\star}$ in (A4.3) is larger than $x^{\star}$ in (A4.1) yielding a higher growth rate for scenario (iii) but this occurs only if public debt is negative.

In scenario (ii) the asymptotic public debt ratio equals zero such that (A4.1) holds for both scenario (i) and for scenario (ii) implying that the two scenarios yield the same balanced growth rate. □

Proof of Corollary 2 To prove this corollary we have to show that $\psi > 0$ implies $b^{\star} < 0$, with ψ given by $\psi = -\phi\omega x^{\alpha-1}\rho/(\rho-\psi)$ from the right hand side in (A4.3) from the proof of Proposition 9. This holds because $\psi > 0$ implies that x which solves (A4.1) is smaller than that x which solves (A4.3), so that the balanced growth rate of scenario (i) is smaller than the balanced growth rate of scenario (iii). From the proof of Proposition 9 we know that $b^{\star}$ on the BGP is given by $b^{\star} = \phi(x^{\star})^{\alpha}/(\rho-\psi)$. It is immediately seen that $b^{\star}$ and ψ have the opposite sign since ω and x are positive. □

The Model with Public Infrastructure and with the Government as a Creditor

If the government is a creditor, public debt B is negative. In this case, there is no need for the government to stick to rule (4.11). It is easy to see that the economy, then, is described by the following equations,

$$\dot{C}/C = -\rho + (1-\tau)(1-\alpha)x^{\alpha}, \qquad \dot{K}/K = x^{\alpha} - c - i_p\omega^{-1},$$
$$\dot{B}/B = (1-\tau)(1-\alpha)x^{\alpha} - \tau x^{\alpha}/b + i_p\omega^{-1}/b, \qquad \dot{G}/G = i_p/x,$$

with $i_p = I_p/K$, public investment relative to private capital and $c = C/K$, $x = G/K$ and $b = B/K$, as above. The dynamics around a BGP are described by,

$$\dot{c} = c(-\rho + (1-\tau)(1-\alpha)x^{\alpha} - x^{\alpha} + c + i_p\omega^{-1}),$$
$$\dot{x} = x(i_p/x - x^{\alpha} + c + i_p\omega^{-1}),$$
$$\dot{b} = b((1-\tau)(1-\alpha)x^{\alpha} - \tau x^{\alpha}/b + i_p\omega^{-1}/b - x^{\alpha} + c + i_p\omega^{-1}),$$

where a BGP is given for $\dot{c} = \dot{x} = \dot{b} = 0$, with $c^{\star} = x^{\star} = 0$ again neglected.

Now, assume that a BGP with $b^{\star} \leq 0$ exists. Then setting $i_p = \omega\tau x^{\alpha} - \epsilon\omega\rho b$, $\epsilon \geq 1$, shows that $\dot{B}/B < (=)\dot{C}/C$, for $\epsilon > (=)1$ and $b^{\star} = (<)0$.

On the BGP, $\dot{C}/C = \dot{K}/K = \dot{G}/G$ holds, so that $b = B/K$ asymptotically converges to zero for $\epsilon > 1$. Hence, $\dot{G}/G$ is given by $\dot{G}/G = \omega\tau x^{\alpha-1}$, for $\epsilon > 1, b = 0$ and by $\dot{G}/G = \omega\tau x^{\alpha-1} - \omega\rho b x^{-1}$, for $\epsilon = 1$, $b < 0$.

This shows that the graph of $\dot{G}/G$ with negative public debt ($b < 0$) is above the graph of $\dot{G}/G$ with zero public debt ($b = 0$). Consequently, $\dot{C}/C$ intersects $\dot{G}/G$, which must hold on the BGP, at a larger value of x with $b < 0$ than with $b = 0$. Therefore, $b^{\star} < 0$ goes along with a higher value of $x^{\star}$, and thus, with a higher balanced growth rate than $b^{\star} = 0$.

Chapter 5
The Role of Real Wage Rigidity and Unemployment

In the last chapter we analyzed the role of public debt and public deficits assuming that the government uses its deficit to finance public investment in a productive public capital stock. In this chapter we again take up that approach, but we suppose that labor markets may be characterized by real wage rigidities and by unemployment. We then consider two cases. First, we analyze the case with flexible real wages as a benchmark implying that the unemployment rate is equal to the natural rate of unemployment. The goal, then, is to analyze the model assuming a balanced government budget and to compare the growth performance to a scenario with persistent deficits. In addition, growth effects of deficit financed public investment are studied as well. In a next step, real wages are assumed to be rigid and the growth rate of the wage rate can be described by a Phillips curve that is derived from trade unions' wage setting behaviour. The section again compares a balanced budget scenario to a scenario with permanent deficits and analyzes growth effects of deficit financed public investment.

The motivation to allow for wage rigidities and unemployment in an endogenous growth model is the observation that many European countries experience persistent unemployment in spite of permanently growing GDPs. Therefore, constructing a growth model featuring that characteristic and analyzing effects of fiscal policy within such a model seems to be justified.

The rest of that chapter is organized as follows. In the next section, we present the basic structure of our model. Then we analyze our model where we assume flexible wages and in the following section we study the model assuming wage rigidities. The following section discusses the economic mechanisms behind the results in detail and compares the outcome to that in the model where unemployment is absent.

5.1 The Growth Model

Our economy consists of three sectors: A household sector which receives labor income and income from its saving, a productive sector and the government. First, we describe the household sector.

A. Greiner, B. Fincke, *Public Debt and Economic Growth*,
Dynamic Modeling and Econometrics in Economics and Finance 11,
DOI 10.1007/978-3-642-01745-2_5, © Springer-Verlag Berlin Heidelberg 2009

5.1.1 The Household Sector

The household sector is represented by one household which maximizes the discounted stream of utility arising from per-capita consumption, $C(t)$, over an infinite time horizon subject to its budget constraint, taking factor prices as given. The utility function is assumed to be logarithmic, $U(C) = \ln C$, and the household inelastically supplies L units of labor of which L^d is demanded by the productive sector. The rest $L - L^d$ is unemployed and the household receives unemployment benefits of ϱw per unemployed labor, where w is the wage rate and $\varrho \in (0, 1)$.[1] We assume that unemployment payments in our economy are strictly positive and sufficiently high so that unemployed can lead dignified lives. In addition, unemployed must pursue simple activities, organized by the government, that are skill preserving. Hence, unemployment does not lead to a loss of human capital and unemployed labor can again be employed in the production process in the economy. Total labor supply L is constant over time. The maximization problem of the household can be written as,

$$\max_C \int_0^\infty e^{-\rho t} \ln C dt, \tag{5.1}$$

subject to

$$(1-\tau)(wL^d + rK + r_B B) + \varrho w(L - L^d) = \dot{W} + C + \delta K. \tag{5.2}$$

The coefficient ρ is the household's rate of time preference, r is the return to capital and r_B is the interest rate on government bonds. $W \equiv B + K$ gives wealth which is equal to public debt, B, and private capital, K, which depreciates at the rate δ. Finally, $\tau \in (0, 1)$ is the constant income tax rate and we assume that unemployment benefits are not subject to the income tax. The dot over a variable again gives the derivative with respect to time.

A no-arbitrage condition requires that the return to capital equals the return to government bonds yielding $r_B = r - \delta/(1-\tau)$. Thus, the budget constraint of the household can be written as

$$\dot{W} = (1-\tau)(wL^d + rW) + \varrho w(L - L^d) - \delta W - C. \tag{5.3}$$

To solve this problem we formulate the current-value Hamiltonian which is written as

$$\mathcal{H} = \ln C + \lambda\big((1-\tau)(wL^d + rW) + \varrho w(L - L^d) - C - \delta W\big). \tag{5.4}$$

Necessary optimality conditions are given by

$$C^{-1} = \lambda, \tag{5.5}$$

$$\dot{\lambda} = (\rho + \delta)\lambda - \lambda(1-\tau)r. \tag{5.6}$$

[1] From now on we again omit the time argument t if no ambiguity arises.

If the transversality condition $\lim_{t\to\infty} e^{-\rho t} W/C = 0$ holds, which is fulfilled for a time path on which assets grow at the same rate as consumption, the necessary conditions are also sufficient.

5.1.2 The Productive Sector and the Labor Market

The productive sector is represented by one firm which behaves competitively and which maximizes static profits. The production function of the firm is

$$Y = K^{1-\alpha}(GL^d)^\alpha. \tag{5.7}$$

Y is output, G denotes public capital and $\alpha \in (0, 1)$ gives the elasticity of output with respect to public capital and $(1 - \alpha)$ is the private capital share. With this formulation public capital is labor augmenting implying that it raises the productivity of labor input. Profit maximization gives the interest rate as

$$r = (1 - \alpha)(Y/K). \tag{5.8}$$

In case of flexible wages, implying a vertical Phillips curve, labor demand equals its natural level, L^n, and the wage rate is determined by the marginal productivity rule. Thus, we get

$$w = \alpha(L^n)^{\alpha-1}K^{1-\alpha}G^\alpha. \tag{5.9}$$

The unemployment rate, then, is equal to its natural rate and is given by $1 - L^n/L$. At this point we should like to point out that we assume that labor supply exceeds labor demand, that is $L \geq L^d$ holds. Thus, there is no rationing of the productive sector in the economy.

In case of rigid real wages, labor demand is again obtained from the firm maximizing profits. This leads to

$$L^d = \alpha^{1/(1-\alpha)}(w/K)^{1/(\alpha-1)}(G/K)^{\alpha/(1-\alpha)}. \tag{5.10}$$

The reason for rigid wages are labor market imperfections due to trade unions setting the wage rate. As concerns the wage setting process we follow Raurich et al. (2006) and assume that there is a large number of unions that set the wage rate in order to maximize the following expression:

$$\max_w ((1 - \tau)w - w^s)^\gamma L^d(\cdot) \tag{5.11}$$

with $L^d(\cdot)$ given by (5.10), w^s denoting the reference wage and the coefficient $\gamma \in (0, 1)$ gives a measure of the weight gap in the unions' objective function. Hence, trade unions maximize the difference between the net wage rate and the reference wage times labour demand. The solution to the optimization problem yields the wage rate as

$$w = \frac{w^s}{(1-\tau)(1-\gamma(1-\alpha))}. \tag{5.12}$$

As concerns the reference wage w^s there exist several approaches in the literature (see for example Layard et al. 1991; Blanchard and Katz 1999; Blanchard and Wolfers 2000; Collard and de la Croix 2000, or Raurich et al. 2006; Greiner and Flaschel 2009). We follow Raurich et al. (2006) and posit that the reference wage equals workers' cumulated past average labor income where income further back in time contributes less than more recent labor income. In particular, we assume exponentially declining weights put on average labor income further back in time. Hence, the reference wage can be written as

$$w^s = \theta \int_{-\infty}^{t} e^{-\theta(t-s)} x(s) ds, \tag{5.13}$$

with x the workers' average income given by $x = (1-\tau)wL^d/L + \varrho w(L - L^d)/L$. The parameter $\theta > 0$ determines the weight attributed to more recent income. The higher θ, the larger the weight given to more recent levels of average income compared to income further back in time.

Differentiating (5.12) with respect to time and using (5.13) yields the growth rate of the wage rate as

$$\frac{\dot{w}}{w} = \theta \frac{(1-\tau)L^d/L + \varrho(L - L^d)/L}{(1-\tau)(1-\gamma(1-\alpha))} - \theta. \tag{5.14}$$

Defining

$$\frac{\bar{L}}{L} = \left(\frac{(1-\tau)(1-\gamma(1-\alpha)) - \varrho}{(1-\tau) - \varrho} \right) \quad \text{and} \quad \beta_L = \frac{\theta(1-\tau) - \theta\varrho}{(1-\tau)(1-\gamma(1-\alpha))}$$

the evolution of the wage rate can be written as[2]

$$\frac{\dot{w}}{w} = \beta_L \left(\frac{L^d - \bar{L}}{L} \right), \tag{5.15}$$

with $\bar{L}$ the normal level of employment in the labor market in the sense that there is no tendency for a change in the wage rate if labor demand is equal to that value. The parameter $\beta_L > 0$ gives the speed of adjustment determining how strongly actual labor demand relative to the normal level of employment affects the growth rate of the wage rate.

[2]Note that $(1-\tau) > \varrho$ must hold for $\beta_L > 0$ and, thus, $(1-\tau)(1-\gamma(1-\alpha)) > \varrho$ for $\bar{L}/L > 0$.

Hence, given the unions' wage setting behaviour, the evolution of the wage rate can be described by a simple Phillips curve relationship where the change in the wage rate negatively depends on the rate of unemployment.[3]

We should also point out that there is one good in our economy that can be either consumed or invested. Consequently all variables are real including the return to capital and the wage rate so that (5.15) describes the evolution of the real wage rate. Next, we describe the public sector.

5.1.3 The Government

The government in our economy receives tax revenues from income taxation and has revenues from issuing government bonds. Public spending is composed of public investment, I_p, spending for unemployment benefits, $\varrho w(L - L^d)$, and of public consumption, C_p, that is neither productive nor welfare enhancing. Further, the government sets the primary surplus such that it is a positive linear function of public debt which guarantees that public debt is sustainable. The accounting identity describing the accumulation of public debt in continuous time is given by,

$$\dot{B} = r_B B(1 - \tau) - S, \qquad (5.16)$$

where S is government surplus exclusive of net interest payments.

The inter-temporal budget constraint of the government is fulfilled if

$$B(0) = \int_0^\infty e^{-\int_0^\mu (1-\tau) r_B(\nu) d\nu} S(\mu) d\mu \leftrightarrow \lim_{t\to\infty} e^{-\int_0^t (1-\tau) r_B(\mu) d\mu} B(t) = 0 \qquad (5.17)$$

holds. Equation (5.17) is the present-value borrowing constraint which states that public debt at time zero must equal the future present-value surpluses.

Again, we assume that the ratio of the primary surplus to GDP ratio is a positive linear function of the debt to GDP ratio and of a constant. The primary surplus ratio, then, can be written as

$$\frac{S}{Y} = \phi + \psi \, \frac{B}{Y} = \frac{\tau Y - I_p - C_p - \varrho w(L - L^d)}{Y}, \qquad (5.18)$$

where $\phi \in \mathbb{R}$, $\psi \in \mathbb{R}_{++}$ are constants. The parameter ψ determines how strongly the primary surplus reacts to changes in public debt and ϕ determines whether the level of the primary surplus rises or falls with an increase in GDP.

Using (5.18) the differential equation describing the evolution of public debt can be written as

$$\dot{B} = (r_B(1 - \tau) - \psi) B - \phi Y. \qquad (5.19)$$

[3] An extensive discussion of the role of the Phillips curve in dynamic macroeconomics can be found for example in Flaschel et al. (1997).

Using that the evolution of public debt is given by $\dot{B} = r_B B(1-\tau) + I_p + C_p + \varrho w(L - L^d) - \tau Y = r_B B(1-\tau) - \psi B - \phi Y$ public investment can be written as

$$I_p = \omega(\tau - \phi)Y - \omega\psi B - \omega\varrho w(L - L^d), \tag{5.20}$$

where we assumed that public consumption relative to public investment is constant, $C_p/I_p = \kappa = \text{constant}$, $\omega = 1/(1+\kappa)$.

Denoting by δ_G the depreciation rate of public capital, the differential equation describing the evolution of public capital, then, is written as

$$\dot{G} = \omega(\tau - \phi)Y - \omega\psi B - \omega\varrho w(L - L^d) - \delta_G G. \tag{5.21}$$

5.1.4 The Balanced Growth Path

The description of our economy is completed by deriving the growth rate of consumption and by deriving the economy wide resource constraint. The growth rate of consumption is obtained from (5.5) and (5.6) as

$$\frac{\dot{C}}{C} = -(\rho + \delta) + (1-\tau)(1-\alpha)(Y/K) \tag{5.22}$$

with Y/K given by $Y/K = (L^n)^\alpha (G/K)^\alpha$ in case of a vertical Phillips curve and by $Y/K = \alpha^{\alpha/(\alpha-1)}(w/K)^{-\alpha/(1-\alpha)}(G/K)^{\alpha/(1-\alpha)}$ if the Phillips curve has a negative slope, where the latter is obtained by using the optimality condition (5.10).

The economy wide resource constraint is derived by combining the budget constraint of the household with that of the government as

$$\frac{\dot{K}}{K} = \frac{Y}{K} - \frac{C}{K} + \psi\frac{B}{K} + (\phi - \tau)\frac{Y}{K} + \varrho(L - L^d)\frac{w}{K} - \delta, \tag{5.23}$$

with $L \geq L^d$.

Hence, the economy is completely described by (5.19), (5.21), (5.22) and (5.23), with r given by (5.8). The wage rate is either determined by (5.9) or by (5.15) with L^d given by (5.10), depending on whether the Phillips curve is vertical or negatively sloped.

A balanced growth path (BGP) is given when the conditions shown in Definition 5 are fulfilled.

Definition 5 A balanced growth path (BGP) is a path such that consumption, private capital, public capital and the wage rate grow at the same strictly positive constant growth rate, that is $\dot{C}/C = \dot{K}/K = \dot{G}/G = \dot{w}/w = g$, $g > 0$, $g = \text{constant}$, and either

(i) $\dot{B} = 0$ or
(ii) $\dot{B}/B = g$.

This definition shows that, as usual, consumption, private capital, public capital, and thus output, as well as the wage rate grow at a constant and strictly positive rate over time on the BGP. Public debt may also grow the same rate as output or it may be constant. The latter holds when the government pursues a balanced budget. However, in contrast to the last chapter, we do not consider the case where public debt grows but less than all other economic variables.

In the next two sections we analyze our model, first for the case of a vertical Phillips curve and, second, assuming that the Phillips curve is negatively sloped.

5.2 Analysis of the Model with Real Wage Flexibility

In this section we study the structure of our model assuming that labor demand equals its natural level, $L^d = L^n$, such that the unemployment rate equals its natural rate, $1 - L^n/L$. The wage rate is determined by the marginal productivity rule (5.9).

In this case, the economy is completely described by (5.19), (5.21), (5.22) and (5.23), with r and w given by (5.8) and (5.9), with $L^d = L^n$. To analyze our economy around a BGP we define the new variables $c \equiv C/K$, $b \equiv B/K$ and $x \equiv G/K$. Differentiating these variables with respect to time leads to a three dimensional system of differential equations given by

$$\dot{c} = c\big((1-\alpha)x^{\alpha}(L^n)^{\alpha}(1-\tau) - \rho + c - x^{\alpha}(L^n)^{\alpha} - (\phi-\tau)x^{\alpha}(L^n)^{\alpha} - \psi b\big) + (-c)(\varrho\alpha x^{\alpha}(L^n)^{\alpha-1}(L-L^n)), \quad (5.24)$$

$$\dot{b} = b((1-\alpha)x^{\alpha}(L^n)^{\alpha}(1-\tau) - \psi - \phi x^{\alpha}(L^n)^{\alpha}/b - x^{\alpha}(L^n)^{\alpha} - (\phi-\tau)x^{\alpha}(L^n)^{\alpha}) - b(\psi b + \varrho\alpha x^{\alpha}(L^n)^{\alpha-1}(L-L^n) + c), \quad (5.25)$$

$$\dot{x} = x(\omega(\tau-\phi)(L^n)^{\alpha}x^{\alpha-1} - \omega\psi b/x - \omega\varrho\alpha x^{\alpha-1}(L^n)^{\alpha-1}(L-L^n) - x^{\alpha}(L^n)^{\alpha}) + x(c + \delta - \psi b - (\phi-\tau)x^{\alpha}(L^n)^{\alpha} - \varrho\alpha x^{\alpha}(L^n)^{\alpha-1}(L-L^n) - \delta_G). \quad (5.26)$$

A solution of $\dot{c} = \dot{b} = \dot{x} = 0$ with respect to c, b, x gives a BGP for our model and the corresponding ratios $x^{\star}, b^{\star}, c^{\star}$ on the BGP.[4]

In the following we consider two situations. First, we analyze the economy with a balanced budget, then for the case of permanent deficits.

5.2.1 *Balanced Government Budget*

The balanced budget scenario, scenario (i), is obtained by setting the reaction coefficient ψ equal to the net return on capital, $(1-\tau)r - \delta$, making ψ an endogenous variable. Further, ϕ is set equal zero for all times, that is $\phi = 0$, for $t \in [0, \infty)$. For

[4]The $\star$ denotes BGP values and we exclude the economically meaningless BGP $x^{\star} = c^{\star} = 0$.

this scenario, Proposition 10 gives results as concerns uniqueness and stability of a balanced growth path.

Proposition 10 *Assume that there exists a balanced growth path for scenario* (i). *Then, the balanced growth path is unique and saddle point stable.*

Proof See the appendix to this section. □

This proposition demonstrates that the balanced budget scenario is characterized by a unique BGP which is saddle point stable, in case of ongoing growth. The fact that the existence of a BGP cannot be shown for the analytical model is due to unemployment benefits paid by the government and due to depreciation of public capital. Thus, if unemployment benefits exceed a certain threshold sustained growth may not be feasible because public resources devoted to growth enhancing public investment are not sufficiently large.

It should also be pointed out that saddle point stability implies, in case of a vertical Phillips curve, that there exists a unique value $c(0)$ such that the economy converges to the balanced growth path. If one takes both $x(0)$ and $b(0)$ as given, since both x and b are state variables, this means that the economy is determinate, implying that two economies with identical initial capital stocks and the same initial level of public debt have the same transitional growth rates.

5.2.2 Permanent Public Deficits

As concerns scenario (ii), the deficit scenario, where public debt grows at the same rate as consumption and capital in the long-run, the analytical model turns out to be quite complicated and no unambiguous results can be derived. But it is possible to derive a result as concerns the public debt to private capital ratio for the analytical model. This is done in Proposition 11.

Proposition 11 *Assume that there exists a balanced growth path in scenario* (ii). *Then, the ratio of public debt to private capital is given by*

$$b^\star = \frac{\phi (x^\star)^\alpha (L^n)^\alpha}{\rho - \psi}.$$

Proof See the appendix to this section. □

From Proposition 11 one can realize that in case of a relatively low reaction coefficient ψ, so that $\psi < \rho$, the coefficient ϕ must be positive for sustained growth with a positive government debt to be feasible.[5] This implies that the primary surplus must rise as GDP increases if the reaction of the government to higher public

[5]In this chapter we limit our consideration to $b \geq 0$.

debt is relatively small. If the reverse holds, that is for $\psi > \rho$, the coefficient ϕ must be negative. In this case, the reaction of the government to higher debt is relatively large implying that the government pays too much attention to stabilizing debt and does not attach sufficient weight to fostering economic growth through public investment. Therefore, the primary surplus must decline with a higher GDP, implying that public investment rises, so that sustained growth is feasible.

An interesting result can be obtained when the deficit scenario is compared to the balanced budget scenario. Analogously to the last chapter, it turns out that the balanced budget scenario always is associated with a higher growth rate. Proposition 12 gives the result.

Proposition 12 *The balanced growth rate in scenario* (ii), *the deficit scenario, is lower than the balanced growth rate in the balanced budget scenario, scenario* (i).

Proof See the appendix to this section. □

From an economic point of view, the result in Proposition 12 is due to the fact that in the deficit scenario the government must devote resources to the debt service that cannot be used for productive public investment. The latter does not hold for the balanced budget scenario so that this scenario goes along with a higher balanced growth rate.

In order to get additional insight in our model we perform simulations. We should like to point out that our model is a highly stylized one so that we do not intend to make calibration exercises or replicate real economies. The simulations are intended to derive results that cannot be obtained for the analytical model. In particular, we are interested in growth effects of deficit financed public investment and in the question of how the reaction coefficient, ψ, affects stability of the model in order to compare this model to the one of the last chapter, where we performed the same exercise.

In the simulations, the subjective discount rate is set to 3.5 percent and the depreciation rates of private and of public capital are 3.5 and 7.5 percent, respectively, that is $\rho = 0.035$, $\delta = 0.035$, $\delta_G = 0.075$. Labor supply is normalized to one, $L = 1$, and the natural rate of employment is 0.98 giving a natural rate of unemployment of 2 percent. The parameter ω is set to $\omega = 0.65$ implying that the ratio of public consumption to public investment is about 55 percent. The income tax rate is set to 10 percent and the unemployment benefit is 80 percent of the wage rate, that is $\tau = 0.1$, $\varrho = 0.8$. The elasticity of output with respect to public capital is set to 30 percent. It must be pointed out that this implies that the elasticity of output with respect to labor is also 30 percent while the elasticity of output with respect to capital is 70 percent. This can be justified by supposing that labor is raw labor and that capital is interpreted in a broad sense so that capital comprises both private physical and human capital.[6]

[6] We made the simulations also with $\alpha = 0.6$. Qualitatively, the results are identical to those presented here.

Table 5.1 Balanced growth rate, g, and eigenvalues for different ϕ with $\psi = 0.01$

	$\phi = 0.065$	$\phi = 0.055$	$\phi = 0.045$
g	5%	11.8%	15.2%
Eigenvalues	$+; -; +$	$-; +; +$	$-; +; +$

In Table 5.1 we report the balanced growth rate, g, and the signs of the eigenvalues of the Jacobian for different values of ϕ, with ψ set $\psi = 0.01$.

In order to interpret Table 5.1 we note that a deficit financed increase in public investment is modelled by a decline in ϕ which can be seen from (5.20). Hence, Table 5.1 shows that a deficit financed increase in public investment leads to a higher balanced growth rate with the parameters underlying the simulation. However, it can also be seen that only one eigenvalue is negative implying that the economy is unstable in this case. Consequently, the government must levy an additional non-distortionary tax in order to control public debt so that the economy can converge to the BGP.

If ϕ is further increased in Table 5.1, the balanced growth rate declines and for $\phi \geq 0.068$ no BGP exists any longer. If ϕ is decreased, the balanced growth rate rises and for $\phi \to 0$ the balanced growth rate approaches its maximum value of about 24 percent which is equal to the growth rate obtained in the balanced budget scenario.

Next, we choose a higher value for ψ and set $\psi = 0.05$ so that $\rho < \psi$ holds. Table 5.2 gives results for this example.

Table 5.2 shows that with a larger reaction coefficient ψ the economy is stable. For $\psi = 0.05$ there are either two negative real eigenvalues or two complex conjugate eigenvalues with negative real parts. But in this case, a deficit financed increase in public investment reduces the balanced growth rate. The reason is that the initial deficit financed increase in public investment is compensated by the strong reaction of the government to the higher public debt so that the economy ends up with a smaller growth rate. Hence, there is again a trade-off between stability and positive growth effects of deficit financed public investment.

If ϕ is increased the growth rate rises and again approaches its maximum value for $\phi \to 0$. If ϕ is decreased, the balanced growth rate declines and it turns out that for $\phi \leq -0.036$ the balanced growth path becomes unstable, that is the Jacobian matrix has only positive eigenvalues or eigenvalues with positive real parts. For $\phi \leq -0.041$, finally, no BGP exists any longer.

In order to see that a lower reaction coefficient ψ destabilizes the economy, we set $\phi = -0.03$ and continuously decrease ψ starting from $\psi = 0.05$. Doing

Table 5.2 Balanced growth rate, g, and eigenvalues for different ϕ with $\psi = 0.05$

	$\phi = -0.01$	$\phi = -0.02$	$\phi = -0.03$
g	21.5%	18.3%	13.8%
Eigenvalues	$+; -; -$	$+; -a \pm bi, a, b > 0$	$+; -a \pm bi, a, b > 0$

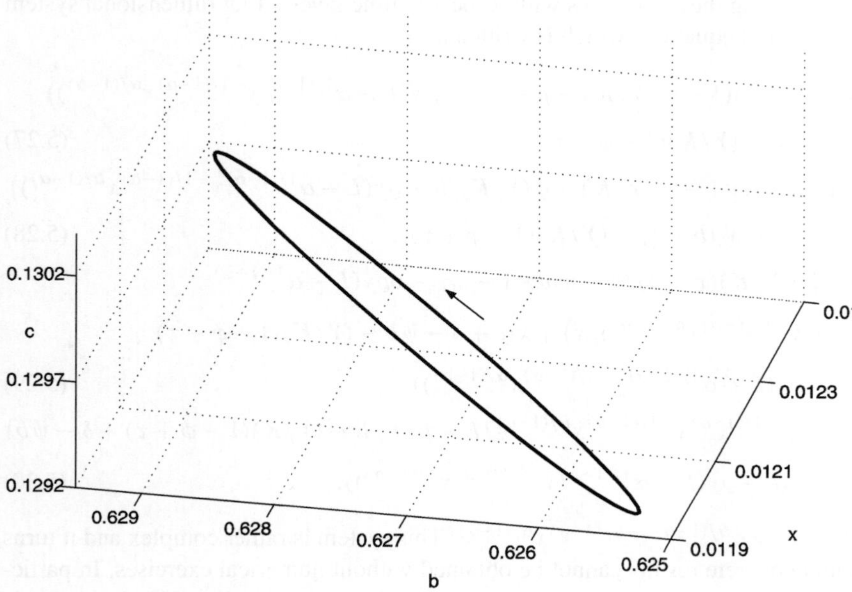

Fig. 5.1 Limit cycle in the $(x-b-c)$ phase space

so shows that for $\psi = \psi_{crit} \approx 0.048$ two eigenvalues are purely imaginary and for values of ψ smaller than ψ_{crit} one eigenvalues is positive and two are complex conjugate with positive real parts, implying that the BGP looses stability. In addition, a Hopf bifurcation can be observed at $\psi = \psi_{crit}$ leading to limit cycles. At the bifurcation point the first Lyapunov coefficient l_1 is negative, $l_1 \approx -1.089$, indicating that the emerging limit cycles are stable.[7]

Figure 5.1 shows a limit cycle in the $(x-b-c)$ phase space. The orientation of the cycle is as indicated by the arrow.

5.3 The Model with Real Wage Rigidities

In case of real wage rigidities, labor demand is given by (5.10) and the wage adjustment is described by the Phillips curve (5.15). This implies that the growth rate of the wage rate is a negative function of the unemployment rate. In this case, the economy is completely described by (5.15), (5.19), (5.21), (5.22), and (5.23), with r given by (5.8) and L^d given by (5.10).

In order to analyze the economy around a BGP we proceed as in the last section and define the variables $c \equiv C/K$, $b \equiv B/K$, $x \equiv G/K$ and, in addition, $y = w/K$.

[7]For those computations as well as for the depiction of the limit cycle we used the software CL_MATCONT, see Dhooge et al. (2003).

Differentiating these variables with respect to time gives a four dimensional system of differential equations which is written as,

$$\dot{c} = c\big((1-\alpha)(1-\tau)(Y/K) - \rho - \psi b - \varrho y(L - \alpha^{1/(1-\alpha)} y^{-1/(1-\alpha)} x^{\alpha/(1-\alpha)})\big)$$
$$+ c(c - (Y/K)(1-\phi+\tau)), \tag{5.27}$$
$$\dot{b} = b\big((1-\alpha)(1-\tau)(Y/K) - \phi(Y/K)/b - \varrho y(L - \alpha^{1/(1-\alpha)} y^{-1/(1-\alpha)} x^{\alpha/(1-\alpha)})\big)$$
$$+ b(c - \psi(b+1) - (Y/K)(1-\phi+\tau)), \tag{5.28}$$
$$\dot{x} = x\big(\omega(Y/K)(\tau-\phi)/x - w\omega b/x - \delta_G - \omega\varrho y(L - \alpha^{1/(1-\alpha)}$$
$$\times y^{-1/(1-\alpha)} x^{\alpha/(1-\alpha)})/x\big) + x(c + \delta - \psi b - (Y/K)(1-\phi+\tau)$$
$$- \varrho y(L - \alpha^{1/(1-\alpha)} y^{-1/(1-\alpha)} x^{\alpha/(1-\alpha)})), \tag{5.29}$$
$$\dot{y} = y\big(\beta_L \alpha^{1/(1-\alpha)} y^{-1/(1-\alpha)} x^{\alpha/(1-\alpha)}/L - \beta_L \bar{L}/L - (Y/K)(1-\phi+\tau) + \delta - \psi b\big)$$
$$+ y(c - \varrho y(L - \alpha^{1/(1-\alpha)} y^{-1/(1-\alpha)} x^{\alpha/(1-\alpha)})), \tag{5.30}$$

with $Y/K = \alpha^{\alpha/(1-\alpha)} y^{-\alpha/(1-\alpha)} x^{\alpha/(1-\alpha)}$. This system is rather complex and it turns out that concrete results cannot be obtained without numerical exercises. In particular, we are again interested in the question of how fiscal policy affects economic growth and stability of the economy. First, we analyze the balanced budget scenario.

5.3.1 Balanced Government Budget

As in the last section, the balanced budget scenario, scenario (i), is obtained by setting the reaction coefficient ψ equal to the net return on capital, $(1-\tau)r - \delta$, and by setting $\phi = 0$. For this scenario, Proposition 13 gives information about stability properties of the dynamic system.

Proposition 13 *Assume that there exists a balanced growth path for scenario* (i). *Then, there is at least one negative real eigenvalue.*

Proof See the appendix to this section. □

If there is exactly one negative real eigenvalue the economy is unstable. In this case, the government again has to levy a non-distortionary tax and use the revenue to control public debt such that the economy can converge to the BGP in the long-run. If there are two negative eigenvalues or two eigenvalues with negative real parts, there exist unique initial values of consumption and of the wage rate, the economy can choose, such that it converges to the BGP. In case of more than two negative real eigenvalues, the economy is indeterminate in the sense that the initial consumption and the initial wage rate are not uniquely determined. Next, we study the deficit scenario and try to find how fiscal policy can affect the economy.

5.3.2 Permanent Public Deficits

To analyze the economy with this scenario we again use numerical examples and take the same parameter values as in the last chapter and we set the parameter β_L, determining the adjustment speed of wages, to $\beta_L = 0.07$ and $\bar{L}$ is set to $\bar{L} = 0.75$. This corresponds to $\gamma = 0.04$ in (5.11) and to $\theta = 0.6$ in (5.13). In Table 5.3 we study effects of raising deficit financed public investment with a relatively small reaction coefficient ψ.

Table 5.3 shows that for a relatively small value of the reaction coefficient ψ, the model is unstable. In addition, it can be seen that a deficit financed increase in public investment, modelled by a decrease in ϕ, reduces the balanced growth rate and raises the unemployment rate.

If the parameter ϕ is further decreased in Table 5.3, the growth rate becomes negative for $\phi \leq 0.0094$. If ϕ is still further reduced, the balanced growth rate continues to decline and it converges to the value of the balanced budget scenario which is -0.3% for $\phi \to 0$. Thus, a balanced budget would go along with a negative balanced growth rate and an unemployment rate of 28.9%. The Jacobian has exactly one negative eigenvalue implying that the BGP is unstable. If ϕ is increased the economy reaches the full employment state for $\phi = 0.0524$ with a growth rate of 2.1%.

If we set the reaction coefficient ψ to a higher value, implying that the government raises the primary surplus to a larger degree as public debt increases, the situation changes. Then, the economy becomes stable and a deficit financed increase in public investment leads to a higher balanced growth rate and a smaller unemployment rate. Table 5.4 shows the results with ψ set to $\psi = 0.05$.

Table 5.4 shows that the economy is saddle point stable with a larger value of ψ. The outcome that a higher reaction coefficient stabilizes the economy is equivalent to the result of the last section with flexible wages and a vertical Phillips curve. But, in contrast to the last section, the trade-off between positive growth effects of deficit financed public investment and stability does not seem to exist any longer when real wages are rigid. As Table 5.4 demonstrates, a deficit financed rise in public

Table 5.3 Balanced growth rate, g, unemployment rate, u, and eigenvalues for different values of ϕ with $\psi = 0.01$

	$\phi = 0.065$	$\phi = 0.055$	$\phi = 0.045$
g	1.5%	1.2%	0.8%
u	3.1%	8.3%	13%
Eigenvalues	+; −; +; +	+; −; +; +	+; −; +; +

Table 5.4 Balanced growth rate, g, unemployment rate, u, and eigenvalues for different values of ϕ with $\psi = 0.05$

	$\phi = -0.01$	$\phi = -0.02$	$\phi = -0.03$
g	0.07%	0.5%	1%
u	24%	17.9%	10.7%
Eigenvalues	+; −; +; −	+; −; +; −	+; −; +; −

investment, modelled by a decline in the parameter ϕ, raises the balanced growth rate and the economy is stable.

If we increase the parameter ϕ in Table 5.4 it turns out that for $\phi \geq -0.008$ the balanced growth rate becomes negative. If ϕ is reduced the growth rate rises and for $\phi = -0.0422$ it attains 1.7% that goes along with an unemployment rate equal to zero. It should also be mentioned that the increase of the balanced growth in Table 5.4 goes along with a higher debt to private capital ratio, in contrast to the latter chapter where a higher balanced growth rate was associated with a smaller debt to capital ratio.

The difference to the outcome of the last section is clearly due to the difference in wage flexibility that determines the shape of Phillips curves. In the next section, we discuss in detail the economic mechanisms behind the different results.

5.4 Discussion and Comparison to the Model Without Unemployment

In the last two sections we have derived results for our model and we have seen that the outcome partly depends on the flexibility of the real wage rate, that is on whether the Phillips curve is vertical or whether it has a negative slope. In this section we want to identify economic mechanisms that generate the different results.

One result we derived was a trade-off between positive growth effects of higher deficit financed public investment and stability of the model when the Phillips curve is vertical. The reason for that outcome is that a high reaction coefficient ψ implies that the increase in the primary surplus is large as public debt rises, which stabilizes the economy. But, with a large ψ, the initial increase in deficit financed public investment is more than compensated by the rise in public debt implying that public investment declines again, so that the economy is characterized by a smaller growth rate in the long-run. Thus, the higher public debt requires more resources for the debt service which reduces public investment in the end.

If wages are rigid and the Phillips curve has a negative slope, the trade-off does not exist. In this case, when the reaction of the primary surplus to public debt ψ is sufficiently large, a deficit financed increase in public investment raises the ratio of public to private capital and labor demand. As a consequence, unemployment declines reducing unemployment payments of the government which raises public investment. Thus, lower unemployment spending prevents a decline in public investment as public debt rises, even if the reaction coefficient ψ is large. Further, a large reaction coefficient ψ has a positive effect on the growth rate of private capital, which can be seen from the economy wide resource constraint (5.23). Therefore, a deficit financed increase in public investment raises the balanced growth rate for a large ψ, even if it goes along with a higher debt to private capital ratio in the long-run.

With a small ψ, the positive effect of less unemployment payments on public investment, as a result of higher deficit financed public investment, would be amplified. But, in this case, the crowding-out effect of an increase in public investment dominates in the economy wide resource constraint so that private investment declines. This is again seen from the economy wide resource constraint (5.23), where we recall that the initial deficit financed increase in public investment is modelled by a lower ϕ. Therefore, a deficit financed increase in public investment reduces the balanced growth, where $\dot{K}/K = \dot{G}/G$ holds, for a small reaction coefficient ψ in case the Phillips curve has a negative slope.

Hence, the different effects of higher deficit financed public investment in our model are due to the fact that employment is equal to its natural level with flexible wages whereas employment varies if real wages are not flexible when deficit financed public investment is increased. It should also be mentioned that a higher balanced growth rate goes along with a higher wage to private capital ratio if wages are flexible. In case of rigid real wages, the reverse holds. In this case, a higher balanced growth rate goes along with a smaller ratio of the wage rate to private capital implying a higher employment share and, thus, less unemployment.

Finally, comparing our model with the model where unemployment is not considered, analyzed in the last section, it can be realized that, from a qualitative point of view, the model with flexible wages produces the same results as the model without unemployment. This holds although the differential equations in the two models are of course different, due to unemployment in this model leading to unemployment payments from the government to the household sector. Nevertheless, if wages are flexible and the Phillips curve is vertical, employment is fixed at its natural rate and the wage rate equals the marginal product of labor. Only if wages are rigid and the Phillips curve has a negative slope, fiscal policy affects the unemployment rate and unemployment payments. Then, the model gives rise to different outcomes, as mentioned above.

5.5 Conclusion

Should the government run deficits and finance productive public spending in order to promote growth and employment in an economy? The answer to this question crucially depends on whether real wages are flexible and the Phillips curve is vertical or whether wages are rigid and the Phillips curve has a negative slope.

With flexible real wages, there is a trade-off between stability and positive growth effects of deficit financed increases in public investment. If a deficit financed increase in public investment raises the balanced growth rate, the government has to levy a lump-sum tax in order to control public debt. Otherwise, convergence to the balanced growth path cannot be assured. If real wages are rigid and the Phillips curve has a negative slope, this trade-off does not exist. The reason for this is that fiscal policy affects the level of employment in this case and, therefore, the feedback effect of higher public debt is different from the situation where employment is fixed at its natural level.

A result that holds independent of the flexibility of real wages, is that a stronger reaction of the government to higher public debt stabilizes the economy. Hence, if the reaction of the government to higher debt is large, the economy is stable and converges to the balanced growth path asymptotically, independent of whether real wages are flexible or rigid.

Appendix

Proof of Proposition 10 The strategy of the proof is analogous to that of the proof of Proposition 7. Hence, we set $\phi = 0$, $\psi = (1-\tau)(1-\alpha)x^\alpha (L^n)^\alpha - \delta$ and $b = 0$. Setting $\dot{x}/x = \dot{c}/c$ gives $q(x,\cdot) = (1-\alpha)x^\alpha (L^n)^\alpha (1-\tau) - (\rho + \delta) + \delta_G - \tau x^{\alpha-1}(L^n)^\alpha + \varrho\alpha x^{\alpha-1}(L^n)^{\alpha-1}(L - L^n)$. In case of sustained growth we have $g = \tau x^{\alpha-1}(L^n)^\alpha - \delta_G - \varrho\alpha x^{\alpha-1}(L^n)^{\alpha-1}(L - L^n) > 0$ which is only possible for $\tau > \varrho\alpha(L - L^n)/L^n$. With this, it is easily seen that $\lim_{x\to 0} q(x,\cdot) = -\infty$ and $\lim_{x\to\infty} q(x,\cdot) = +\infty$. Further, we have $\partial q(\cdot)/\partial x > 0$. Thus, uniqueness of a BGP is shown.

To show saddle point stability, we compute the Jacobian matrix evaluated at the rest point of (5.24)–(5.26). The Jacobian is given by

$$\mathrm{J} = \begin{bmatrix} c & \partial\dot{c}/\partial b & \partial\dot{c}/\partial x \\ 0 & \partial\dot{b}/\partial b & 0 \\ x & \partial\dot{x}/\partial b & \partial\dot{x}/\partial x \end{bmatrix},$$

with $c = c^\star$ and $x = x^\star$. One eigenvalue of this matrix is given by $\varrho_1 = \partial\dot{b}/\partial b = -\dot{K}/K = -g < 0$. Thus, we know that one eigenvalue, ϱ_1, is negative. Further, $c(\partial\dot{x}/\partial x) - x(\partial\dot{c}/\partial x)$ can be computed as follows, $c(\partial\dot{x}/\partial x) - x(\partial\dot{c}/\partial x) = -\alpha(1-\alpha)x^{\alpha-1}(L^n)^\alpha(1-\tau) + (\alpha-1)x^{-1}(\tau x^{\alpha-1}(L^n)^\alpha - \varrho\alpha x^{\alpha-1}(L^n)^{\alpha-1}(L-L^n))$. $g > 0$ implies $\tau x^{\alpha-1}(L^n)^\alpha - \varrho\alpha x^{\alpha-1}(L^n)^{\alpha-1}\,(L - L^n) > \delta_G > 0$. Consequently, the determinant of J is negative. Since the product of the eigenvalues equals the determinant, $\lambda_1 \cdot \lambda_2 \cdot \lambda_3 = \det \mathrm{J} > 0$, and because of $\lambda_1 < 0$, we know that two eigenvalues are negative and one is positive. □

Proof of Proposition 11 To prove Proposition 11, equation $\dot{b}/b = 0$ is solved with respect to c giving $c = c(x, b, \cdot)$. Inserting $c = c(x, b, \cdot)$ in $\dot{c}/c$ and solving $\dot{c}/c = 0$ with respect to b gives $b^\star$ as in Proposition 11. □

Proof of Proposition 12 To prove this proposition we note that we set $\phi = 0$, $\psi = (1-\tau)(1-\alpha)x^\alpha(L^n)^\alpha - \delta$ and $b = 0$ to get scenario (i). Further, the balanced growth rate is given by $\dot{C}/C = -(\rho+\delta) + (1-\tau)(1-\alpha)x^\alpha(L^n)^\alpha$. Along a BGP we have $\dot{C}/C = \dot{G}/G$ which implies

$$\begin{aligned}(1-\tau)(1-\alpha)x^\alpha(L^n)^\alpha - (\rho+\delta) \\ = \omega\tau x^{\alpha-1}(L^n)^\alpha - \omega\varrho\alpha x^{\alpha-1}(L^n)^{\alpha-1}(L - L^n) - \delta_G. \qquad \text{(A5.1)}\end{aligned}$$

A value $x_i^\star$ such that the left hand side in (A5.1) equals the right hand side gives a BGP for scenario (i).

Using that b on the BGP is given by $b = \phi \cdot (x^\star)^\alpha (L^n)^\alpha / (\rho - \psi)$, the condition $\dot{C}/C = \dot{G}/G$ can be written for scenario (ii) as

$$(1-\tau)(1-\alpha)x^\alpha (L^n)^\alpha - (\rho + \delta)$$
$$= \omega\tau x^{\alpha-1}(L^n)^\alpha - \omega\varrho\alpha x^{\alpha-1}(L^n)^{\alpha-1}(L - L^n) - \delta_G - \rho\omega b/x. \quad \text{(A5.2)}$$

A value $x_{ii}^\star$ such that the left hand side in (A5.2) equals the right hand side gives a BGP for scenario (ii).

The function on the left hand side of equation (A5.1) and of equation (A5.2) are identical. The graph of the function on the right hand side of (A5.1), however, is above the graph of the function on the right hand side of (A5.2) for all $b > 0$. Therefore, the left hand side and the right hand side in (A5.1) intersect at a larger value of x than the left hand side and the right hand side in (A5.2), giving a higher balanced growth rate for scenario (i). □

Proof of Proposition 13 To prove this proposition, we compute the Jacobian matrix evaluated at the rest point of system (5.27)–(5.30). The Jacobian has the following form,

$$\mathrm{J} = \begin{bmatrix} c & \partial\dot{c}/\partial b & \partial\dot{c}/\partial c & \partial\dot{c}/\partial y \\ 0 & \partial\dot{b}/\partial b & 0 & 0 \\ x & \partial\dot{x}/\partial b & \partial\dot{x}/\partial c & \partial\dot{x}/\partial y \\ y & \partial\dot{y}/\partial b & \partial\dot{y}/\partial c & \partial\dot{y}/\partial y \end{bmatrix},$$

with $c = c^\star$, $x = x^\star$ and $y = y^\star$. One eigenvalue of this matrix is given by $\lambda_1 = \partial\dot{b}/\partial b = -\dot{K}/K = -g < 0$. □

Chapter 6
Conclusion

In this book we have studied effects of public debt. Starting point of our analysis was the conjecture that an increase in the public debt to GDP ratio must be accompanied by a rise in the primary surplus to GDP ratio such that public debt can be sustainable. In analogy to Bohn (1995) who used discrete time, it was shown that a linear increase in the primary surplus relative to GDP as public debt relative to GDP rises, assures sustainability of public debt. However, such a policy does not necessarily imply that the debt to GDP ratio remains bounded if the reaction is not sufficiently strong. But, in the long-run, a rising debt to GDP ratio is not compatible with a sustainable debt policy so that, sooner or later, the public debt ratio must become constant. The reason for the latter is that a rise in the debt to GDP ratio requires an increase in the primary surplus to GDP ratio, as just mentioned. Since the primary surplus relative to GDP must be financed out of GDP and, therefore, cannot exceed the GDP of a country, the primary surplus relative to GDP is bounded by above. Consequently, once the upper bound of the primary surplus has been reached, the debt to GDP ratio must be constant. An immediate consequence of this is that it may be impossible for public debt to be sustainable, simply if it is too large relative to GDP so that it exceeds the present value of future primary surpluses that can be maximally achieved.

The empirical estimations with which we tested whether the primary surplus relative to GDP is positively and statistically significantly correlated with the debt to GDP ratio indeed gave evidence that this holds true for developed economies. Most estimations yielded a positive reaction coefficient on average showing that governments raise the primary surplus relative to GDP as the debt to GDP ratio increases. Allowing for time variation of the reaction coefficient also demonstrated that this coefficient is not constant in most cases. Instead, this coefficient is characterized by variations over time, where the reaction coefficient has clearly declined in some countries. It should also be pointed out that the debt to GDP ratio in most of the euro area countries under consideration has increased over the last decades although the reaction coefficient was positive. Hence, our empirical analysis has shown that the reaction coefficient was positive but it was not large enough to stabilize the debt to GDP ratio. However, as pointed out in the previous paragraph, the debt to GDP ratio

A. Greiner, B. Fincke, *Public Debt and Economic Growth*,
Dynamic Modeling and Econometrics in Economics and Finance 11,
DOI 10.1007/978-3-642-01745-2_6,

must become constant sooner or later. Otherwise, sustainability of public debt will not be given.[1] For the developing countries considered in our study, the results are not so good. With the exception of the two economies Botswana and Rwanda, none of the estimated reaction coefficient was positive and statistically significant and in one case it was even negative and statistically significant.

Given the empirical evidence for developed countries that the primary surplus relative to GDP rises as the public debt to GDP ratio increases, we then analyzed endogenous growth models where this rule was integrated. In all of our models we posited that the tax rate is fixed. Hence, when the primary surplus is to be increased, this can be achieved by reductions in public spending or by a higher total tax revenue as the result of increases in GDP. In analyzing our models, it turned out that a crucial aspect as concerns growth effects of public debt is whether wages are flexible guaranteeing full employment or the natural rate of employment or whether real wages are rigid implying that the economy is suffering from unemployment.

In the models with flexible real wages and full employment it turned out that a zero public debt to GDP ratio always goes along with a higher balanced growth rate, compared to the case where the debt to GDP ratio is positive in the long-run. This holds independent of whether public spending is unproductive or whether the government invests in a productive public capital stock. In the latter case, it is the debt service associated with a positive public debt to GDP ratio that prevents public resources from being used for productive spending so that the economy ends up with a smaller growth rate in the long-run, compared to the situation with a zero debt to GDP ratio. In the first case, when public spending is unproductive, the shadow price of wealth is smaller if the debt to GDP ratio is positive because this implies that less of the household's savings is used for the formation of productive private capital. That leads to a lower return to capital and, thus, to a smaller investment share leading to a lower balanced growth rate.

But the fact that a zero public debt to GDP ratios yields the highest balanced growth rate, unless the government is a lender to the private sector, does not imply that deficit financed productive public investments always reduce the long-run growth rate. Instead, we could find numerical examples where a deficit financed rise in public investment leads to a higher balanced growth rate. In this case, public investment is productive implying that GDP, and thus, the tax revenue strongly increase. As a consequence, the long-run debt to GDP ratio is reduced by this fiscal policy and the increase in the debt ratio, through the deficit financing of the public investment, is only transitory. However, in this situation, the economy turned out to be unstable meaning that the government has to levy an additional non-distortionary tax, possibly at a later point in time, in order to control public debt. Thus, there is a trade-off between stability and positive growth effects of deficit financed increases in public investment in the class of models considered in this book.

From the perspective of maximizing welfare our analysis has shown that a fiscal policy that implies a zero debt to GDP ratio in the long-run also yields higher welfare compared to a fiscal policy that goes along with a strictly positive public debt

[1]It goes without saying that the outcome of our study only alludes to the time period considered and does not automatically hold for future periods as well.

ratio. Hence, if a government starts out with a positive public debt to GDP ratio it should perform a fiscal policy that leads to a zero debt to GDP ratio asymptotically. It can do this in two ways. It can either run a balanced budget at any point in time or it can run a deficit that, however, grows less than GDP. In both cases, the debt to GDP ratio converges to zero. Comparing the latter two policies from a welfare theoretic perspective suggests that the balanced budget scenario performs worse. The reason for that outcome[2] is that public deficits imply a higher level of initial consumption in the scenario where public debt grows, but less than GDP, compared to the balanced budget scenario and the higher level of consumption implies a positive welfare effect.

If we allow for unemployment and the government pays unemployment benefits the qualitative results do not change when real wages are flexible such that the natural level of employment is realized in the economy. But when real wages are rigid the outcome changes. Then, the trade-off between stability and positive growth effects of deficit financed increases in public investment does not exist any longer. The reason for this result is that fiscal policy affects the level of employment in this case and, therefore, the feedback effect of higher public debt is different from the situation where employment is fixed at its natural level. Hence, a deficit financed increase in public investment can lead to a higher balanced growth rate, a lower unemployment rate and a higher debt ratio. If unemployment is reduced, unemployment payments decline and, thus, raise productive public spending so that the negative effect of a higher debt ratio can be compensated.

Consequently, the decisive aspect determining growth effects of public debt is whether real wages are sufficiently flexible so that in the long-run the economy realizes its natural rate of employment or whether wages are rigid so that unemployment is persistent. In the first case, a zero debt to GDP ratio yields a higher balanced growth rate compared to a situation with a positive stock of outstanding government bonds. This does not necessarily hold when unemployment is persistent because then a positive stock of public debt, with the deficits used to finance productive public spending, can go along with a lower level of unemployment and, thus, less unemployment spending. Due to less unemployment spending, more resources are available for productive public spending in spite of the higher debt service. But it must be pointed out that a prerequisite for this outcome is that the government does invest available resources in a productive public capital stock and does not use them for unproductive purposes. In addition the employment effects of public spending must be sufficiently large so that resources for productive public spending are set free. Whether these two aspects hold in reality must be carefully checked if that result is to be used as a policy recommendation.

A result that is independent of whether real wages are flexible or rigid, is that a stronger reaction of the government to higher public debt stabilizes the economy. Hence, if the primary surplus of the government rises to a large extent as public debt increases, the economy is stable and converges to the balanced growth path

[2]Of course, this result is also obtained when public spending is welfare enhancing and yields immediate utility for households, cf. Greiner (2009).

asymptotically. Otherwise, if the reaction of the primary surplus is small, the government must levy an additional non-distortionary tax and use the revenue to control the stock of outstanding public debt. It could also be shown that for certain critical values of the reaction coefficient that determines how strongly the primary surplus rises as public debt increases, the economy may be characterized by endogenous cycles implying that the economy does not converge to a balanced growth path but, instead, is characterized by cyclically oscillating growth rates.

Appendix A
Non-parametric Estimation

The subsequent algorithm is based on Wood (2000) and implemented in the public domain software package R (see Ihaka and Gentleman 1996). The program and more information about it can be downloaded from http://www.r-project.org/. We exemplify the fit with the simplified model (see also Greiner and Kauermann 2008)

$$s_t = \phi_0 + \psi_t b_{t-1} + \varepsilon_t.$$

Let s_t and b_{t-1} be the observed values for $t = 2, 3, \ldots$. For fitting we replace the functional shape ψ_t by the parametric form

$$\psi_t = \psi_{00} + \psi_{01} t + Z(t)\boldsymbol{\gamma}, \tag{A.1}$$

where $Z(t)$ is a high dimensional basis in t. A typical setting is to choose $Z(t)$ as cubic spline basis functions allocated at the observed time points $t = 2, 3, \ldots$. However, numerically more efficient is to work with a reduced basis as suggested in O'Sullivan (1986) or Wood (2000). The latter proposal is implemented in R. The idea is to construct only those basis functions corresponding to the largest eigenvalues of $Z(t)Z(t)^T$ (see Wood 2000 for more details).

In principle, with replacement (A.1) one ends up with a parametric model. However, fitting the model in a standard OLS fashion is unsatisfactory due to the large dimensionality of $Z(t)$ which will lead to highly variable estimates. This can be avoided by imposing an additional penalty term on γ, shrinking its values to zero. To be more specific, we obtain an estimate by minimizing the penalized OLS criterion

$$\sum_t \{s_t - d_t \psi_d - Z(d_t)\gamma\}^2 + \lambda \gamma^T P \gamma$$

with λ called the smoothing or penalty parameter and $\gamma^T P \gamma$ as penalty. Matrix P is thereby chosen in accordance to the basis and for cubic splines the penalty corresponds to the integrated square derivative of ψ_t (see also Ruppert et al. 2003, for more details). It is easy to see that choosing $\lambda = 0$ yields an unpenalized OLS

A. Greiner, B. Fincke, *Public Debt and Economic Growth*,
Dynamic Modeling and Econometrics in Economics and Finance 11,
DOI 10.1007/978-3-642-01745-2,

fit, while $\lambda \to \infty$ typically implies $\gamma = 0$ depending on the choice of P. Hence, λ steers the amount of smoothness of the function with a simple linear fit as one extreme and a high dimensional parametric fit as the other extreme.

Let $\boldsymbol{\psi} = (\psi_1, \psi_2, \ldots)^T$ be the time varying effect stacked up to a column vector and assume for simplicity of presentation that $\phi_0 \equiv 0$. Let $\mathbf{t}$ be the vector of observed points in time and $Z(\mathbf{t})$ the spline basis evaluated at these points. With the spline approximation we set $\boldsymbol{\psi} = B(\mathbf{t})\boldsymbol{\theta}$ where $B(\mathbf{t}) = (\mathbf{1}, \mathbf{t}, Z(\mathbf{t}))$ and $\boldsymbol{\theta} = (\psi_{00}, \psi_{01}, \boldsymbol{\gamma})^T$. The estimate $\hat{\boldsymbol{\psi}}$, say, is then available in analytic form via $\hat{\boldsymbol{\psi}} = H(\lambda)\mathbf{s}$, with $\mathbf{s} = (s_1, s_2, \ldots)^T$ and $H(\lambda)$ as hat or smoothing matrix, respectively, defined through

$$H(\lambda) = B(\mathbf{t}) \left(B^T(\mathbf{t}) B(\mathbf{t}) + \lambda \begin{pmatrix} 0 & 0 \\ 0 & P \end{pmatrix} \right)^{-1} B^T(\mathbf{t}).$$

Note that $H(0)$ and $H(\infty)$ are classical hat matrices while $H(\lambda)$ for $0 < \lambda < \infty$ is a penalized version. The trace of $H(\lambda)$ is usually understood as the degree of the fit where $2 = \mathrm{tr}(H(\infty)) \le \mathrm{tr}(H(\lambda)) \le \mathrm{tr}(H(0)) = p + 2$ with p as dimension of $Z(\mathbf{t})$. The linear operator also allows to easily calculate variances of the estimate via

$$\mathrm{Var}(\hat{\boldsymbol{\psi}}) = H(\lambda)\Sigma(s)H^T(\lambda)$$

with $\Sigma(s)$ as covariance matrix of $\mathbf{s}$. Assuming uncorrelated and homoscedastic residuals we get $\mathrm{Var}(\hat{\boldsymbol{\psi}}) = \hat{\sigma}^2 H(\lambda) H^T(\lambda)$ with $\hat{\sigma}^2$ as residual variance estimate. Finally, if additional covariates are in the model, like in (2.9) or in (2.13), we pursue the same estimation like above but with hat matrix $H(\lambda)$ being supplemented by the additional covariate vectors.

To obtain a reliable fit, λ should be chosen data driven. One possibility is to use a generalized cross validation criterion defined through

$$\mathrm{GCV}(\lambda) = \sum_t \left(\frac{s_t - \phi_0 - \hat{\psi}_t b_{t-1}}{1 - \mathrm{tr}(H)/n} \right)^2$$

with n as overall sample size. A suitable choice for λ is achieved by minimizing $\mathrm{GCV}(\lambda)$. This can be done iteratively using a Newton-Raphson algorithm, as has been pointed out and implemented by Wood (2000, 2001). In principle there are numerous other routines to select λ, like an Akaike Information Criterion or Cross Validation (see e.g. Hastie and Tibshirani 1990). The generalized cross validation however has proven to be numerically quite stable and is therefore the default choice used in the implemented version in `R`.

Appendix B
Some Useful Theorems from Dynamic Optimization

In this book we have assumed that economic agents are rational, behave inter-temporally and perform dynamic optimization. In this appendix we present some basics of the method of dynamic optimization using Pontryagin's maximum principle and the Hamiltonian.

Let an inter-temporal optimization problem be given by

$$\max_{u(t)} W(x(0), 0), W(\cdot) \equiv \int_0^\infty e^{-\rho t} F(x(t), u(t))dt \tag{B.1}$$

subject to

$$\frac{dx(t)}{dt} \equiv \dot{x}(t) = f(x(t), u(t)), x(0) = x_0 \tag{B.2}$$

with $x(t) \in \mathbb{R}^n$ the vector of state variables at time t and $u(t) \in \Omega \in \mathbb{R}^m$ the vector of control variables at time t and $F : \mathbb{R}^n \times \mathbb{R}^m \to \mathbb{R}$ and $f : \mathbb{R}^n \times \mathbb{R}^m \to \mathbb{R}^n$. ρ is the discount rate and $e^{-\rho t}$ is the discount factor.

$F(x(t), u(t))$, $f_i(x(t), u(t))$ and $\partial f_i(x(t), u(t))/\partial x_j(t)$, $\partial F(x(t), u(t))/\partial x_j(t)$ are continuous with respect to all $n + m$ variables for $i, j = 1, \ldots, n$. Further, $u(t)$ is said to be admissible if it is a piecewise continuous function on $[0, \infty)$ with $u(t) \in \Omega$.

Define the current-value Hamiltonian $\mathcal{H}(x(t), u(t), \lambda(t), \lambda_0)$ as follows:

$$\mathcal{H}(x(t), u(t), \lambda(t), \lambda_0) \equiv \lambda_0 F(x(t), u(t)) + \lambda(t) f(x(t), u(t)) \tag{B.3}$$

with $\lambda_0 \in \mathbb{R}$ a constant scalar and $\lambda(t) \in \mathbb{R}^n$ the vector of co-state variables or shadow prices. $\lambda_j(t)$ gives the change in the optimal objective functional W^o resulting from an increment in the state variable $x_j(t)$. If $x_j(t)$ is a capital stock $\lambda_j(t)$ gives the marginal value of capital at time t. Assume that there exists a solution for (B.1) subject to (B.2). Then, we have the following theorem.

Theorem 1 *Let $u^o(t)$ be an admissible control and $x^o(t)$ is the trajectory belonging to $u^o(t)$. For $u^o(t)$ to be optimal it is necessary that there exists a continuous*

A. Greiner, B. Fincke, *Public Debt and Economic Growth*,
Dynamic Modeling and Econometrics in Economics and Finance 11,
DOI 10.1007/978-3-642-01745-2,

vector function $\lambda(t) = (\lambda_1(t), \ldots, \lambda_n(t))$ *with piecewise continuous derivatives and a constant scalar* λ_0 *such that*:

(a) $\lambda(t)$ *and* $x^o(t)$ *are solutions of the canonical system*

$$\dot{x}^o(t) = \frac{\partial}{\partial \lambda}\mathcal{H}(x^o(t), u^o(t), \lambda(t), \lambda_0),$$

$$\dot{\lambda}(t) = \rho\lambda(t) - \frac{\partial}{\partial x}\mathcal{H}(x^o(t), u^o(t), \lambda(t), \lambda_0),$$

(b) *For all* $t \in [0, \infty)$ *where* $u^o(t)$ *is continuous, the following inequality must hold*: $\mathcal{H}(x^o(t), u^o(t), \lambda(t), \lambda_0) \geq \mathcal{H}(x^o(t), u(t), \lambda(t), \lambda_0)$,

(c) $(\lambda_0, \lambda(t)) \neq (0, 0)$ *and* $\lambda_0 = 1$ *or* $\lambda_0 = 0$.

Remarks

1. If the maximum with respect to $u(t)$ is in the interior of Ω, $\partial\mathcal{H}(\cdot)/\partial u(t) = 0$ can be used as a necessary condition for a local maximum of $\mathcal{H}(\cdot)$.
2. It is implicitly assumed that the objective functional (B.1) takes on a finite value, that is $\int_0^\infty e^{-\rho t} F(x^o(t), u^o(t)) < \infty$. If x^o and u^o grow without an upper bound[1] $F(\cdot)$ must not grow faster than ρ.
3. Working with the present-value Hamiltonian that contains the discount factor $e^{-\rho t}$ gives necessary conditions that are equivalent to those of Theorem 1 after suitable transformation. Working with the current-value Hamiltonian instead of the present-value Hamiltonian implies that the differential equations are autonomous and do not explicitly depend on time.

Theorem 1 provides us only with necessary conditions. The next theorem gives sufficient conditions.

Theorem 2 *If the Hamiltonian with* $\lambda_0 = 1$ *is concave in* $(x(t), u(t))$ *jointly and if the transversality condition* $\lim_{t\to\infty} e^{-\rho t}\lambda(t)(x(t) - x^o(t)) \geq 0$ *holds, conditions* (a) *and* (b) *from Theorem* 1 *are also sufficient for an optimum. If the Hamiltonian is strictly concave in* $(x(t), u(t))$ *the solution is unique.*

Remarks

1. If the state and co-state variables are positive the transversality condition can be written as stated in the above chapters, that is as $\lim_{t\to\infty} e^{-\rho t}\lambda(t)x^o(t) = 0$.
2. Given some technical conditions it can be shown that the transversality condition is also a necessary condition.

Theorem 2 requires joint concavity of the current-value Hamiltonian in the control and state variables. A less restrictive theorem is the following.

[1] Note that in the book we did not indicate optimal values by ^{o}.

Theorem 3 *If the maximized Hamiltonian*

$$\mathcal{H}^o(x(t), \lambda(t), \lambda_0) = \max_{u(t)\in\Omega} \mathcal{H}(x(t), u(t), \lambda(t), \lambda_0)$$

with $\lambda_0 = 1$ *is concave in* $x(t)$ *and if the transversality condition* $\lim_{t\to\infty} e^{-\rho t}\lambda(t)$ $(x(t) - x^o(t)) \geq 0$ *holds, conditions* (a) *and* (b) *from Theorem* 1 *are also sufficient for an optimum. If the maximized Hamiltonian* $\mathcal{H}^o(x(t), \lambda(t), \lambda_0)$ *is strictly concave in* $x(t)$ *for all* t, $x^o(t)$ *is unique (but not necessarily* $u^o(t)$*).*

Since the joint concavity of $\mathcal{H}(x(t), u(t), \lambda(t), \lambda_0)$ with respect to $(x(t), u(t))$ implies concavity of $\mathcal{H}^o(x(t), \lambda(t), \lambda_0)$ with respect to $x(t)$, but the reverse does not necessarily hold, Theorem 3 may be applicable where Theorem 2 cannot be applied.

The above three theorems demonstrate how optimal control theory can be applied to solve dynamic optimization problems. The main role is played by the Hamiltonian function (B.3). It should be noted that in many economic applications, as in this book, interior solutions are optimal so that $\partial\mathcal{H}(\cdot)/\partial u(t) = 0$ can be presumed. For further reading and more details concerning optimal control theory we refer to the books by Feichtinger and Hartl (1986), Seierstad and Sydsæter (1987) or Beavis and Dobbs (1990).

Data Sources

International Statistical Yearbook (2006). IMF database. *DSI data service & information.*
International Statistical Yearbook (2007). IMF database. *DSI data service & information.*
OECD (2003). *OECD economic outlook statistics and projections.* Databasis: OECD economic outlook 73, June 2003, especially all "Government Account" data.
OECD (2007a). Gross domestic product. http://www.oecd.org/statsportal/0,2639,en_2825_293564_1_1_1_1_1,00.html. Last access November 2nd, 2007.
OECD (2007b). OECD statistical compendium, Volumes 1/2007 and 2/2007. *OECD Publications.*
World Bank (2008a). Data & statistics, country at a glance tables, 9/28/07. http://go.worldbank.org/3516WI4UM0. Last access on September 9th, 2008.

A. Greiner, B. Fincke, *Public Debt and Economic Growth,*
Dynamic Modeling and Econometrics in Economics and Finance 11,
DOI 10.1007/978-3-642-01745-2, © Springer-Verlag Berlin Heidelberg 2009

Bibliography

Afonso, A. (2005). Fiscal sustainability: the unpleasant European case. *Finanzarchiv*, *61*, 19–44.

Aghion, P., & Howitt, P. (1992). A model of growth through creative destruction. *Econometrica*, *60*, 323–351.

Arrow, K. J., & Kurz, M. (1970). *Public investment, the rate of return, and optimal fiscal policy*. Baltimore: John Hopkins Press.

Bajo-Rubio, O., Diaz-Roldan, C., & Esteve, V. (2004). Searching for threshold effects in the evolution of budget deficits: an application to the Spanish case. *Economic Letters*, *82*, 239–243.

Ballabriga, F. C., & Martinez-Mongay, C. (2005). *Sustainability of EU public finances*. European Economy. Economic Papers, No. 225, April 2005, European Commission, Brussels.

Barro, R. J. (1979). On the determination of public debt. *Journal of Political Economy*, *87*, 940–971.

Beauchemin, K. R. (2001). Growth or stagnation? The role of public education. *Journal of Development Economics*, *64*, 389–416.

Benhabib, J., & Perli, R. (1994). Uniqueness and indeterminacy. *Journal of Economic Theory*, *63*, 19–41.

Beavis, B., & Dobbs, I. M. (1990). *Optimization and stability theory for economic analysis*. Cambridge: Cambridge University Press.

Blanchard, O. J., & Fischer, S. (1989). *Lectures on macroeconomics*. Cambridge: MIT Press.

Blanchard, O., & Katz, L. F. (1999). Wage dynamics: reconciling theory and evidence. *American Economic Review*, *89*, 69–74.

Blanchard, O., & Wolfers, J. (2000). The role of shocks and institutions in the rise of European unemployment: the aggregate evidence. *The Economic Journal*, *110*, C1–C33.

Blankenau, W. F., & Simpson, N. B. (2004). Public education, expenditures and growth. *Journal of Development Economics*, *73*, 583–605.

Bohn, H. (1990). Tax smoothing with financial instruments. *American Economic Review*, *80*, 1217–1230.

Bohn, H. (1995). The sustainability of budget deficits in a stochastic economy. *Journal of Money, Credit and Banking*, *27*, 257–271.

Bohn, H. (1998). The behaviour of U.S. public debt and deficits. *Quarterly Journal of Economics*, *113*, 949–963.

Bohn, H. (2008). The sustainability of fiscal policy in the United States. In R. Neck & J.-E. Sturm (Eds.), *Sustainability of Public Debt* (pp. 15–50). Cambridge: MIT Press.

Buiter, W. H. (1982). *Predetermined and non-predetermined variables in rational expectation models*. Technical Paper No. 21, National Bureau of Economic Research, Cambridge, MA.

Buiter, W. H. (2002). The fiscal theory of the price level: a critique. *The Economic Journal*, *112*, 459–80.

Canzoneri, M. B., Cumby, R. E., & Diba, B. T. (2001). Is the price level determined by the needs of fiscal solvency? *American Economic Review*, *91*, 1221–1238.

A. Greiner, B. Fincke, *Public Debt and Economic Growth*,
Dynamic Modeling and Econometrics in Economics and Finance 11,
DOI 10.1007/978-3-642-01745-2, © Springer-Verlag Berlin Heidelberg 2009

Collard, F., & de la Croix, D. (2000). Gift exchange and the business cycle: the fair wage strikes back. *Review of Economic Dynamics*, *3*, 166–193.

Correia, M. D. R., Neck, R., Panagiotidis, T., & Richter, C. (2008). An empirical investigation of the sustainability of the public deficit in Portugal. *International Economics and Economic Policy*, *5*, 209–223.

Dickey, D. A., & Fuller, W. A. (1981). Likelihood ratio statistics for autoregressive time series with a unit root? *Econometrica*, *49*, 1057–1072.

Dhooge, A., Govaerts, W., Kuznetsov, Y. A., Maestrom, W., & Riet, A. M. (2003). CL_MATCONT: a continuation toolbox in Matlab. http://users.ugent.be/~ajdhooge/, Ghent University. Last access October 17th, 2008.

Embassy of the Republic of Mauritius (2008). Economy of Mauritius. http://www.mauritius-embassy.de/economy.php. Last access on September 3rd, 2008.

Enders, W. (2005). *Applied econometric time series* (2nd ed.). New York: Wiley.

European Union (1992). Treaty on European Union. http://europa.eu.int/eur-lex/lex/en/treaties/dat/11992M/htm/11992M.html. Last access November 27th, 2007.

Feichtinger, G., & Hartl, R. F. (1986). *Optimale Kontrolle Ökonomischer Prozesse: Anwendungen des Maximumprinzips in den Wirtschaftswissenschaften*. Berlin: De Gruyter.

Fincke, B., & Greiner, A. (2008). *How to assess debt sustainability? Some theory and empirical evidence for selected euro area countries*. Working Paper No. 148, Center for Empirical Macroeconomics, Bielefeld University.

Fincke, B., & Greiner, A. (2009, forthcoming). Do governments in developing countries pursue sustainable debt policies? Empirical evidence for selected countries in Africa and Latin America. *Journal of Development Studies*.

Flaschel, P., Franke, R., & Semmler, W. (1997). *Dynamic macroeconomics: instability, fluctuations and growth in monetary economies*. Cambridge: MIT Press.

Fuller, W. A. (1976). *Introduction to statistical time series*. New York: Wiley.

Futagami, K., Morita, Y., & Shibata, A. (1993). Dynamic analysis of an endogenous growth model with public capital. *Scandinavian Journal of Economics*, *95*, 607–625.

Futagami, K., Iwaisako, T., & Ohdoi, R. (2008). Debt policy rule, productive government spending, and multiple growth paths. *Macroeconomic Dynamics*, *12*, 445–462.

Ghosh, S., & Mourmouras, I. (2004). Endogenous growth, welfare and budgetary regimes. *Journal of Macroeconomics*, *26*, 363–384.

Glomm, G., & Ravikumar, B. (1992). Public versus private investment in human capital: endogenous growth and income distribution. *Journal of Political Economy*, *100*, 818–834.

Gong, G., Greiner, A., & Semmler, W. (2001). Growth effects of fiscal policy and debt sustainability in the EU. *Empirica*, *28*, 3–19.

Government of Botswana (2008). Economic Information. http://www.gov.bw/index.php?option=com_content&task=view&id=63&Itemid=74. Last access on September 3rd, 2008.

Granger, C. W. J. (2008). Non-linear models: where do we go next—time varying parameter models? *Studies in Nonlinear Dynamics & Econometrics*, *12*(3), 1–9.

Greiner, A. (2007a). An endogenous growth model with public capital and sustainable government debt. *Japanese Economic Review*, *58*, 345–361.

Greiner, A. (2007b). *Budget rules and macroeconomic stability with endogenous growth*. SSRN Working Paper. http://ssrn.com/abstract=984881.

Greiner, A. (2008a). *Sustainability of public debt: some theoretical considerations*. SSRN Working Paper. http://ssrn.com/abstract=1266042.

Greiner, A. (2008b). Does it pay to have a balanced government budget? *Journal of Institutional and Theoretical Economics*, *164*, 460–476.

Greiner, A. (2008c). Human capital formation, public debt and economic growth. *Journal of Macroeconomics*, *30*, 415–427.

Greiner, A. (2009). *Economic growth, public debt and welfare: comparing three budgetary rules*. SSRN Working Paper. http://ssrn.com/abstract=1354035.

Greiner, A., & Flaschel, P. (2009). *Public debt and public investment in an endogenous growth model with real wage rigidities*. SSRN Working Paper. http://ssrn.com/abstract=1334542. *Scottish Journal of Political Economy*, forthcoming.

Greiner, A., & Kauermann, G. (2008). Debt policy in Euro-area countries: empirical evidence for Germany and Italy using penalized spline smoothing. *Economic Modelling*, *25*, 1144–1154.

Greiner, A., & Semmler, W. (2000). Endogenous growth, government debt and budgetary regimes. *Journal of Macroeconomics*, *22*, 363–384.

Greiner, A., Köller, U., & Semmler, W. (2007). Debt sustainability in the European monetary union: theory and empirical evidence for selected countries. *Oxford Economic Papers*, *59*, 194–218.

Guo, J.-T., & Harrison, S. G. (2004). Balanced-budget rules and macroeconomic (in)stability. *Journal of Economic Theory*, *119*, 357–363.

Haber, G., & Neck, R. (2006). Sustainability of Austrian public debt: a political economy perspective. *Empirica*, *33*, 141–154.

Hamilton, J. D., & Flavin, M. (1986). On the limitations of government borrowing: a framework for empirical testing. *The American Economic Review*, *76*, 808–819.

Hassard, B. D., Kazarinoff, N. D., & Wan, Y.-H. (1981). *Theory and applications of Hopf bifurcation*. Cambridge: Cambridge University Press.

Hastie, T. J., & Tibshirani, R. J. (1990). *Generalized additive models*. London: Chapman and Hall.

Heinemann, F. (2002). *Factor mobility, government debt and the decline in public investment*. ZEW Discussion Paper, No. 02-19. http://zew.de/.

Ihaka, R., & Gentleman, R. (1996). R: a language for data analysis and graphics. *Journal of Computational and Graphical Statistics*, *5*, 299–314.

International Monetary Fund (1995). IMF approves stand-by credit for Panama. IMF Press Release No. 95/60. http://www.imf.org/external/np/sec/pr/1995/pr9560.htm. Last access on September 3rd, 2008.

International Monetary Fund (2008). Heavily indebted poor countries (HIPC) debt initiative all publications. http://www.imf.org/external/np/hipc/index.asp. Last access on September 5th, 2008.

Krueger, A. B., & Lindahl, M. (2001). Education for growth: why and for whom? *Journal of Economic Literature*, *39*, 1101–1136.

Layard, P. R. J., Nickell, S. J., & Jackman, R. (1991). *Unemployment: macroeconomic performance and the labor market*. Oxford: Oxford University Press.

Leeper, E. M. (1991). Equilibria under 'active' and 'passive' monetary and fiscal policies. *Journal of Monetary Economics*, *27*, 129–147.

Levine, R., & Renelt, D. (1992). A sensitivity analysis of cross-country growth regressions. *American Economic Review*, *82*, 942–963.

Lucas, R. E. (1998). On the mechanics of economic development. *Journal of Monetary Economics*, *22*, 3–42.

Martin, G. M. (2000). US deficit sustainability: a new approach based on multiple endogenous breaks. *Journal of Applied Econometrics*, *15*, 83–105.

McCallum, B. C. (2003). Is the fiscal theory of the price level learnable? *Scottish Journal of Political Economy*, *50*, 634–649.

McCallum, B. C., & Nelson, E. (2006). *Monetary and fiscal theories of the price level: the irreconcilable differences*. Working Paper 2006-010A, Federal Reserve Bank of St. Louis.

Minkner-Buenjer, M. (1999). Costa Rica: Internationalisierung der Wirtschaft mit Bananen und Mikroprozessoren. *Brennpunkt Latainamerika. Politik Wirtschaft Gesellschaft, Institut für Iberoamerika-Kunde Hamburg*, *19*, 162–172.

Neck, R., & Getzner, M. (2001). Politico-economic determinants of public debt growth: a case study for Austria. *Public Choice*, *109*, 243–268.

Neck, R., & Sturm, J.-E. (2008). Sustainability of public debt. Introduction and overview. In R. Neck & J.-E. Sturm (Eds.), *Sustainability of public debt* (pp. 1–14). Cambridge: MIT-Press.

Ni, S., & Wang, X. (1994). Human capital and income taxation in an endogenous growth model. *Journal of Macroeconomics*, *16*, 493–507.

Nsouli, S. M., Eken, S., Duran, P., Bell, G., & Yucelik, Z.M. (1993). *The path to convertibility and growth the Tunisian experience*. IMF Occasional Paper 109.

O'Sullivan, F. (1986). A statistical perspective on ill-posed inverse problems (C/R:P 519–527). *Statistical Science*, *1*, 502–518.

Oxley, H., & Martin, J. P. (1991). Controlling government spending and deficits; trends in the 1980s and prospects for the 1990s. *OECD Economic Studies*, *17*, 145–189.

Paul, E. C. (1987). *Fisheries development and the food needs of Mauritius*. Rotterdam: A.A. Balkema.

Payne, J. E., Mohammadi, H., & Cak, M. (2007). Turkish budget deficit sustainability and the revenue-expenditure nexus. *Applied Econometrics*, *7*, 823–830.

Pfaff, B. (2006). *Analysis of integrated and cointegrated time series with R*. New York: Springer.

Raurich, X., Sala, H., & Sorolla, V. (2006). Unemployment, growth, and fiscal policy: New insights on the hysteresis hypothesis. *Macroeconomic Dynamics*, *10*, 285–316.

Rebelo, S. (1991). Long-run policy analysis and long-run growth. *Journal of Political Economy*, *99*, 500–521.

Romer, P. M. (1986). Increasing returns and long-run growth. *Journal of Political Economy*, *94*, 1002–1037.

Romer, P. M. (1990). Endogenous technological change. *Journal of Political Economy*, *98*, S71–S102.

Ruppert, R., Wand, M. P., & Carroll, R. J. (2003). *Semiparametric regression*. Cambridge: Cambridge University Press.

Sawada, Y. (1994). Are the heavily indebted countries solvent?: tests of intertemporal borrowing constraints. *Journal of Development Economics*, *45*, 325–337.

Schmitt-Grohé, S., & Uribe, U. (1997). Balanced-budget rules, distortionary taxes, and aggregate instability. *Journal of Political Economy*, *105*, 976–1000.

Seierstad, A., & Sydsæter, K. (1987). *Optimal control with economic applications*. Amsterdam: North-Holland.

Sims, C. A. (1994). A simple model for study of the determination of the price level and the interaction of monetary and fiscal policy. *Economic Theory*, *4*, 381–399.

Stork, J. (1990). Europe's other frontier: North Africa faces the 1990s. *Middle East Report*, *163*(44), 4–8.

Trehan, B., & Walsh, C. E. (1991). Testing inter-temporal budget constraints: theory and applications to U.S. Federal budget and current account deficits. *Journal of Money, Credit and Banking*, *23*, 206–223.

Uzawa, H. (1965). Optimum technical change in an aggregative model of economic growth. *International Economic Review*, *6*, 18–31.

van Ewijk, C. (1991). *On the dynamics of growth and debt*. Oxford: Oxford University Press.

Westerlund, J., & Prohl, S. (2008, forthcoming). Panel cointegration tests of the sustainability hypothesis in rich OECD countries. *Applied Economics*.

Wilcox, D. W. (1989). The sustainability of government deficits: implications of the present-value borrowing constraint. *Journal of Money, Credit and Banking*, *21*, 291–306.

Wood, S. N. (2000). Modelling and smoothing parameter estimation with multiple quadratic penalties. *Journal of the Royal Statistical Society, Series B*, *62*, 413–428.

Wood, S. N. (2001). mgcv: GAM's and generalized ridge regression for R. *R News*, *1*(2), 20–25.

Woodford, M. (1994). Monetary policy and price level determination in a cash-in-advance economy. *Economic Theory*, *4*, 345–380.

World Bank (2008b). Data & statistics, country classification. http://web.worldbank.org/WBSITE/EXTERNAL/DATASTATISTICS/0,,contentMDK:20420458~menuPK:64133156~pagePK:64133150~piPK:64133175~theSitePK:239419,00.html. Last access on March 13th, 2008.

MIX
Papier aus verantwortungsvollen Quellen
Paper from responsible sources
FSC® C105338

If you have any concerns about our products,
you can contact us on
ProductSafety@springernature.com

In case Publisher is established outside the EU,
the EU authorized representative is:
Springer Nature Customer Service Center GmbH
Europaplatz 3, 69115 Heidelberg, Germany

Printed by Libri Plureos GmbH
in Hamburg, Germany